REBECCA M. STAHL, JD, LLM, AND ⸺ STAHL, PHD

REPRESENTING CHILDREN IN DEPENDENCY AND FAMILY COURT

BEYOND THE LAW

Cover design by Kelly Book/ABA Design.

Library of Congress Cataloging-in-Publication Data

Names: Stahl, Rebecca M., author. | Stahl, Philip M., author.
Title: Representing children in dependency and family court : beyond the
   law / Rebecca M. Stahl, JD, LLM and Philip M. Stahl, PhD, ABPP (Forensic).
Description: Chicago : American Bar Association, [2018] | Includes
   bibliographical references and index.
Identifiers: LCCN 2018008916 (print) | LCCN 2018010085 (ebook) | ISBN
   9781641051477 (e-book) | ISBN 9781641051460 (pbk. : alk. paper)
Subjects: LCSH: Legal assistance to children—United States. |
   Children—Legal status, laws, etc.—United States. | Custody of
   children—United States. | Domestic relations courts—United States. |
   Juvenile justice, Administration of—United States.
Classification: LCC KF3735 (ebook) | LCC KF3735 .S67 2018 (print) | DDC
   346.7301/7—dc23
LC record available at https://lccn.loc.gov/2018008916

Dedication

To the children and families who have been a part of the Dependency and Family Courts, and to our AFCC friends and family, who have inspired and taught us so much.

Contents

Acknowledgments

We are grateful for the assistance, inspiration, encouragement, and support of many colleagues with whom we share professional and personal relationships. Thanks go out to Honorable Amy Pellman, Stacy Heard, JD, Prof. Paul Bennett, Daniel Harkins, JD, and Michael Kretzmer, JD, for their review of previous versions of portions of this manuscript. The comments of these esteemed colleagues have been immensely helpful.

We appreciate the support and guidance provided by Allen Bailey and Jeff Salyards and the entire publication Board of the Family Law Section of the American Bar Association. Their support of our project has allowed us to develop a book that might seem counterintuitive for lawyers.

Rebecca would like to thank her law school professors, especially Barbara Atwood and Paul Bennett, who inspired her during law school, taught her how to work with children, and continue to be friends and colleagues to this day. She would like to thank her early mentors, including The Honorable Sarah Simmons and Edith Croxen, who reminded her she had to practice to better understand the needs of children, to The Honorable Karen Adam, who has been a guide, mentor, and friend since Rebecca's first year of law school, and to Mark Henaghan whose visionary mindset helped Rebecca hold a similar vision for children's representation. Finally, Rebecca thanks former colleagues at the Office of Children's Counsel and her current colleagues at the Children's Law Center of California, who support, encourage, and challenge her every day. Rebecca also needs to make clear that her opinions as expressed in this book are hers alone and not those of the Children's Law Center of California, nor of any past or future employment.

Phil would like to thank Joy Lyngar and the administration of the National Judicial College who have supported his work with judges, especially in developing his understanding of domestic violence, and recent Chairs of the ABA Family Law Section, including Scott Friedman, Lori Nelson, Greg Ortiz, Mary Vidas, and Roberta Batley for supporting his participation with the Section over the last five years.

We both acknowledge the leadership of the Association of Family and Conciliation Courts in advocating for the well-being of children who experience the breakup of their families and for providing us a home, nay a family, of supportive and inspirational colleagues to remind us every day why we do the work we do.

On a personal level, many thanks to our family, blended as it is. To Andrea and Tim Dapper, Rebecca's mother and stepfather. Also to Ruth Stahl, Phil's wife and Rebecca's stepmother, who has encouraged us along every step of the way with this project and so many others. Also to Jason, Phil's son and Rebecca's brother, and Jason's partner, Jennie, and their son, Damon, all of whom have been with us during each step of our work, in spirit or as cheerleaders.

And finally, the biggest thanks must go to the children we have served over the years. It is our passion for their well-being and their stories that have brought us to this work and kept us "in the trenches" for all these years. We thank them for sharing so much of themselves and for their bravery despite the challenges life has given them.

About the Authors

Rebecca M. Stahl is a lawyer for children who is currently working at the Children's Law Center of California in Los Angeles County, representing children in dependency cases. She previously represented children in both family and dependency cases in Tucson, Arizona, at the Pima County Office of Children's Counsel. Rebecca was a Fulbright Scholar in New Zealand and during her Fulbright year earned a Master of Law degree from the University of Otago in Dunedin, New Zealand, where she studied the role of lawyers for children in family court cases. Rebecca attended the University of Arizona College of Law and has presented at a variety of international conferences focused on children's rights and family law on topics ranging from yoga and stress management to the role of lawyers for children in both family and juvenile court and has published articles on the role of children's representation. She is also a yoga instructor and currently a somatic experiencing student.

Contact Information:
Rebecca Stahl
Email address:
rmstahl@gmail.com

Philip M. Stahl, PhD, ABPP (Forensic), is a board-certified forensic psychologist in private practice living in Maricopa County, Arizona, who conducts child custody evaluations and provides consultation and expert witness testimony throughout the United States. He has conducted trainings both nationally and internationally for attorneys, child custody evaluators, and others working with high-conflict families of divorce. He has presented workshops for judges throughout the country and is on the faculty of the National Judicial College and the National Council of Juvenile and Family Court Judges. He has cowritten and taught a program with the National Institute for Trial Advocacy (NITA) titled "Modern Divorce Advocacy."

As a former Board member of AFCC, he was on the task force that drafted AFCC's original "Model Standards of Practice for Child Custody Evaluation," as well as their revision in 2006. He was a member of the American Bar Association Wingspread Task Force on High Conflict Families in 2000. He testified by invitation to the Ohio Task Force for Family Law Reform and a New York State Commission regarding child custody evaluations and was appointed by the Arizona Supreme Court to participate in the revisions to *Planning for Parenting Time: A Guide for Separating Parents* (2009). Dr. Stahl is on the Editorial Review Board of AFCC's journal, *Family Court Review*. Along with his teaching, Dr. Stahl has written extensively on various issues in high-conflict divorce and custody evaluations. He is the author of several books and articles associated with custody evaluations and high-conflict parents, including *Forensic Psychology Consultation in Child Custody Litigation: A Handbook for Work Product Review, Case Preparation, and Expert Testimony* (coauthor with Dr. Robert Simon—Family Law Section of the American Bar Association, 2013), *Conducting Child Custody Evaluations: From Basic to Advanced Issues* (Sage Publications, 2010), *Parenting After Divorce, 2nd Edition* (Impact Publishers, 2008), *Relocation Issues in Child Custody Cases* (coeditor with Dr. Leslie Drozd—Haworth Press, 2006), and "Emerging Issues in Relocation Cases," published by the *Journal of American Academy of Matrimonial Law*. His child custody evaluation was cited by the California Supreme Court in its recent landmark decision modifying eight years of relocation case law following Burgess (*In re Marriage of LaMusga* (2004) 32 Cal.4th 1072, 12 Cal.Rptr.3d 356, 88 P.3d 81).

Contact Information:
Philip M. Stahl, Ph.D., ABPP (Forensic)
18521 E. Queen Creek Road
Suite 105-448
Queen Creek, AZ 85142

Voicemail 925-394-4062 / 602-235-0946
Philipstahlphd@gmail.com
www.parentingafterdivorce.com

Introduction

The Purpose of This Book

Rebecca and Phil began conceptualizing this book when Rebecca first became a lawyer, when she recognized all the issues she never learned in law school that were important in a dependency court or family court practice. Phil is a psychologist who has worked with children in the courts since the mid-1980s. Phil is a life member of the Association of Family and Conciliation Courts, an interdisciplinary association focused on the well-being of children, and Rebecca joined AFCC while in law school. At AFCC and other meetings, Rebecca started to learn about family issues and their impact on children whose cases are in the court system. We kept talking about what children's representatives needed to know and how to expose them to these issues.

While in New Zealand studying for her LLM, Rebecca researched various ways the New Zealand court system guided children's representatives in their practice. She developed a model, which we identify in this book as the child's representative being equivalent to the child's imaginary friend. This is discussed more fully in Chapter 3.

Since the end of 2011, Rebecca has worked almost exclusively as a children's lawyer in dependency court matters—first in Tucson, Arizona, and now in Los Angeles, California. Through her work and her attendance at conferences, she has learned a great deal about child development and attachment, about domestic violence, and, most importantly, about trauma. Her work in understanding the impact of trauma on children in the court system has been a central component in her understanding of the children she represents in dependency court. As a trained yoga instructor and a somatic experiencing student, Rebecca has also become highly sensitized to the somatic experience of those who are traumatized and how trauma stays within the body and nervous system long after the initial events. As her skills developed, we returned to the idea of our book so that we could share what we both have learned about children, trauma, and various considerations about how to represent children in the court system.

This is not a book about the law. You learned the law while attending your law school classes and while studying for the Bar in your jurisdiction. The American Bar Association Family Law Section is also publishing a companion book on the law in representing children in dependency court, written by our colleague and friend Melissa Kucinski, titled *A Practical Handbook for the Child's Attorney: Effectively Representing Children in Custody Cases.* We urge you to read that book as well.

Rather, this book is unique. The title, *Representing Children in Dependency and Family Court: Beyond the Law*, reflects the various issues that Rebecca has learned are critical for working with child clients in dependency and family court settings. Some children's representatives work exclusively in this area and may already be aware of some of the family dynamics we discuss but want to delve deeper into. Some children's representatives occasionally work with children's cases and have had limited or no exposure to these issues. And some lawyers may be considering working with children and need to know where to start. *Representing Children in Dependency and Family Court* is the place to start.

"I'm a Lawyer, Not a Social Worker"

A comment that both Rebecca and Phil hear from children's representatives is that they are lawyers, not social workers or psychologists. They do not understand why the dynamics discussed in this book are so critical. Many lawyers who practice in family and juvenile court state that their job is to practice law and not to practice social work. This refrain from lawyers is heard across the family-juvenile law divide. It is true that lawyers should not practice social work. Lawyers, however, are more than the law they practice; that is the very essence of being a good lawyer. The best advice Rebecca ever received as a young lawyer came from a retired securities lawyer who said, in paraphrase, "I had to understand my clients' businesses better than they did, or I would not be able to advise them and represent them." In other words, the lawyer must understand the client on all levels that affect the legal representation. In family and dependency law, that means issues that society more traditionally believes to be social work or psychology.[1]

---

1. We are not advocating you become the social worker on a case and enroll children in services, find therapists for them, or drive them to their appointments. We understand there is a difference between understanding the psychological issues your client faces outside the legal realm and practicing social work. You are still a lawyer and not an actual

We believe the need to fully understand the client increases with respect to children who are less legally sophisticated and psychologically aware clients. The lawyers who represent children must understand them, the system in which they are engaged, the services available to them, the schools they attend, their ethnic and cultural issues, any special needs they have, the legal issues they face outside of family and juvenile courts, etc. In addition, lawyers for children, even if their only clients are children, need to understand the issues their parents face, whether that be the emotional strain a separation poses on parents or the issues parents need to address (e.g., complying with court-ordered therapy and parent education) to reunify with their children. Children in family and dependency law cases do not exist in a vacuum; thus, it is necessary to understand the adults with whom they live. For this reason, the imaginary friend concept described later views each child from his perspective.

Law school does not train lawyers how to engage with children. Instead, lawyers learn to ask about objective facts and to keep emotions out of the conversation. Knowing that, we ask lawyers reading this book to step out of law school training for a moment and refocus on how to interact with your child clients. We will circle back to how to bring this work into a legal practice, but for now, we ask you to turn off the focus on objective facts and admissible evidence in order to see children and your role from a different perspective.

We believe the most important question a lawyer for children can ask is "Why?" Curiosity is your most important attribute as a children's lawyer; someone may have given you information, but that does not mean there is not always more to learn and understand about your clients' lives. And patience may be the second most important attribute; it takes time to have a safe and strong relationship with child clients. We often hear about children's behaviors, whether they excel in school despite egregious circumstances at home or they have been kicked out of five different preschools. All children respond in different ways to their life circumstances,[2] and we know "hurt people hurt people." A person who feels hurt can, in turn, hurt others. Children, even more than adults, respond to life from an emotional place. They feel and act on impulse before they stop and think about their responses. And when they have experienced trauma, they feel and act

---

social worker, but sometimes the line can feel blurry, and one of the goals of this book is to help you understand your client from a psychological or social work perspective.

2. We will discuss trauma and its effect on behavior in Chapter 4. Here, we are discussing how to begin to see past the legal training to another way of seeing children and their actions.

from that place, which can result in circumventing their ability to control their actions.[3] Understanding the "why" is vital to understanding the "what"—the behaviors children use to express themselves.

Despite the importance of knowing why and asking why, depending on the child can be counterproductive. Too often, when we ask why, children respond with "I don't know." There are other ways of exploring the why without asking that specific question. Instead, ask other questions to understand as much as you can about your client's life, her history, the source(s) of her troubles, and the nature of her feelings. Being curious and asking relevant questions about her life enables you to learn as much as you can about your client, even if you can't ask her "why" she feels or acts in certain ways.

Another reason to be able to understand the why is to be able to speak to our individual clients differently based on their experiences. Just as we learn to do our job differently with different judges, we learn to speak to child clients differently based on their life experiences and why they act in certain ways. Life experiences may be case related, and they may be external to the case. For example, in what culture was your client raised? Is the child being bullied in school because of her sexual orientation? Was the child in a car accident that caused trauma that is now affecting everything else, including his issues in the case?

Rebecca had a child client while in law school who she went four years without seeing after her graduation from law school. But when his case reactivated for the third time in juvenile court, his case was randomly assigned to her again. Although to others he was an angry, obstinate, gang-related teenager who would blow up at the smallest issue, Rebecca knew him well enough that she could often calm him down. She usually could get him to come back from those outbursts by mentioning his siblings. Rebecca knew the "why" because she had known him for so long, so his behaviors became an expression from the "why," not from the place of an out-of-control teenager. From that place, they were better able to discuss his legal options.

The ability to create this level of understanding in a relationship is limited in legal representation. Although it happens, it is rare, and unfortunate, when we know our clients for long periods of time. But this relationship with one client has always guided Rebecca's interaction with every other client. By asking different questions and being the person in their lives not asking about the behaviors, but instead asking about the underlying issues, we can begin to shift the

---

3. In addition, children who were exposed to drugs may be more hindered in their ability to respond because their brain development can be affected by in utero drug exposure.

conversation, often back to what we needed to discuss initially to do the legal work. This simple question and deeper awareness, with the interest it conveys to your client, also helps create a feeling of safety, a topic we will discuss in depth in Chapter 4. This curiosity also helps convey to your clients that you are not going to make assumptions about them. We have both seen lawyers assume they know the why when they have never asked. We will discuss bias in Chapter 11, but one of the most important ways to control for bias is to be curious without judgment. Thus, taking a more holistic approach, and understanding all the issues that affect our clients, does not make one a social worker; it makes one a good lawyer.

Understanding your clients on a deeper level includes recognizing that the children will likely change throughout the proceedings. One of the many arguments over the years as to why children should have less say in their lives involves the fact they are children and will change their mind anyway. Some see this as a negative aspect of childhood, but in truth, it is how humans are. We change. We grow. As lawyers for children, we must be ready and open to all possibilities children's lives present. If our clients' views change, that is to be expected, and understanding *why* they change is as important as understanding *that* they change. It may be that a child has been manipulated or wants to manipulate a situation.[4] It also may be that the child has grown and changed and sees things in a different light and from broader perspectives. Sometimes we never know exactly what is happening, but the curiosity to ask the "why" question helps guide our next moves as their legal representatives.

Understanding the "why" for children's actions helps lawyers advise child clients to ask for what they need in a particular situation. Understanding these issues is vital for two reasons: first, it is important to advise our clients directly. As the securities lawyer instructed, only by understanding our clients can we offer them solutions. Second, the interventions may be required legally. In situations where children refuse to see a parent, for example, it may be necessary to understand the why in order to determine what interventions are necessary to attempt to resolve the problem. As we will discuss later, these are complex issues, but looking at the broader perspective is vital to advising clients and helping them get the services they need in order to meet the legal and moral obligations these cases entail.

Services available to clients is one area where juvenile and family law differ dramatically. When there is child welfare intervention, federal law requires child

---

4. Suggestibility and the variables that contribute to internal or external influence of what children say will be examined more fully in Chapter 5.

welfare agencies to provide the family with reasonable services aimed at reunification of the family. Those services often include providing therapeutic intervention for the children as well as ensuring children live as normal a life as possible. Family law, by contrast, has no automatic state intervention, so there is no one to provide the services except the parents who are often so embroiled in their own emotional turmoil they are not as present as they should be to provide appropriate services to their children. Thus, it is vital that lawyers who represent children in family law cases understand how to help children so they may ask for orders appropriate for the children's mental health. In an era of increasingly diminishing resources, the job of the lawyer to solve problems is that much greater.

While it is true that lawyers cannot be responsible for arranging the services, they must understand the services available, and the issues children face, in order to advocate strongly for those services that best benefit the children. (For a more detailed look at the variety of therapeutic interventions, see the website associated with the book.) Judges who rotate between benches and parents who are experiencing their own turmoil may not have the necessary resources to know what the children need. It is vital that lawyers for children understand what may help children in order to ask for appropriate orders for services for their child clients.

Cultural Issues to Consider

Finally, perhaps the most important aspect of the recognition of your role as more than just a legal lawyer is understanding that your clients and you are likely from different cultures. Culture can be defined broadly, and here we define it to include race, ethnicity, religion, socioeconomic level, language, country of origin, and sexual orientation. It likely includes many other aspects as well, and we hope you will consider all of them in your representation. While this book was being written and these issues of culture were being discussed, Canada announced millions of dollars in reparations to native cultures for taking children from native homes to be adopted by white Canadians.[5] In other words, even from a legal perspective, these issues are still front and center in the work you do with children. Also, during the writing of this book, a major New Zealand newspaper posted

---

5. Ian Austen, *Canada to Pay Millions in Indigenous Lawsuit Over Forced Adoptions*, N.Y. Times, Oct. 6, 2017, https://www.nytimes.com/2017/10/06/world/canada/indigenous-forced-adoption-sixties-scoop.html?_r=0.

an article about how recognizing culture, and using culture, can help heal trauma differently, and maybe better, than other techniques.[6]

From a personal and relationship standpoint with your child clients, however, it is important to recognize and honor the differences we all share. How your clients view you and your willingness to work with their unique culture can affect whether they feel comfortable enough with you to have the necessary professional relationship required for you to adequately represent them. For example, the day after the 2016 presidential election, Rebecca was speaking to a 16-year-old client who asked Rebecca who she had voted for the day before. Hoping to instill a little civic education into the conversation and not realizing why the child had asked, Rebecca responded, "That's a private matter." The child replied, "If you voted for Trump, I'm walking out of the room." In that moment, that child would not have been comfortable having a lawyer who had voted for Donald Trump.

These cultural issues can also show up in other areas. For example, should Jewish foster children be forced to go to church with their foster parents? Obviously, a First Amendment argument is that the answer is no, but what about something more difficult for you to accept personally? But what if a child does not want to be around a different race? Is that a sufficient reason to ask for a child to be removed from a home? Is putting a cultural belief about acceptance on a foster child acceptable just because that is what you believe is right?

We believe it is important to learn as much as you can about other cultures, but you cannot learn everything. We will discuss bias more in Chapter 11, but here it is important to discuss how bias affects what you see in front of you. Rebecca once had a situation where she was asking for her 17-year-old female client to be removed from her mother's custody as the client wanted. The judge made it very clear she was not going to order the removal that day. Rebecca's client dressed like society's view of a boy and, upon superficial glance, could have looked like a boy to other people. When she entered the courtroom, the judge changed her mind and ordered the removal of the child without any explanation as to why. The only difference is the judge may have thought the child was being treated poorly by her mother not because she was an out-of-control teenager, but because she was not expressing herself and her sexuality the way her mother believed was appropriate. To the judge, the mother's conduct was inexcusable.

---

6. Michelle Duff, *In Narrative Therapy, Maori Creation Stories Are Being Used to Heal*, Stuff.co.nz, Mar. 9, 2018, https://www.stuff.co.nz/national/102115864/in-narrative-therapy-mori-creation-stories-are-being-used-to-heal.

Neither Rebecca nor the child welfare agency had mentioned these issues to the court because they are rarely legally relevant, but they were culturally relevant to the court that day. And ultimately, they became legally relevant because the judge took the necessary protective measures for the child.

The issue of children's emerging sexual orientation and sexuality in general can be difficult for you, as their lawyer, to address. Culturally, LGBTQ issues sometimes seem to change daily, and it can be difficult for cisgender,[7] heterosexual individuals to know the right way to talk about these issues. And even over the past five to ten years, children express themselves differently and more fluidly than ever before, particularly on either coast within the United States. It can be difficult to keep up. Being curious, being open to anything, and asking questions can be very helpful. Be polite. Neither of us has ever had a child become upset when we asked a question incorrectly or used the wrong term because we were polite. And if you do not know what terms to use for your clients, just ask. Ask about pronouns. Ask about names. In other words, ask about everything about which you are not certain. Phil suggests saying something like, "You are talking about something that often has different meanings for different people. Please help me understand what you mean."

Another way cultural issues can emerge that affect legal representation immediately is how different cultures respond to government officials. If you grew up with no reason to fear the police or child welfare agencies, you will likely respond to them differently than someone who has never felt safe trusting these officials. People from many cultures, however, fear government officials, so they withhold information. One of Rebecca's biases is honesty. If people are honest about making mistakes, Rebecca believes the problem can be addressed, but when people lie and cover up, she believes it is far more difficult for the situation to be resolved. But what happens when a parent is from a culture that is leery of government officials and hides the truth as a form of protection? How does that bias interact with a cultural norm Rebecca does not share? It requires asking questions.

And while you know you are a safe person for your clients, they often do not know that. They often see you as different than they are, and therefore, they believe you are unable to understand them and their circumstances. Rebecca once had a case where she really liked the mom, but the mom could not stop using drugs. In court, Rebecca stated, "I understand why." After court, the mother's lawyer said

---

7. Merriam Webster defines *cisgender* as "of, relating to, or being a person whose gender identity corresponds with the sex the person had or was identified as having at birth," https://www.merriam-webster.com/dictionary/cisgender.

to Rebecca, "Of all the things you said, that upset her the most. She asked how you could understand if you had never been an addict." Many people believe if you have not experienced something, you cannot understand it. This book is not a place to debate that, but what is important is your clients may believe that and therefore might not trust you as much as you would like them to trust you.

There are likely hundreds, if not thousands, of stories of how culture, broadly defined, impacts your relationship with your child clients and your legal arguments. What is important to remember is you do not know how your culture, or how children's views of your culture, affect them and their willingness to trust you. The more you ask about these issues and get to know what matters to your clients, the better. Sometimes they will tell you; other times they will not. And if you are not sure whether your own misunderstanding of a culture is interfering with your ability to read a case correctly, ask questions. Ask people who are culturally different from you. Ask people with whom you generally disagree.

The takeaway here is to stay curious and ask questions. Never stop asking questions. Even when you think you understand, ask more questions. No matter what your cultural background, it will likely be different from that of your client. The only way to begin to understand is to ask. Learn about cultures different from your own. But also learn what it is like for the child sitting in front of you. This is the takeaway of this entire book, but it begins with trust—and that trust begins by asking questions.

Language Used in This Book

We have attempted to avoid two main problems with writing texts such as this. First, we do not want to presume a particular gender for attorneys or children. We also do not like to use *s/he* or *he/she* or *they* for grammatical reasons. Instead, periodically we alternated between the use of *he* and *she* in the book. We recognize there are more than two genders, but for clarity of writing, we have chosen to limit ourselves to these two. We thank you, the reader, for indulging us in this choice.

Further, we often use the word *data* when discussing both research and the information you obtain in your cases. It is a plural word, and we use it as such. We also alternate between *lawyer* and *representative*. We recognize that not all people who represent children are legally trained, and we hope this book can be beneficial to them as well. For those trained in the legal profession, there are issues specific to you, and we will address them as such.

Throughout this book, we refer to all children as children, from birth until 18 years of age. We recognize that older teenagers, in particular, are very different from other children, but we believe it is important to remember no matter the age of child clients, they remain children in the court system. They do not have the same rights as parents, and their development is not complete. We do not use the word as a form of disrespect, but instead as a form of the highest respect for these people in our lives.

Also note that we often refer to ourselves in the first person. Phil is a psychologist whose significant work experience is in Family Court, and Rebecca is an attorney whose significant work experience is in Dependency Court. We have both experienced working in both types of courts. We regularly provide examples from our work and our lives to help in sharing our information, and most of them come from these experiences. We use our first names to differentiate whose experiences we are citing so you, the reader, can better understand this. Sometimes these examples have been altered slightly to protect confidentiality.

Citations in This Book

We want this book to lead you to accessible information. Although we cite many research articles and books, and the online resources section is full of them, we also recognize it is the twenty-first century and information is readily available that can help you in your practice. Therefore, when we believe the information is beneficial in a more accessible source, we have linked to that. This includes online resources provided by research agencies, professors, and even mainstream articles when the topic we are discussing involves mainstream topics. Some of the articles we reference will also be available in the online materials if they are readily available online without being behind a pay wall.

A Final Note

We urge you, the reader, to consider things you wish we had discussed, problems you encounter, and suggestions you have for our next edition of this book. We know this book is unique, and if you have ideas of topics we need to include or different ways of interacting with child clients, please let us know. We are encouraged by the goal we all share, i.e., improving the representation of children and improving the lives of children in the court system. Feel free to contact either of us if you have ideas, dilemmas, suggestions, or problems you have encountered so we can continue to help those in the field grow and learn from our early writing, as well as practical experiences along the way. Thank you, in advance, for your contributions to our next project.

The Role of Children's Representatives as They Stand Today

This chapter sets the stage for the entire book. We begin by focusing on the various similarities and differences between representing children in family and dependency courts and then outlining the important information you likely never learned in law school about representing children. As you will see, we believe representing children requires an understanding of various psychological and legal principles that will prepare you for each of your cases.

Family and Dependency Law Overlap

A common belief among most family and dependency law lawyers and judicial officers is that there is an impassable chasm between dependency and family law. More recently, there have been endeavors to create unified family courts that include child welfare cases, but those efforts remain isolated, and in practice, professionals still talk about them as though they exist separately from one another and the issues at stake are entirely different. This book aims to dispel that myth and focus on the similar issues that affect children's representation. Therefore, this section discusses the similarities but also the differences so when we do speak of the differences, it is from a place of understanding, not of disrespect of a different kind of law.[8]

Differences between Family and Dependency Law

The fundamental difference between family and dependency law is the involvement, or lack of involvement, by the State. In private family law cases, there is an underlying presumption by society and the court system the child's two parents are "good enough." Dependency law, by contrast, presupposes that either one or both parents is somehow inadequate, potentially unable to parent because of abuse, neglect, or another form of inability such as medical incapacitation. This raises two main differences for lawyers representing children. First, children generally are not allowed to be present in family law courtrooms. By contrast, many dependency courts have begun to allow children over the age of 12—and in some jurisdictions, all children—to be present at all court hearings. Having a client sitting at counsel table with the lawyer changes the dynamics of the case and the argument.

The second major difference is the child's presumptive position in each court system. In family court, it may be presumed the child loves both of his parents and wants to spend as much time as possible with each even when those two parents are in significant conflict. In dependency court, however, children generally are not conflicted between the parents and the State. This is not true in all situations, of course. In many situations, children are removed from their parents and placed with relatives or even foster parents, and the child prefers that to living with her parents. But the underlying assumption is that the child will not feel pulled in multiple directions. This is generally the explanation as to why children more often have the right to be present in dependency court proceedings than they do in family court proceedings.[9]

Perhaps the most important legal difference between family and dependency law is the vague concept of best interests of the children. In family law, because the issue is generally between two parents, the question of best interests of the

---

8. Of course, this will not cover all similarities and differences between the two types of courts. This is simply an overview of why there are similar and different roles for the lawyers to better outline the variety of reasons this book is written as it is.

9. Another difference between the two courts is potentially in how they deal with children who are refusing contact with a parent. That issue will be addressed in Chapter 8.

children is the core tenet in the case. By contrast, in dependency law, reunification and a parent's right to parent is the core interest, so there are times when the best interests of the children is not the central question. While child safety is often the central concern, best interests is not. For example, one could argue that after eighteen months of being in a foster home and visiting a parent only twice a week for the first year of her life, it is in the child's best interests to remain in the foster home. Parents' rights and federal law in the United States, however, trump that analysis and require children to be returned to parents when those parents have taken the necessary steps to minimize the risk to the children when returned.

Although these legal differences can have serious repercussions for the outcome of the case, they do not, in fact, change the way children's representatives should generally act, particularly at the beginning of a case. The underlying similarities between family and dependency law far outweigh the differences when we look at them from a psychological, and not a legal, standpoint.

Similarities between Family and Dependency Law

From a legal perspective, the most common similarity between the two courts is that parents have constitutionally protected rights to parent their children in the United States but children's rights are not constitutionally, or even generally statutorily, protected in the same manner. The underlying legal assumption is, therefore, that legal parents should parent their children with as little interference from the State as possible and each parent should have as much contact as possible when the parents are separated. Legally, parents' rights are fundamental to every aspect of the law, including how to interpret the effects of all the psychological issues addressed.

From a psychological perspective, family and dependency law both revolve around psychological issues such as trauma, domestic violence, abuse (physical, sexual, and emotional), neglect, mental health issues, child development, attachment, resistant children, and substance abuse. Although family law requires an understanding of child development in order to create the most appropriate parenting plans, when children's representatives are appointed in family law cases, it is generally because of some variety of high conflict involving one of the above issues. Thus, from the perspective of representing children, family and dependency law are even more similar than in cases where a child's representative is deemed legally unnecessary in family court.

Perhaps the most obvious similarity, and the one that exists regardless of the intensity of the conflict between the parents, is that all family and dependency law cases begin with some form of trauma. Understanding how to work with children in shock from recent trauma, and a more in-depth analysis of the ACE study and other trauma studies, will be a focus of Chapter 4. We address it here simply to recognize the similarities for the children's experiences between family and dependency courts. In practice, dependency court professionals often balk at cases with undertones of family law, expressing a desire they be handled elsewhere. When cases end and a residential schedule for the children is needed, dependency court professionals use as few judicial and attorney resources as possible to just get the cases out of the courthouse.[10]

Most importantly, family and dependency law are similar in how they differ from other areas of law.

Family Law and Dependency Law Are Different from Other Areas of Law

Family and dependency law, as areas of practice, are fundamentally different from other areas of the law. Children's representatives must understand these underlying differences because they affect the very nature of how the parties and professionals interact when engaged in the court process. Moreover, they also underlie how representation of a child, a nonparty to family law proceedings, in these areas is unique in the legal profession and does not always fit within the confines of what it means to be a lawyer as most children's representatives were trained to be.

Family and Dependency Law Fundamental Differences

Perhaps the most fundamental difference between family law and other areas of the law is that "[j]udgments in child custody cases are, literally, human interest stories."[11] The same is true of dependency law. Thus, instead of fact finders determining whether the facts of the case fulfill the elements of a statute or those outlined in a precedential case, the judge in family and dependency courts must gather the story of a family and determine how that story influences the nebulous concepts of the child's best interests, safety, and welfare, which are influenced by

---

10. This is not true in all jurisdictions, but in jurisdictions where the chasm continues to exist between family and dependency courts, it remains the normal practice.

11. GRAEME AUSTIN, CHILDREN: STORIES THE LAW TELLS 8 (Victoria University Press 1994).

societal and personal biases. There was a time when family law tried to apply presumptions and rules, like other areas of law. The two most notable of these rules have been the father's rights presumption and the tender years' doctrine.[12]

These rules and presumptions were easy to apply, but they prohibited judges from deciding cases differently regardless of the evidence to support a different outcome.[13] What is most interesting is these rules and presumptions created opposite results, more proof that such rules are merely indications of their time and not what works for each family. These rules even appeared in popular culture in the film *Kramer vs. Kramer*, likely a precursor to the changing law— as society saw how inappropriate these rules were, the legal system began to change. As a result, family law evolved beyond these presumptions toward a focus on the child's best interests and welfare. The best interests standard has sparked debate for years:[14]

> The best interests of the child doctrine is at once the most heralded, derided and relied upon standard in family law today. It is heralded because it espouses the best and highest standard; it is derided because it is necessarily subjective; and it is relied upon because there is nothing better.

The concerns raised about its subjectivity are valid, and there are examples of outrageous decisions,[15] but the best interests standard allows judges to see each family and child as an individual story to be written and ultimately allows them to consider each child individually.[16] The standard removed family law from specific rules to human-interest stories. It has, therefore, fundamentally changed everyone's role. It also created a very difficult job for the children's representative, an issue we will discuss in Chapter 10.

---

12. *Id.* at 13–15.

13. *Id.*

14. Lynne Marie Kohm, *Tracing the Foundations of the Best Interests of the Child Standard in American Jurisprudence*, 10 J.L. & FAM. STUD. 337, 337 (2008).

15. *Id.* at 370–76.

16. Austin, *supra* note 11, at 12.

Dependency law is also a nebulous mix of stories masquerading as legal concepts. When children are removed from their parents, there is generally a period of time before they are returned, and in that period of time, parents usually must complete a case plan designed by child welfare professionals and ordered by the judge. While it is generally easy to determine whether someone has attended classes, it is far more difficult to determine whether parents have made the necessary changes such that their children will now be safe in their home. These determinations require more of the crystal ball approach than the past determination of inappropriate conduct. Some jurisdictions might attempt to alleviate some of this confusion with strict rules and timelines, but those approaches tend to miss the mark and result in either draconian removal of children or placement of children back with parents who are fundamentally unable to care for their children because they participated in some classes but failed to show they benefited from them. As you will read further and as some of the critical psychological issues are addressed, this nuanced approach will make more sense.

The traditional Anglo adversarial model of jurisprudence outside of family and dependency law is fundamentally unable to address the full needs of the family. The adversarial model is a zero-sum approach, which requires a winner and a loser. Families, however, are not zero-sum. Children are not property to be won or lost by their parents either between parents or between safety and the love of a family. In other areas of law, litigants may leave the courtroom and never interact again, but families are living entities that continue to exist, albeit in a new form, after the final judgment. This is true even in cases where children are adopted or reunify with their parents; their time away from their new families, even if only the first few hours of life, inherently changes how they interact with their new families in the future.

In addition, the adversarial model focuses almost exclusively on past events. Family and dependency law, by contrast, focus on the future. It is more like informed fortune-telling than a win-lose legal battle. The current family law system, however, asks parents and families to predict and enter an unknown future without giving them the proper tools to do so. It pits them against each other and then expects them to get along once the court orders have been signed. It severs relationships at one moment in time, usually the moment with the most unresolved animosity within the family, and instead of resolving the problems from the past, the past becomes irrelevant and is never addressed.[17] Thus, these

---

17. Clare Huntington, *Repairing Family Law*, 57 Duke L.J. 1245, 1249 (2008).

unresolved issues permeate the process, and they often continue to permeate the newly structured family going forward.[18]

Here exists another difference between family and dependency law. While certainly broken, the goal of dependency courts is to reunify and repair a broken family. Services are offered throughout the case in the hope the family can repair the pain caused by the trauma prior to the State's intervention as well as the trauma caused by the State's intervention. Of course, it is impossible to undo the previous damage entirely, but the underlying intention to heal—as opposed to break apart—makes exiting a successful dependency court case sometimes less damaging than exiting a family law case. Of course, many dependency court cases begin while parents are together and end with them separated, so the outcome of cases is often similar.

These emotional issues, which the law prides itself on finding irrelevant, are far from irrelevant to the families. Instead, every decision parents make originates from an emotional response. This is only natural, and the effects of the trauma on child clients will be more fully addressed in a later chapter, but here it is important to recognize that in a separation, the only basis parents have to stand on is emotion. The decision about how to raise children and where they should live has not, until very recently in human evolution, been made in a courtroom. Instead, the rearing of children has been an instinct passed down through generations, one we feel before we think. The legal system, however, does not work on that level. Instead, it prides itself on logic and rules, the opposite of how families operate.

Children in family law cases are removed from the legal system by an additional layer; they are not parties to the case. This is not necessarily true in dependency court cases. In family law cases, children's best interests are central, but children have no legal standing in the case. Thus, the most legally significant person is not a party and traditionally has had no model for integrating into the system. When representing children in family law cases, therefore, the child's representative must consider how a nonparty to a case must navigate a legal system that makes little sense to the parties and almost no sense to the children involved. That would be difficult enough, but there are additional procedural differences between lawyers for adults and lawyers for children appointed in family and dependency court cases that make this navigation significantly more nontraditional.

---

18. *Id.* at 1250.

The Procedural Differences of a Lawyer for the Child[19]

The procedural aspects of lawyering consider how lawyers are appointed and how they interact with their clients. These procedural differences significantly influence the lawyer-client relationship and the lawyer's role vis-à-vis the court.

The major procedural differences between lawyers for children and lawyers for adults immediately flip the lawyer-client model upside down. Generally, adults are in court either by their choosing or through their own alleged or real actions.[20] The parents in family law cases choose to have children, and when they are unable to agree on the best parenting model, they must go to court.[21] Parents in dependency court cases have generally made a parenting mistake that renders the child unsafe.[22] Thus, the children in both family and child welfare cases are involved because of their parents' actions. They do not choose to enter the system that will eventually determine their fate. A lawyer appointed to represent these children must first explain to the client why the court is part of his life before reaching the substantive issues regarding the actual lawyer-client relationship. It is not uncommon for children to become bewildered as to why they are in a courthouse or why so many strange adults have spoken to them about things society generally teaches children not to discuss with strangers.[23]

Adults usually choose their own lawyers, except in cases of indigence where they might have a lawyer appointed for them. When choosing a lawyer, adults

---

19. Although much of this book will address all manner of children's representatives, including GALs, this section specifically looks at these roles from the perspective of lawyers and legal ethics.

20. For example, a business client brings a suit against another business or the government charges a person with a crime.

21. Parents involved in the court process may argue they do not specifically choose to disagree about their children, but their entry into the court process is a choice on some level.

22. In jurisdictions where a child welfare case can go forward with a non-offending parent, this is not entirely true.

23. This is especially true in cases of sexual abuse of one sibling when there are no allegations of sexual abuse of the other siblings. The representative for the non-abused siblings has a very difficult road to navigate—how to explain to a child the court is involved in his life for safety reasons when the child has never experienced a feeling of not being safe, and the representative does not want to inform the child that his sibling has been sexually abused. From a procedural aspect, these are some of the most difficult cases for children's representatives to navigate.

presumably take the time to find the most qualified person to represent them and with whom they will personally interact well. In contrast, the first time a child client meets his lawyer occurs after the lawyer's appointment. Rather than a client walking into the lawyer's office seeking services, the lawyer appears to the child and announces, "Hello, I am your lawyer." The child may not even know what a lawyer is. Thus, before any explanation of the role has occurred and before the relationship has started, the presumptive balance between lawyer and client has been inverted. The potential confusion to your child client is enormous, and recognition of this inherent disconnect before you enter the child client's life is critical. Adults who choose their lawyers choose them because they trust them. Children have no reason to trust their representatives, and often they have every reason not to trust adults outside their familial circle.

In addition, children's representatives first learn about their clients from outside sources, including the child's parents and court documents written by other professionals. Sometimes children's representatives speak with teachers, grandparents, and counselors before meeting the child. They seek out and obtain records and information regarding the child. Thus, at the first meeting with a child client, the representative has already learned about the child, but never from the child's perspective—always from the point of view of someone else involved in the system, and as we will discuss later in the book, all people bring biases to their work.[24] Thus, the first information children's representatives receive about their child clients begins from a biased perspective provided by others.[25] As we will discuss throughout this book, learning about your child client from his perspective is critical to your representation.

In contrast, lawyers who represent adults usually obtain case information directly from their client when their client enters their office for the first time and explains his version of the facts. A lawyer for an adult first understands his client influenced only by his client's views. This dynamic undermines one of the cornerstones of the lawyer-client relationship by asking the lawyer to learn about

---

24. Bias is not used here as a judgment about the person's views of the child. Everyone's views are tainted by his own perceptions about the world. It is used simply to point out that the lawyer learns about the child from the ways other people see the child rather than learning about the child from his own interaction with the child. A more complete description of different types of bias and its potential influence in our work will be discussed in Chapter 11.

25. This oddity of representation also appears frequently for parents' attorneys in child welfare cases.

the client from people other than the client, including some people who have their own agenda in the case that may not correlate with that of the child client.

Similarly, adult clients generally determine the goals and scope of representation. The lawyer advises and counsels the client, but the client generally makes the final determination about the goals to be achieved,[26] though not necessarily about the best path for achieving those goals. The academic literature on lawyers for children suggests that at least with respect to children who are old enough to direct counsel, they should be able to determine the goals of the representation.[27] In addition, the American Bar Association's Rules of Professional Conduct state that lawyers should attempt to have as normal a relationship as possible with child clients.[28] This argument, however, ignores how substantive law controls the lawyer's role, even a child client old enough to direct counsel.

For example, in the United States, many states have statutes providing for the appointment of a "best interests attorney," so even if the lawyer and the child client prefer the lawyer to fill a different role, the lawyer's duty is to provide evidence to the court and advocate for the child's best interests. This is also true in dependency law where federal law requires the appointment of a GAL for the child. Many states interpret that to mean only best interests representation or some form of "dual" role. Therefore, the two people engaged in the relationship generally cannot determine the lawyer-client relationship.

Lawyers for adults usually represent only one client in any particular case, and before they can represent multiple clients, they must reasonably believe they can navigate the potential conflicts and have consent from all of the involved clients.[29] By contrast, lawyers presumptively represent all siblings in a case regardless of client consent. This issue will be examined more fully in Chapter 10, but we mention it here as a procedural difference of representing child clients.

The courtroom provides another venue where the roles between lawyers for children and lawyers for adults differ procedurally. Adult clients usually come to court for hearings. Children, by contrast, rarely come to court in family law cases, and often their presence is prohibited. In dependency court cases, they are more likely allowed to be present, but each jurisdiction handles children's presence in court differently. The child's lack of physical presence in the courtroom

---

26. Of course, if the goals are illegal, the lawyer is not bound to follow them.

27. Barbara A. Atwood, *Representing Children Who Can't or Won't Direct Counsel: Best Interests Lawyering or No Lawyering at All?*, 53 ARIZ. L.R. 381, 382–83 (2011).

28. MODEL RULES OF PROF'L CONDUCT R. 1.14 (2009).

29. *Id.*, R. 1.7.

changes the lawyer's role in two significant ways. First, lawyers cannot consult with the client as the case progresses in the courtroom, so if new evidence arises or new ideas are proposed, the lawyer cannot consult with his client. Lawyers for children, therefore, must understand their child clients' complete perspectives better than they understand their adult clients with whom they can consult continuously. Second, the lawyer must ensure the child's lack of presence does not result in a situation where the child is "out of sight, out of mind." It is easy to generalize about someone who is not physically present, so the lawyer must continually remind the Court (and perhaps the parties) about the specific child involved. When a child is in the courtroom and emotionally reacting to what is happening, judges and parties respond differently.

Finally, the process of becoming a lawyer for children is more involved than becoming a lawyer generally. In many jurisdictions, to be appointed as a lawyer for children, you need to go through a process that places you on a list to represent children. It is never a mistake that someone is appointed to represent a child; instead, it is the culmination of not only completing law school, becoming a member of the Bar, and completing required training but also of consciously choosing to work with children and represent them. This appointment process helps ensure that lawyers who represent children want to be there. It also helps ensure they expect the difficulties such appointment entails.

These procedural differences between lawyers for children appointed by the Court and lawyers for adults chosen by the adults impact every aspect of the role, and children's lawyers must always be conscientious of them. Thus, when discussing the role of lawyers for children, one must start by recognizing these differences while also recognizing that lawyers must act as lawyers within the legal parameters of these cases.

These procedural differences influence substantive law and vice versa. The following section examines an overview of the substantive law that lawyers and courts must follow and its impact on the role of the child's lawyer.

The Tired Debates

The role of children and their lawyers in family and dependency law cases has been debated for decades. As legislation has moved away from rules and presumptions, the question must be answered, "How does a court effectively determine a child's best interests?" Thus, the debates regarding lawyers for children do not always start and end with the actual role. They also focus on the child's participation in the system and whether the child should have a lawyer at all.

These tangential discussions have pigeon-holed the discussion about the actual role of the lawyer for the child into one focused almost exclusively on the child's views and wishes rather than a holistic lawyer for the child. The next chapter provides background on these basic assumptions before looking at how they have influenced the legislation and guidelines.

Unique Questions Related to Our Work with Children | 2

Children are inherently different from adults. The legal system recognizes this in numerous ways. But it also tries to fit children into a system not designed for them. This chapter examines several ways children's unique situations affect your representation. While this book is not specifically about the academic debates about representing children and when children should have representatives, these are important issues to discuss to lay a foundation for why it is important you understand the issues we address in Sections II and III of the book.

Should Children Have a Voice?

No one would ever ask whether an adult central to a legal case should have a voice in that process. The question of children's voice, however, dates back over sixty years. The question over whether children should have a voice at all in family and dependency cases in most of the world is no longer an issue because of the United Nations Convention on the Rights of the Child (UNCRC). Article 12 of the UNCRC provides children the right to be heard in all judicial proceedings that affect them, and countries around the world have found ways to implement it for purposes of family and dependency cases.[30] In addition, although the United States has not ratified the UNCRC, the factors judges consider in most states include some reference to the child's wishes or preferences,[31] and federal law requires all children have a guardian *ad litem* (GAL) appointed in all dependency court cases to give voice to the children involved.

The disagreement over the weight to afford children's voice rests on two major presumptions, neither of which can be fully supported. First, children may not be sufficiently mature to express views, wishes, or preferences. This argument concludes that it is a pointless exercise to attempt to consider the child's voice when the child can contribute nothing to the decision maker. Even preverbal children, however, can shed light on the case through their actions, and understanding the child's unique circumstances "may lead to creative solutions in the child's interest."[32] We will address these issues in depth in later chapters with more specific examples.

A second argument assumes the concept of voice means children are afforded the choice, which some people argue causes more harm than good.[33] Research, however, continues to show that children want to be involved in the process.[34] Similarly, there is concern, especially in the United States, that affording children too much say can undermine parents' rights to raise their children as they deem appropriate.[35] But "there does not have to be a conflict."[36] Children's voice, in

---

30. Rebecca M. Stahl, *Don't Forget about Me: Implementing Article 12 of the United Nations Convention on the Rights of the Child*, 24 ARIZ. J. INT'L & COMP. L. 803 (2008).

31. *See, e.g.,* ARIZ. REV. STAT. § 25-403(A) ("The court shall consider . . . (2) The wishes of the child as to the custodian."); Rev. CODE OF WASH. ANN. § 26.09.187(3)(a)(vi).

32. *American Bar Association Section of Family Law Standards of Practice for Lawyers Representing Children in Custody Cases*, 37 FAM. L.Q. 129, 135 (2003) [hereinafter ABA Guidelines].

33. PATRICK PARKINSON & JUDY CASHMORE, THE VOICE OF A CHILD IN FAMILY LAW DISPUTES 8 (Oxford University Press 2008); Richard A. Warshak, *Payoffs and Pitfalls of Listening to Children*, 52 J. FAM. REL. 373 (2003); Robert E. Emery, *Children's Voices: Listening—And Deciding—Is an Adult Responsibility*, 45 ARIZ. L. REV. 621 (2003).

34. Nicola Taylor, *What Do We Know about Involving Children and Young People in Family Law Decision Making? A Research Update*, 20 AUSTL. J. OF FAM. L. 5 (2006).

35. Linda D. Elrod, *Client-Directed Lawyers for Children: It Is the "Right" Thing to Do*, 27 PACE L. REV. 869, at 889 (2007).

36. *Id.*

whatever form, is only one piece of the evidence judges consider,[37] so when children have voice, they simply participate; they do not decide.

Moreover, some children may not want to choose between their parents. The problem in United States family law cases is that many statutes have the child's wishes regarding parenting time as one of the factors the judge must consider.[38] By contrast, in New Zealand, the legislation focuses on views, not preference between parents.[39] Understanding the distinction between views and wishes is fundamental to understanding the role the lawyer for the child should have, so the New Zealand approach is examined in more detail than it otherwise would be. This distinction opens the door to moving beyond the outdated debate between client-directed and best interests representation and into a place where the debate surrounding lawyers for children exists in a more holistic manner. We believe, except in extreme circumstances, it is not appropriate to ask children with whom they want to live, and certainly never as an opening question to a child.

Instead, the word *views* opens the door to greater participation by the child without having to make a decision between two opposing outcomes. Judge Peter Boshier, from New Zealand, defines the distinction between views and wishes as:[40]

> The term "wishes" is somewhat whimsical in its connotations, and detracts from giving weight to the child's perspective. The term "views" implies the child has a greater capacity to understand their situation and form legitimate "views." The term "view" can also be less qualitative than a "wish." It implies children have a perspective, without implying that they want something to happen—such as choosing one parent over another.

---

37. PARKINSON & CASHMORE, *supra* note 33, at 116.

38. *See, e.g.,* ARIZ. REV. STAT. § 25-403.

39. CARE OF CHILDREN ACT (2004), *available at* www.legislation.govt.nz/act/public/2004/0090/latest/whole.html.

40. Judge Peter Boshier "Involving Children in the Family Court" (paper presented to New Zealand Law Society Conference Family Law: The New Era—Professionalism in the Family Court, Wellington, October 2005).

More appropriate than views, even, is the term *perspectives*:[41]

> First, it provides information which will help to assess how the competing proposals for parenting arrangements will impact upon the children without needing to ask them, even obliquely, to express a view about the different options and choices. . . . Second, children's perspectives may assist in resolving the dispute. . . . Third, focusing on children's perspectives rather than their wishes avoids the pitfalls involved in making children de facto decision-makers or placing upon them the intolerable burden of choice between their parents' proposals. . . . Fourth, seeing the issue of participation in terms of perspectives rather than wishes allows the child's voice to be heard at whatever age and stage they may have reached without worrying about their maturity. . . . Finally, seeing children's participation in terms of children's views and perspectives rather than children's wishes offers a potential resolution about the role of children's legal representatives in family law proceedings.

A child's unique perspective is important, not the child's decision-making capabilities. Thus, the discussion must shift to a focus on the child's perspectives rather than wishes or preferences and perhaps even views. Then it does not matter what developmental age the child is; what matters is the child's ability to express feelings, a subject we will cover throughout this book. Further, focusing on perspectives rather than wishes works in dependency cases as well; more is at stake than only with whom a child will be living.

When discussing the role of representing children, it is important to determine the perspectives, views, and wishes you need to present to the court. Understanding specific jurisdictions' approaches is necessary, but the children's representative can greatly affect how judges interpret children's positions by changing the language used to express it. This is, potentially, the single greatest effect children's representatives can have on the in-court process—providing a container in which the judge can best understand how the child sees the world. Thus, understanding the psychological issues affecting your ability to do this is the focus of Section II of this book.

By focusing on perspectives rather than wishes, the issue moves from one of a zero-sum question to a view of the child's unique position in the family and the world. When statutes focus on wishes and preferences, children's representatives

---

41. Parkinson & Cashmore, *supra* note 33, at 203–04.

focus their role on one aspect of lawyering, which makes it more difficult, though not impossible, to provide holistic representation. It ultimately places the child in a bind between participating in ways he may not want or be left out completely. The concept of voice must continue to be examined, and even though the debate about whether children should have a voice seems to be diminishing, the role of that voice in the legal process, in both family and dependency courts, continues to percolate.

Children in dependency cases face a similar issue. While it is true that many of them want to be returned to their parents, their perspectives on how their parents are doing is crucial to the case, and rarely do their views on the case come into play. Adults often want to protect children from the issues in the case, but they usually understand what is going on and have the most pertinent information to how their family has changed, or not. Rebecca often asks clients, including some very young clients, whether they have noticed a difference in how their parents have behaved since the beginning of the case.

The next debate focuses on how to get the child's voice before the court. Should a lawyer be appointed to fill that role? If appointed, what is the proper role of that lawyer, and is it limited by the child's voice?

Should Children Have Lawyers?

Adults involved in legal proceedings either have legal counsel or represent themselves. But there remains an ongoing debate about whether children should have lawyers, and therefore a seat at the table, in family law cases. In dependency cases, the question is answered, but only in terms of GALs. Not every jurisdiction provides lawyers for children in dependency cases. This section argues that children's lawyers, and therefore representation, serves a unique and valuable purpose in both family and dependency cases, although we recognize that in family cases, children would likely need representation only in cases that are high conflict or have critical issues (e.g., domestic violence, substance use/abuse, serious mental health issues, or relocation) before the court. We believe this conversation is an important part of the book because understanding why children have lawyers helps you better understand what your role ultimately should be.

Before tackling the question of whether lawyers are appropriate for children in family and dependency cases, it is important to understand lawyers' general substantive roles.[42] Lawyers are central to our modern view of jurisprudence,

---

42. All children will have some form of representative in dependency cases, but many jurisdictions continue to use non-legally trained GALs. The question of whether these people should, instead, be legally trained, is the focus of this section for dependency cases.

but they are a relatively recent phenomenon.[43] In general, people hire lawyers when they have a problem they cannot solve on their own.[44] For example, a criminal defendant needs someone to protect his rights, a business owner needs help writing employment contracts, and heirs need help navigating the probate process. In all those situations, lawyers are asked to be educators, counselors, and advocates.

In addition, lawyers are the bridge between citizens and the law. Law can be described as rules created by legislatures, which makes the lawyer's role "simply to advise the unfortunate individuals [the client] to whom these often arbitrary, inconsistent, antiquated, threatening rules apply, as to precisely what their options are, and provide educated guesses as to the likely results of a given course of action."[45] Stated differently, lawyers are the bridge between the client and this arbitrary system of laws by helping clients understand their rights within the system. Lawyers also help the legal system understand the clients by preparing the clients to present the appropriate information to the Court in the appropriate manner.

Thus, lawyers are educators, advocates, and a two-way bridge between the client and the legal process. As noted above, children in family and dependency cases present a different scenario. Traditionally, a child's parents are his educator, advocate, and bridge to the adult world. But when children are involved with the legal profession, the parents often lose sight of their children's needs or have had their parental rights limited in some fashion. Thus, the question is whether the government will enter the family and appoint a lawyer to represent the child. Jurisdictions around the world offer different answers and provide different rationales for their conclusions.

In the United States, even though every state has a provision for appointing a representative for children in family law cases, rarely is that person appointed automatically and even more rarely is the person appointed as a traditional lawyer.[46] Most commonly, statutes allow for the appointment of a GAL, whose only duty is to present evidence on the best interests of the child when certain parameters are met and usually within the judge's discretion. GALs are not considered beneficial by everyone, and there are many arguments that they create more harm than good.[47]

---

43. Suri Ratnapala, Jurisprudence 195 (Cambridge University Press 2009).

44. Michael Lamb, *It's No Joke*, 24 Mont. Lawyer 1, at 7 (1999).

45. *Id.* at 6.

46. Sometimes the person appointed is not legally trained and is a lay advocate.

47. Richard Ducote, *Guardians Ad Litem in Private Custody Litigation: The Case for Abolition*, 3 Loy. J. Pub. Int. L. 106, at 115–16 (2002).

All children in the United States are appointed a GAL in dependency court cases as prescribed by the Child Abuse Prevention and Treatment Act (CAPTA). The CAPTA does not, however, define the role to be performed by the GAL. Instead, it requires either the appointment of an attorney or a Court Appointed Special Advocate (CASA) to obtain a first-hand, clear understanding of the situation and provide recommendations regarding the child's best interests. It further requires the GAL be provided training in child development. Jurisdictions differ in whether they appoint legally trained GALs or CASAs to the role of CAPTA GAL.

The American Academy of Matrimonial Guidelines [AAML Guidelines], issued in 2009, argue that the lack of children's representation is good for family law. They state lawyers for children should be the exception rather than the rule because litigation is already too costly, which creates a disparity between those who can afford lawyers and those who are self-represented.[48] The AAML focuses attention on the problems arising from lawyers for children who may be the only lawyer in a case, and it believes too many lawyers slow down the system, which creates harm and causes an unnecessary increase in cost.[49]

The AAML raises the traditional arguments against lawyers for children. Practitioners often specify an additional argument that there is an "overlap between the functions performed by some professionals," so lawyers for children are not always necessary.[50] In addition, the litany of professionals children encounter when involved in these cases can become extreme, so the addition of the lawyer for the child is often viewed as one more professional who adds nothing except another person the child needs to see.

We believe these concerns are valid, but they do not offer a complete picture. Most importantly, they are exacerbated when lawyers do not have a clear indication of the child's role or their own role in representing the child.[51] Thus, the first step to ameliorating the problems is to define the lawyer's role clearly, and it must include roles not served by other professionals that also benefit everyone involved.

---

48. *American Academy of Matrimonial Lawyers Representing Children: Standards for Attorneys for Children in Custody or Visitation Proceedings with Commentary*, 22 J. Am. Acad. Matrimonial Lawyers 227, at 229 (2009) [hereinafter AAML Standards].

49. *Id.* at 230.

50. *Id.* at 16.

51. Barbara A. Atwood, *Representing Children: The Ongoing Search for Clear and Workable Standards*, 19 J. Am. Acad. Matrimonial L. 183, at 183 (2005).

Unlike the AAML Guidelines, the American Bar Association Guidelines [ABA Guidelines], issued in 2003, suggest there are specific times when lawyers for children are useful—and perhaps even necessary.[52] The ABA Guidelines enumerate factors to determine whether a lawyer should be appointed for children.[53] The ABA Guidelines suggest considering avenues to avoid appointment, but the following types of cases may require the appointment of a lawyer for the child:[54]

a: Consideration of extraordinary remedies such as supervised visitation, terminating or suspending parenting time, or awarding custody or visitation to a non-parent;

b: Relocation that could substantially reduce the child's time with a parent or sibling;

c: The child's concerns or views;

d: Harm to the child from illegal or excessive drug or alcohol abuse by a child or a party;

e: Disputed paternity;

f: Past or present child abduction or risk of future abduction;

g: Past or present family violence;

h: Past or present mental health problems of the child or a party;

i: Special physical, educational, or mental health needs of a child that require investigation or advocacy;

j: A high level of acrimony;

k: Inappropriate adult influence or manipulation;

l: Interference with custody or parenting time;

m: A need for more evidence relevant to the best interests of the child;

n: A need to minimize the harm to the child from the processes of family separation and litigation; or

o: Specific issues that would best be addressed by a lawyer appointed to address only those issues, which the court should specify in its appointment order.

---

52. ABA Guidelines, *supra* note 32.

53. These factors apply when state law does not require, but still permits, appointment of a lawyer for the child.

54. ABA Guidelines, *supra* note 32, at 152–53.

Although this list covers a broad range of cases, the commentary specifies that a failure to appoint is not a violation of the child's rights.[55] Therefore, the ABA Guidelines do not prioritize appointing a lawyer for the child. While they appear more open to the idea, they still operate on the assumption that lawyers are only necessary sometimes and only when the legal issues are most difficult. These assumptions ignore the benefit to the child the lawyer provides. Moreover, research suggests that most children react negatively to their parents' divorce, at least during the litigation phase of the case, even if such a reaction is more likely in many of the types of cases enumerated by the ABA Guidelines.[56] Thus, a lawyer for the child could be important in many cases.

There are, of course, benefits that lawyers for children bring to the entire process:[57]

> Children's attorneys can enhance the court's understanding of the child's perspective, facilitate the introduction of evidence, sharpen the presentation of factual and legal issues, promote dispute resolution, and protect the child from the harms of litigation itself.

These benefits will be more specifically addressed in the next chapter, but here it is important to point out that from the family and children's perspectives, each child's personality and situation is unique. Having someone provide that unique perspective to the court should be important in any case.

This section addresses why a lawyer is the best person to fill that role, especially if people believe lawyers for children provide services similar to those of other professionals in the system. Unlike other professionals, lawyers may present evidence in court and call witnesses, and they have the training to determine what is necessary to navigate the legal system.[58] Professor Barbara Atwood's research of Arizona judges suggests judges prefer when legally trained people help them focus the evidence, specifically in cases where neither of the parents

---

55. "Appointment of a lawyer is a tool to protect the child and provide information to help assist courts in deciding a case in accordance with the child's best interests. A decision not to appoint should not be regarded as actionably denying a child's procedural or substantive rights under these Standards, except as provided by state law." *Id.* at 154.

56. Stahl, *supra* note 30, at 45.

57. Atwood, *supra* note 27, at 385.

58. Atwood, *supra* note 27, at 397.

have lawyers.[59] In addition, lawyers appointed to represent children are the only people in the case whose only agenda is the child.[60]

Others argue lawyers are not necessary if a psychologist is involved. However, those are two distinct roles, as it is the lawyer's duty to present the child's views to the Court and a custody evaluator's duty to evaluate the family and the child's perspectives. A similar argument can be made for all aspects of the lawyer for the child's role. The lawyer's duty is to help the Court make sense of the child's world from the child's perspective within the context of the law. Therefore, it is essential that the person appointed for the child be a lawyer, one who understands the child but who also understands the underlying legal issues involved and can present the child's individuality to the Court as well as navigate the legal system.

Most importantly, lawyers for children are the only professionals in the court process whose sole focus is the child.

Best Interests

No book on representing children can be complete without a discussion about the differences between representing children's best interests and representing their wishes. Some of this conversation will take place in Chapter 10 on ethics, but we wanted to place it here at the beginning because so many people believe it to be such a crucial piece of the discussion about lawyers for children. It is important to note this is the only area of the law where this is a question. Except in cases of competency, which would typically occur with severe cognitive problems or severe mental illness, lawyers are always client-directed. It is only children's unique situation, and society's beliefs about children's abilities and value, that create this debate.

To begin, we believe this conversation is important, and Rebecca has written on it and presented on it numerous times at CLE conferences. But in the day-to-day life of being a lawyer for children, especially with respect to the model we are presenting here, the two types of practice end up being very similar. Research

---

59. *Id.* at 398 ("As one judge put it, 'I want a lawyer, someone who can present evidence, file motions, cross-examine witnesses. That's essential.'").

60. Arguably, the court could appoint a lay advocate to fulfill the role of being the only person whose agenda is the child, but generally people who have no legal training misunderstand the legal process, which may lead to more miscommunication between the court, the parties, and the child.

done in Tucson supports this as well.[61] The majority of a lawyer's work is the same regardless of the type of appointment. For example, the lawyer can subpoena evidence, write motions, examine witnesses, and gather information about his client regardless of whether he is appointed as a client-directed or best interests lawyer.

The rest of this book focuses on the importance of getting to know your child clients and understanding their perspectives. These issues are important regardless of your role. Yes, your ultimate job in the courtroom might change depending on the type of appointment, but there are pros and cons to both roles, which will be discussed in Chapter 10. What is important here is to understand that the main purpose of the best interests role is because there is a societal belief that children are not mature enough to direct counsel or they will act in ways that are not in their best interests.

Let us be clear—everyone has moments of immaturity, and most humans make decisions against their best interests nearly every day. How many of us eat the wrong foods, fail to exercise, drive too fast, and fight with our loved ones despite knowing it is not healthy? Why should children be treated differently only because their brains are not fully developed?

And yet, family and juvenile law themselves, as described in the previous chapter, are unique within the law and require a fundamentally different understanding of what the legal system does. These two types of law have a way of putting children in situations unique not only to childhood but also to these situations. They put children in the middle in ways unlike no other parties in other cases. Thus, the best interests model can be used as a shield, a way to protect the child from the parties in the case who could use the children as pawns in their games.

Despite years of study, gut instincts that tell her one thing, and years of practice in a variety of jurisdictions and roles, Rebecca has concluded there are pros and cons to both roles. Unique aspects of each make it beneficial to the lawyer and the child. The debates will continue, and you likely have your preference of roles, but for the rest of the book, before we come back to these issues in Chapter 10, we invite you to set those preconceived notions aside and change your perspective to one of connecting to your child clients as themselves regardless of what role you think is best. This book is not about that issue. This book is about ways to help you get to know your clients, and the various psychological issues

---

61. Jennifer Duchschere et al., *Guardians* Ad Litem *and Children's Attorneys in Arizona: A Qualitative Examination of the Roles*, 68 Juv. & Fam. Ct. J. 33–50 (2017).

they face better, so no matter what role you play, you can do it from a more informed and more connected place.

Children are unique. Family and dependency law are unique. These facts raise issues that make representing children one of the most debated issues in the legal profession. But perhaps the most important aspect to remember throughout this book and throughout your practice is that it is an honor afforded to few. Regardless of whether society, or even the legal profession, believes children should have a voice at the table or whether they believe your job should exist, the truth is it does. And you have an opportunity to work with some of the most interesting people in the system in a type of law that bridges stories and psychology and the law. Most importantly, from our perspective, you have the opportunity to help children at a time in their lives when they are particularly vulnerable. You are the one person there solely to listen, honor, and help your client through her struggles, just when she needs it most. We hope the rest of this book provides you with better insight and perspective for doing that job no matter the role your particular jurisdiction has chosen for you.

Imagining a New Role | 3

This chapter presents a new paradigm for the role of the lawyer for the child in both family and dependency law cases. It views the role from a conceptual model based upon the lawyer as the child's imaginary friend and focuses on reaching beyond the debates between best interests and client-directed lawyers into a new way of viewing the role to best help your child clients navigate the legal process. This model encompasses the ideas we will present in the rest of the book relating to the underlying issues lawyers for children must understand to fully represent children as clients, but we present it here as a backdrop to the rest of the book.

The concept of an imaginary friend exists in psychological literature as well as popular culture.[62] This chapter first examines the limited

---

62. The psychological literature about imaginary friends often refers to them as imaginary companions or simply as ICs. Although that phrase sounds more sophisticated, it does not cover the underlying rationale for this conceptual model; the child understands what an imaginary friend is. Although adults may attempt to give the concept an adult name, we will refer to the model as the imaginary friend model.

psychological data as well as societal conceptions of imaginary friends and then presents an overview of how to translate the imaginary friend model into a role for lawyers. This fundamental framework relies on the psychological aspects addressed in the rest of the book.

The Imaginary Friend's Role

In popular culture, imaginary friends "are often depicted as the inventions of lonely, unhappy children."[63] Psychological research has grown and developed during the past twenty to twenty-five years.[64] Today the psychological consensus says imaginary friends, although not universal, exist for all types of children and not only in lonely or extremely creative children.[65] Today psychologists believe having an imaginary friend is "healthy and relatively common."[66] Moreover, "[c]hildren with [imaginary friends] are able to distinguish fantasy from reality as well as their peers,"[67] and some research suggests that even some adults have imaginary friends.[68] Thus, imaginary friends exist in a broader range of people than psychologists once thought, and there is no single defining characteristic about who has them. Imaginary friends do, however, often fill similar roles for those who have them.

---

63. Marjorie Taylor, Imaginary Companions and the Children Who Create Them 3 (Oxford University Press 1999).

64. Stephanie M. Carlson et al., *The Characteristics and Correlates of Fantasy in School-Age Children: Imaginary Companions, Impersonation, and Social Understanding*, 40 Dev. Psychol. 1173, at 1173 (2004).

65. Eva Hoff, *A Friend Living Inside Me—The Forms and Functions of Imaginary Companions*, 24 Imagination, Cognition and Personality 151, at 152 (2004–2005); H Rouse et al., *Prevalence of Imaginary Companions in a Normal Child Population*, 27 Child: Care, Health and Dev. 13, at 20–21 (2001); Dr. Karen Majors, *My Pretend Friend*, BBC Radio 4, *available at* news.bbc.co.uk/today/hi/today/newsid_9359000/9359360.stm.

66. Taylor, *supra* note 63, at 4.

67. Lise A. McLewin & Robert T. Muller, *Childhood Trauma, Imaginary Companions, and the Development of Pathological Dissociation*, 11 Aggression and Violent Behavior 531, at 538 (2006).

68. David Pearson et al., *Prevalence of Imaginary Companions in a Normal Child population*, 27 Child: Care, Health and Dev. 15, at 20–21 (2001).

A significant amount of the research conducted on imaginary friends focuses on why children create them and what their role is in the child's life. The defined roles are numerous, but underlying the roles is a more fundamental aspect of imaginary friends. They "are very real to the children who create them,"[69] and they "are assumed to remain within the child's control, and to be used in a beneficial manner for the child."[70] Thus, children use imaginary friends, fully aware of their imaginariness, to benefit them in some way.[71] This understanding is crucial to how lawyers can use them as a model when representing children.

A Variety of Roles

The psychological research regarding imaginary friends emphasizes the variety of roles they have. The variety suggests children find it "easier to achieve different objectives with imaginary support."[72] The core function of an imaginary friend, therefore, is to support the child's objectives regarding why the imaginary friend exists in the first place, and for each child those objectives will be different.

Several researchers have surveyed the available research and compiled the emergent themes and roles for imaginary friends. We will examine the procedural and substantive roles imaginary friends play in children's lives. Each section will consider the psychological research as well as the popular culture understanding of imaginary friends and what makes them different from non-imaginary friends.[73]

---

69. McLewin & Muller, *supra* note 67, at 533.

70. *Id.* at 535.

71. Hoff, *supra* note 65, at 174. Adults, like children, experience imaginary events as real. For example, many adults will imagine a conversation in the future and get nervous symptoms just thinking about it. They know that the conversation is just in their head and has not happened yet, but they experience real and palpable symptoms as a result. Thus, it is not uncommon for people to experience reality through their imagination, whether child or adult.

72. *Id.* at 174.

73. We will not refer to non-imaginary friends as "real" friends because imaginary friends are real to the child, even if the child knows that the friend exists only in his imagination. Therefore, we will refer to them simply as non-imaginary friends.

The Procedural Roles

Imaginary friends appear in a variety of popular culture,[74] and often the imaginary friend has a tangential role or exists in the plot simply as a memory. By contrast, the imaginary friend moves to center stage in the comic strip *Calvin and Hobbes*, in which Calvin, a 6-year-old boy, interacts with his stuffed tiger, Hobbes, as though he were a real being. Sometimes Hobbes embodies the persona of a tiger who can eat people or help Calvin with his homework. Hobbes only appears in his stuffed forms in frames where adults or other characters appear. However, when Calvin and Hobbes are alone, Hobbes grows taller than Calvin, and he walks, talks, and sometimes even physically assaults Calvin. The interaction between Calvin and Hobbes directly reflects the procedural differences between imaginary and non-imaginary friends.

The first procedural implication of imaginary friends is perhaps the most fundamental. The adults in the child's life may know about the imaginary friend,[75] but even if they do, the imaginary friend is the child's friend and no one else's. When other people are nearby, the imaginary friend can be a stuffed tiger, but when he is alone with the child, he becomes animated and has a personality all his own.[76] Accordingly, unlike non-imaginary friends, imaginary friends are always available to the child. No matter where the child is or what is happening in his life, the imaginary friend can appear and stand with the child. Whenever the child decides he needs the imaginary friend, for whatever reason, the imaginary friend is there, and other people in the child's life cannot take that relationship away from the child.

In addition, the relationship between children and their imaginary friends is a one-way street. Imaginary friends exist exclusively for the child. By contrast, non-imaginary friend relationships are two-way streets. Aristotle opined, "[F]ull friendship exists between [two people] in the sense that they want nothing else

---

74. Espen Clausen & Richard H. Passman, *Pretend Companions (Imaginary Playmates): The Emergence of a Field*, 167 J. of Genetic Psych. 349, at 349 (2007) (noting the most common examples of imaginary companions in popular culture from *Sesame Street* to *Calvin and Hobbes*); Taylor, *supra* note 63, at 2–4.

75. Carlson et al., *supra* note 64, at 1183 (noting that many children have imaginary friends of which their parents are unaware).

76. Not all imaginary friends are also stuffed animals. Many have no physical form at all. Some psychologists argue that toys should not be defined as imaginary friends. *Id.*

except the good of the other."[77] In non-imaginary friend relationships, both parties want good for the other. Imaginary friends, by contrast, gain nothing from their friendship with the child, but the child gains exponentially from interacting with the imaginary friend. There is no need for the give-and-take that permeates non-imaginary friendships. This means children control the imaginary friend and gain what they need from the imaginary friend without having to offer something in return, something they may not have the ability to give.

Imaginary friends understand the child from the child's point of view and, therefore, can be a "perfect" friend. Where non-imaginary friendships might be hampered by miscommunications and misunderstandings, the imaginary friend relationship is one in which children are understood on their terms. "Individuals of all ages can experience the discrepancy between what they want to express and what they can express given the general limitations of human language. In relation to imaginary companions, children can re-experience the feeling of total understanding."[78] As we discuss in Chapter 5 with respect to attachment, this feeling of being seen and understood is a necessary aspect of developing self-soothing coping mechanisms. A feeling of total understanding from someone else is nearly impossible to find in the external world, particularly in a court system, but imaginary friends understand the child's world only through the eyes of the child, so he cannot misinterpret the child's view of life. Therefore, the imaginary friend can be fully present with the child.

Similarly, children are in absolute control of the situation with their imaginary friends, including how the imaginary friend acts.[79] The child is in control, and the imaginary friend understands the amount and type of control the child wants to have. Even when imaginary friends act in ways that on the surface appear to upset the child, the action is of the child's own making. It can, therefore, be exactly what the child needs in the relationship. Non-imaginary friends, by contrast, may argue over who gets to have, or who must have, more control in any given situation.[80] Disagreements over these issues can harm non-imaginary

---

77. John Eekelaar, Family Law and Personal Life 36 (Oxford University Press 2006).

78. Hoff, *supra* note 65, at 177.

79. *Id.* at 168.

80. While it is more common to think about children fighting to have control, sometimes children may want to give up control to their non-imaginary friends but their non-imaginary friends do not want the control. They then enter a power struggle over who must take control rather than who gets to have it.

friendships, but with imaginary friends, children can keep or give up control based upon their own needs in the moment. In addition, children control how other people interact with the imaginary friend and whether to invite third parties into the relationship. In *Calvin and Hobbes*, Calvin's parents are aware of Hobbes, but they are not privy to the entire relationship between the two.

When children do share them with the world, other people must interact with the imaginary friend on the child's terms.[81] One article in *Psychology Today* recounts an episode where the author's brother made sure his mom stopped to wait for George, the child's imaginary friend.[82] Similarly, there has been some research regarding how involved parents should be in their children's lives vis-à-vis the imaginary friends. One article summarized the available research:[83]

> Excessive parental involvement violates important privacy and autonomy boundaries. Trespassing these imaginal property lines may cause children to worry that adults are ridiculing them or have abdicated their adult roles. Further, adult interference may rupture the child's vital ownership of the imaginary companion. In sum, it appears best that adults are accepting bystanders rather than intrusive, judgmental, and directive participants in the fantasy.

The research, therefore, suggests that children need the autonomy that having an imaginary friend provides, and parents should support such autonomy and interact with the imaginary friend in ways the child requires. The imaginary friend, after all, exists because, for whatever reason, the child believes it is useful or necessary. Parents must support that need without intruding into the relationship between the child and the imaginary friend except on the child's terms.

Finally, imaginary friends arrive in a child's life and leave a child's life abruptly.[84] This appears to be the one piece of the relationship over which the child has no

---

81. Susan Newman, Imaginary Friends: Any in Your House?, Psychology Today, June 19, 2008, https://www.psychologytoday.com/blog/singletons/200806/imaginary-friends-any-in-your-house.

82. *Id.*

83. Robert D. Friedberg, *Allegorical Lives: Children and Their Imaginary Companions*, 25 Child Stud. J. 1 (1995) (internal citations omitted).

84. Carlson et al., *supra* note 64, at 1183.

control.[85] Although some children have elaborate stories for how their imaginary friends appear, most simply show up in the child's life.[86] Similarly, the imaginary friend simply disappears when it is no longer needed, such as when the child starts school or acquires other friends.[87] Perhaps children gain whatever originally prompted the need to create an imaginary friend, or perhaps they just move on to something else.[88] Although the comic strip ends with *Calvin and Hobbes* riding off into the snow together, most children eventually say goodbye to their imaginary friends when the imaginary friend has served its substantive purpose.

The Substantive Roles

The substantive roles imaginary friends fill in children's lives are too numerous to examine here; they are as numerous as the children who have them. Therefore, this section examines the most common roles researchers have found.

One commentator examined and summarized the available research on all the roles and stated, "The extant literature ostensibly suggests that for most young children an imaginary companion is a relatively benign way of mastering multiple interpersonal and intrapersonal pressures."[89] Put more simply, the psychological research suggests the fundamental role of imaginary friends is to help children cope with difficult situations they might not be able to confront alone. Through engagement with another being, albeit a fantasy being, the child can grow and understand life in new and meaningful ways.

Another researcher stated imaginary friends are "an important aspect of children's development toward independence [and] toward creating a social context of their own outside the realm of parental control."[90] The control children have over their interactions with their imaginary friends supports the independence they gain from engaging with them. Children interact with other people, including their non-imaginary friends, under nearly absolute adult regulation, but children have absolute independence from adults while interacting with their imaginary friends. Autonomy is one of the most important goals of children's

---

85. Hoff, *supra* note 65, at 160 ("Other children could not control whether the imaginary companion would turn up. Suddenly it was just there.").

86. *Id.* at 158.

87. *Id.*

88. Carlson et al., *supra* note 64, at 1183.

89. Friedberg, *supra* note 83.

90. Hoff, *supra* note 65, at 153.

development.[91] Having an imaginary friend helps children gain a certain level of autonomy over their lives because the child gains the tools necessary to become a fully autonomous person while being supported by the imaginary friend in the process.

"Some children explained that their imaginary companions had taught them to be more imaginative. The imaginary companions worked as 'creativity consultants' for the children."[92] Imaginary friends, therefore, can help children think through unique solutions to unusual life events when there are few others around willing to help, whether it is exhibiting a new style of childhood play or navigating the complex world of parental disputes. Imaginary friends allow children to think differently, and they provide a support structure through lonely times.

The consensus used to be that children without siblings were more likely to have imaginary friends, but that is not the accepted understanding today.[93] Instead, children who feel alone as a result of changes in their lives, including the birth of younger siblings, the loss of a parent, or even a divorce, are more likely to "reach out" to imaginary friends.[94] Hoff found, "Imaginary companions may enter children's lives when they feel overlooked in different ways."[95] Thus, as parents overlook their children during a court case, children can turn to an imaginary friend, someone who will not only pay attention to them but also understand them.

Imaginary friends appear in moments of vulnerability because children need the companionship of someone who can always be there. They represent "a number of [children's] mature defenses"[96] by providing the child with a positive outlet rather than responding negatively to the vulnerability. The imaginary friend helps children "distance themselves from 'Bad me' percepts as well as hold onto 'Good me' percepts while simultaneously identifying with parents and adapting to developmental tasks."[97] During difficult times in a child's life, he may internalize the negativity surrounding him.[98] The imaginary friend helps the child master these pressures by externalizing the positivity he needs and then using it to learn

---

91. *Id.* at 156.
92. *Id.* at 163.
93. D Pearson, *supra* note 68, at 13.
94. Newman, *supra* note 81.
95. Hoff, *supra* note 65, at 153.
96. Friedberg, *supra* note 83.
97. *Id.*
98. Stahl, *supra* note 30, at 68–69.

how to grow into that being.[99] This helps children build confidence, internalize those traits, and fully engage with the world in which they find themselves.

Understanding the child serves a substantive, as well as procedural, role, and it cannot be overstated. The need to be understood does not end with childhood:[100]

> Individuals of all ages can experience the discrepancy between what they want to express and what they can express given the general limitations of human language. In relation to imaginary companions, children can re-experience the feeling of total understanding.

In moments when this fundamental need is not met by external forces, children can turn to an imaginary friend.

Imaginary friends do not understand children only because they exist in the child's mind; they understand them because they listen. In a world where children are still sometimes told they should be seen and not heard, having someone listen to a child is important and special. Children need someone to listen to them, and if none of the adults already in the child's life assume the listening role, an imaginary friend can assume it. Good listening begins by being non-judgmental. A good listener does not evaluate or judge what it being said; instead, a good listener simply listens. This ability to listen leads to better understanding.

Being a good listener also requires keeping secrets, a concept familiar to childhood. Imaginary friends are the best friends for keeping secrets because, by definition, they are unable to break a child's confidences. Moreover, imaginary friends listen and keep secrets without judging the child's thoughts and views. Instead of trying to evaluate the child and the validity of the child's world, the imaginary friend listens and hears the child on the child's terms, acting as a witness rather than promoting ideas about how the child should be and act. Thus, the imaginary friend does not decide which secrets to keep based upon what they are about. The imaginary friend simply keeps the secret the child does not want to reveal for any reason.

Having a nonjudgmental listener helps give the child confidence. Children often feel powerless when they are ignored, so the imaginary friend's roles make him a rescuer who helps alleviate some of the powerlessness associated with

---

99. Hoff, *supra* note 65, at 160 ("It is not uncommon that the pretend playmate is a rescuer.").

100. *Id.* at 177.

being a child.[101] Sometimes imaginary friends also have additional powers or strengths children wish they had, including the ability to do better in school; these imaginary friends represent the child's ideal self.[102] Imaginary friends "are often ways to compensate for [a child's] lack of competence or mastery."[103] For example, Hobbes often helps Calvin with his homework, and the idea Hobbes knows the answers when Calvin does not indicates the power children transfer onto their imaginary friends. Children can externalize their ideal selves and then use it as a model to help them grow. This, in turn, can increase their confidence.

These are all very important aspects of an imaginary friend, but one psychologist sums it up nicely:[104]

> Imaginary companions are an integral part of many children's lives. They provide comfort in times of stress, companionship when they're lonely, someone to boss around when they feel powerless, and someone to blame for the broken lamp in the living room. Most important, an imaginary companion is a tool young children use to help them make sense of the adult world.

Thus, imaginary friends may play many varied individual roles in each child's life, but overall, they help children "make sense of the adult world." Put another way, imaginary friends are a bridge between children and the adult world. They are "inner mentors, who appeared to assist the children in their identity formation work."[105]

Occasionally, the imaginary friend also takes on importance for the adults in the child's life. At least once, Calvin's mom hugged Hobbes close and expressed her sadness that a poor raccoon might die. For the briefest of moments, she recognized she also needed the support Hobbes could offer. Hobbes was in his stuffed state, unable to be fully embodied as an imaginary friend, but Calvin's mom needed his support, for the briefest of moments. Of course, in the next frame, she says, "You can tell I'm upset when I start talking to you." But this strip

---

101. *Id.* at 153.

102. *Id.* at 162.

103. Friedberg, *supra* note 83.

104. Lawrence Kutner, *Midnight Monsters and Imaginary Companions*, Psych Central, May 17, 2016, https://psychcentral.com/lib/midnight-monsters-and-imaginary-companions/.

105. Friedberg, *supra* note 83, at 161.

recognizes that sometimes there are situations parents are unable to explain to their children, and the child's imaginary friend serves a purpose for the parents as well, if only for a moment. When the child chooses to share, the imaginary friend can teach the parents about their children in ways they may have overlooked and can serve as a bridge back to the child from the parents.

Thus, the child's expression of an imaginary friend can be a portal into a parent's understanding of her child. When adults understand the roles children create for their imaginary friends, parents are more likely able to understand their children's needs, fears, etc. Children often live in their own worlds, and those worlds can be difficult for adults to penetrate and understand. The imaginary friend, when expressed as a real being, becomes the parent's bridge to the child's world. Therefore, an imaginary friend is a two-way bridge between the child's world and the adult's world. The bridge also remains malleable as the situation, and the child, grow and change.

The Lawyer as Imaginary Friend

This section uses the procedural and substantive roles of imaginary friends to analyze how lawyers can fulfill this role for the children they represent. When lawyers use the imaginary friend model, the child has an advocate and a partner and someone whose job it is to understand him. The parents and the court understand the child and his circumstances in a way they are otherwise unable to do.

The research above provides a perfect analogy for children involved in court processes. Children whose parents argue over them, or those who have been removed from their parents by child welfare agencies, are far more likely to feel vulnerable and alone in the world with no one to understand them, which the research suggests is when children are most likely to have imaginary friends. In high-conflict divorce and dependency cases, parents often put their own needs ahead of their children's needs, and legally parents' rights control legal outcomes. Thus, children are overlooked despite the fact the court system ostensibly exists for the child's sake. Further, courts and families misunderstand the children they say they represent. Children are more likely to need someone who is on their side and who exists only for them when they are dragged into the court system.

The following basic model outlines how the lawyer for the child fulfills the imaginary friend role in a child's life in a family or dependency court case. Overall, lawyers for children can "help [children] make sense of the adult world." In court, lawyers help the child make sense of the adult court world, a world that normally does not exist in a child's life and one that is understandably full of fear, uncertainty, and misunderstanding. A lawyer acting as an imaginary friend can help the child bridge some of these difficulties, which will aid the child's ability to be resilient and respond more positively to the entire court process and its aftermath.[106] The lawyer can also provide information to the child that others may be hesitant to provide. This will be discussed more in Chapter 10.

First, and most importantly, the lawyer is the only person in the case whose only agenda is the child.[107] The lawyer for the child is the only person who may look at the case only from the child's perspective. Everyone else in the system has a different agenda, but the child's representative can be focused exclusively on the child's perspectives. Furthermore, the relationship between lawyers and their child clients is a one-way street.[108] Lawyers support the child, and the child need not give anything in return. This is the key difference between an imaginary friendship and a non-imaginary friendship. Lawyers are in a service profession, so the unidirectional nature of the relationship is one of service.

The imaginary friend lawyer is in a unique position to inform the court as well as the parents about the child's individuality and concerns during the case. It begins with understanding the child. Full understanding occurs under the imaginary friend model when the lawyer sees and understands the child through the child's eyes and the child's perspectives. It requires removing the adult-lawyer hat and replacing it with an understanding hat. It requires the lawyer get to know his child client as a person who has a personality embodying concerns, hopes, dreams, vulnerabilities, fears, and views. Therefore, it is important to understand the psychological issues our clients face in the legal world. If we do not understand how trauma and development affect our clients, we are unable to fully understand their unique perspectives.

---

106. Stahl, *supra* note 30, at 43–46.

107. Lawyers, of course, have duties to the Court, but their purpose in the case is to represent the child. As an officer of the Court, a lawyer must be honest with the Court, but the lawyer for the child remains the only person whose only agenda when interacting with the child is to be there for the child.

108. As discussed below in relation to the survey results, many lawyers do gain benefits from being engaged in this work, and that is probably the reason many people decide to represent children. The point, however, is that for this model to work, the lawyer need not gain anything from interacting with the child. The child, by contrast, gains from the friendship, especially from the fact that the lawyer for the child is the dedicated only to the child.

True understanding allows the lawyer to see the child's perspectives and share them with others. This understanding benefits the child because he feels he is not being ignored, and it benefits the court because the best interests mandate requires an understanding of each child's circumstances rather than a focus on what might work for all children. It further benefits the parents who may have lost sight of what their children need and want because of their own emotional blinding during the process. Thus, this unique and fundamental role of the imaginary friend aids everyone involved in legal proceedings, and the child especially gains the support from knowing that someone understands her position regardless of whether it is later adopted by the court.[109]

Procedurally, the lawyer for the child serves many of the same functions as an imaginary friend. Children with lawyers are not alone during the process. Multiple people other than the lawyer give the child conflicting information about what is happening in the case because multiple people try to influence the child based on their own perceptions about what should happen. The people most expected to protect them are the ones leaving them alone, or worse, trying to influence their views about the other parent or the child's caregiver. Children often feel torn and isolated because they cannot seek solace from their parents. Lawyers for children cannot replace parents, but they can help children feel less isolated and confused by the animosity between their parents or the confusion as to why they are not living with their parents, and they can work to understand the child on his terms. Children may not want to make decisions in the case, but they do want someone to pay attention.[110] Moreover, imaginary friend lawyers can inform the child about other children in similar situations, so the child feels less alone both within and outside the family.

It is vital the lawyer for the child help the child feel less alone, but constant availability is one area where the lawyer for the child cannot be a perfect imaginary friend. The lawyer must, however, still ensure he is sufficiently available to the child in ways that work for the child. This is a fine line lawyers must walk with their clients. As noted in Chapter 1, large caseloads and insufficient time make it impossible for children's lawyers to be present for their child clients on a moment's notice, but being someone the child knows he can trust to call and hear responses from is important to the role.

The child client should retain the sense of control he has in a relationship with an imaginary friend. This may be a difficult concept for children to

---

109. Carlson et al., *supra* note 64, at 19.
110. *Id.* at 19.

understand at first; it is not common for children to be in control of situations with adults, especially under circumstances as adult-centric as court. The lawyer must, therefore, help the child understand what it means to be in control. It may not mean the lawyer for the child does anything and everything the child says, but it does mean the child should have input into each aspect of the case.

Control generally comes with responsibility, and this creates a potential problem from the child's point of view. For children, control may mean decision making or the appearance of decision making. The lawyer for the child must explain the limits on the child's control as well as work with the child to determine how much control the child wants to have over the lawyer for the child and the situation generally. All clients, children and adult alike, ultimately cede some direction of their case to their lawyers, and the lawyer-child client relationship should be no different. The child client may simply need more direction in determining when and how to cede the control.

As noted above, many children give up the control they would otherwise have to the imaginary friend in order to learn from him or when they feel overburdened. They externalize powers they do not believe they have internally. Similarly, in court situations, a child should never have more control than he wants or can psychologically manage. Thus, the lawyer for the child should discuss these issues with the child and, most importantly, inform the child he need not make any choices.[111] Some children do not want to discuss the issues at all; the entire process has become too overwhelming. It is okay for the imaginary friend lawyer to allow the child not to participate in the conversation if that is what the child wants. The child should be in control of the situation on the child's terms, not placed in a bind causing him potential harm.[112] We often ask children if they want to be provided information about the case. Some children say yes, and others say no.

---

111. Of course, the child who adamantly does want to choose between his parents can make that choice known, and the lawyer can ensure him of that as well, but the fear expressed by many people in giving children a voice is that they will feel overburdened by having to choose. Therefore, the lawyer's role as an imaginary friend is to be supportive without forcing the child to choose and nonjudgmental when the child makes a choice strongly known.

112. Emery, *supra* note 33 (noting how too much empowerment can result in a child feeling torn between his parents and harmed by the situation).

Lawyers must also be careful about how they enter and exit the child's life. Like an imaginary friend, many lawyers appear out of nowhere in a child's life and leave just as abruptly. Their functions in between are useful, but their appearance and disappearance happen much too quickly. Upon entering the child's life, the lawyer should explain to the child why he is there and what purposes he will serve in the child's life, including how he is different from the parade of professionals the child might have seen already. The first step is to learn what the child needs from the lawyer and what roles the child needs fulfilled in his life by an imaginary friend lawyer. Second, the lawyer must begin to understand the child's perspectives on the case. These two roles are interrelated and ensure the lawyer can better represent the child going forward.

Leaving the lawyer-client relationship is more difficult, but most children eventually leave their imaginary friends behind when the imaginary friends have served their function, whatever that is for the child. The imaginary friend assists the child through a process in which the child grows, and then the imaginary friend can disappear. Similarly, lawyers must leave a child's life, but they can do it carefully and respectfully by explaining to children that they have served their role and must depart. In addition, they should ensure the child can ask any questions he needs answered and should confirm the child has the lawyer's contact information should additional questions arise. An intentional and clear ending of the lawyer-client relationship will help guarantee the child does not feel abandoned by the lawyer and allow the child the opportunity to fully understand the process that has, with any luck, ended. Further, by providing the child contact details for the future, the child understands that should any additional questions or needs arise, the lawyer will be available.[113]

Substantively, lawyers for children must be imaginary friends to be an effective bridge for the client. Most broadly, the lawyer is the child's bridge to the adult world. The lawyer's role is to support the child as he learns and develops through one of the most difficult situations he may face during childhood. As such, the lawyer for the child enters the child's life, aids the child to make sense of this difficult situation, provides a sounding board for developing creativity, enhancing powers, and mastering pressures, and then leaves the child, just as a scaffold is removed and an imaginary friend leaves the child's life. Thus, of all

---

113. The lawyer must set certain parameters for the child in how and when the child can contact him in the future, especially if the lawyer has decided to engage with the child through social media.

the substantive roles the lawyer fills, the overarching theme is to help the child "make sense of the adult world" he has been forced to enter.

In order to help the child understand the adult world, the lawyer must understand the child's world and the child's perspectives. The first step is to listen to the child without judgment. Nonjudgment is broader than not judging the child in front of her; it means not judging the child's input and developmental awareness. It means not evaluating whether the child's views and thoughts are necessarily in the child's best interests. An imaginary friend does not judge the child's thoughts and experiences as good or bad; they simply exist as they are. This is true even if the lawyer believes the child has been coached. Even when influenced by someone, children have a reason for allowing that influence to determine what they ultimately say to people, and understanding that can be important. It even can be important to allow that story to stand, to allow the child to know she played her part by telling a story, and not judge whether it is true. There are other people in the process to judge the veracity of the statements. This does not mean ignore instincts a child is coached, but instead to look beyond that first instinct to the broader question of why. Why does a child make certain statements? Why might a child want something that is not in her best interest? Why would a child want something I think is unsafe? Asking why allows the lawyer to see the unique child and not children generally.

The imaginary friend lawyer first observes and understands. Although a child, especially a very young child, may not fully understand the implications of his perspectives, they remain true for the child, even when they change. When children's perspectives change, the lawyer for the child should understand why, not assume the change is childhood fantasy and proof that children should not have a voice. Understanding is difficult. It takes time, and it requires letting go of personal beliefs and bias about how children behave and develop.

Understanding the child's perspectives is crucial to the second step where the lawyer assists the child in understanding the implications of his perspectives. From that place of listening and understanding, the lawyer for the child can facilitate the child's increased understanding of the situation, including finding creative and unique solutions to the parents' dilemma, if that is what the child wants to do. Similar to Hobbes providing Calvin with some new ideas for addressing arithmetic problems, the lawyer for the child can offer unique perspectives on how to address the issues the child faces when part of a court case.

These new perspectives, however, must be plausible in the child's view. This corresponds to the most crucial aspect of the imaginary friend lawyer—the lawyer can only be what the child understands. In this way, the lawyer for the child is not merely the child's spokesperson. The lawyer for the child takes an active role in understanding the child and working with the child to formulate new and informed views on various elements of the situation. As the child's externalized powers and positivity, the lawyer can reflect these positive issues back to the child, guiding the child from a place of internalized guilt and fear to a place of creativity and understanding.

In this realm of communication, the lawyer has powers the child does not have. The lawyer can translate between the court and the child, understand the child's needs and views through clear perceptions, and guarantee the child is not overlooked in this process. By modeling this ideal self and helping the child grow into it, the lawyer for the child can help the child "develop toward independence" and "make sense of the adult world" that does not usually make that development possible.

Children can get caught in a belief that they are somehow at fault for their parents' disagreements or the child welfare situation. Thus, sometimes the lawyer's role is to help the child differentiate between the "good me percepts" and "bad me percepts" and help the child understand his non-role in the reasons the family is in the court system. Many parents have open arguments and disagreements about how to discipline or care for children, yet it is important that the child understand she is not to blame. Certainly, lawyers for children are not the only people in the system to help children understand this fundamental issue, but the more people who can help children understand this issue, the better it is for the child. It is also important to refrain from blaming a child's parents. Children come from their parents, so if you blame the parent, you may, in the child's mind, be blaming the child as well. It can be helpful to remind children that everyone makes mistakes and the court system exists to help solve problems, not lay blame on how everyone got to the court system in the first place. Of course, some children are all too happy to blame their parents. That is an issue we address in Chapter 8.

The imaginary friend model opens new ways of looking at the role of the lawyer for the child, but upon first impression, infants continue to present a unique challenge. Under the imaginary friend model, however, the same principles apply to infants as apply to older children. The lawyer continues to exist only for the child and must understand the child on his terms and through his perspectives. This means not getting caught up in general notions of developmental theory, but looking at this child and his unique circumstances. This can be particularly important in dependency court cases where the issue is not whether there is a more appropriate parent, but whether the biological parents are safe. It may mean that what is developmentally appropriate for a child at that point in her life is not what the law and situation will require. Still, it is important for lawyers to help the parties and the court understand how best to reduce the harm caused to the child throughout the stages of the case, especially anytime the child changes placements, including initial removal and return to parents.

A lawyer representing an infant must understand how the infant interacts with all the people in his life and be able to use that information in defining legal positions. This requires understanding the infant's life and personality, which is no different than understanding an older child's life and personality. Most importantly, lawyers cannot get all of their information about the child from the child's parents or other adults whose own views about the child will be tainted by their own biases and perceptions.[114] The lawyer still must get to know the child. The individual characteristics of the child, however young, will provide the judge with insight crucial to deciding what is in the child's best interests.[115] Thus, the most important aspect of the imaginary friend model is understanding. Infants, perhaps more than any child, need someone who understands them fully and who can present unbiased information to the Court.

Therefore, with verbal children, the lawyer for the child can fill the procedural and substantive roles of an imaginary friend, and with infants, he can fill all of the procedural roles. If lawyers for children begin from the imaginary friend framework, they find a role that is broader than presenting the child's views, wishes, preferences, or best interests to the court. The lawyer can benefit the child's growth throughout the legal process as well as benefit the Court and parents by understanding the child's perspectives holistically, assisting the child to understand the process and analyze his perspectives, and bridging the disconnect between the child client and the adult world.

In addition, the imaginary friend lawyer is more useful to the judge's decision-making capabilities. Instead of being either a mouthpiece for the child or presenting his own opinions about the child, the lawyer can present the judge with an understanding of who the child is, unique to this family and his own developmental framework. While not all legislation focuses explicitly on the individual child, the only way to act in a child's best interests is by acting for the individual child.

---

114. There is nothing inherently wrong about their views, but everyone's views are biased, especially when there are intense emotions involved. Thus, the lawyer can enter as an outside perspective on the child and attempt to understand the child from the child's point of view.

115. ABA Guidelines, *supra* note 32, at 135 ("Even nonverbal children can reveal much about their needs and interests through their behaviors and developmental levels.").

Conclusions

The reason for a model that looks at a way of thinking rather than providing exact steps to follow is that it can influence all aspects of the practice. There is no way to prepare for every experience you will face as the child's lawyer. Nearly every week we are confronted with new and sometimes more challenging case experiences than we have ever experienced, but there are certain aspects for which you can prepare regardless of the unique case facts with your client. We will address the specifics of how to do this in Chapter 10, but first, in order to understand how to do this, we want to move into the psychological issues confronting your child clients, including a general overview of trauma. Then we will circle back to specifics of what this model, along with the psychological issues, looks like in a practice representing children.

We hope that by using a new paradigm, without it being a strict rule-based paradigm, you can shift the conversations you have with your clients, allowing you to engage with them on a different level. It allows them to see that you want to know them better than just the legal issues in a case. The reason this is so important with children, and not with adults, is because children tell stories differently than adults do. They talk through emotion and heart.

Ultimately, children can tell when adults are being authentic. When feeling stressed and trying to interview a child in five minutes, no adult will be able to get any useful information from the child. But if you take the time to ask the child about himself, and genuinely want the answers, then children change. The reason we are not describing this as rapport building is not because there is a problem with rapport building, but because we don't want rapport building to be something we check off the list. When it is genuine and part of a greater whole of trying to understand the individual child, the rapport building happens more naturally. That is vital to having a child interact with a strange adult in a strange setting.

Critical Psychological Issues to Understand | II

Whenever you are involved in a dependency or family law matter representing a child client, you are likely to encounter several critical psychological issues. Our discussion in the following chapters comes largely from the psychological research in these various domains.

The most important issue to understand is trauma, what it is, and how it is likely to affect your client. After that, we will focus on key variables, including child development, domestic violence, extreme high conflict in family law, children who refuse to see a parent, and what we are going to call a child's "special circumstances."

Trauma is pervasive in your clients. In dependency court, they have likely been traumatized by the events that led to out-of-home placement, by the placement itself, by meeting so many strangers, and by reliving their experiences whenever they talk about them. In very high-conflict separation or divorce, they are likely traumatized by the polarization and intensity of their parents' emotions. Children in these systems often live in a high state of ongoing stress and trauma because of the uncertainty of what is happening in their lives. We will identify longitudinal research on adverse child experiences and explain the potential negative impact of such trauma on your clients, including the various ways in which such trauma may be manifest, both psychologically and physically. Noting that trauma is likely to intensify nearly everything your client experiences, we will suggest some strategies for dealing with child clients and their trauma experiences, as well as describe resiliency and ways to help ease the traumatic experience for your client.

Representing a child who is an infant or a toddler is quite different than representing a child who is a school-age or teenage child. We will provide considerable information about how the psychological and chronological age of the child affects your interaction and representation. We will focus on ways to speak with and listen to children of different ages and explain how children often respond to various types of questions. Finally, we will introduce the importance of being curious, exploring for depth and breadth in your interactions with your child client.

Many think of domestic violence as "one size fits all" dynamics in which all family violence is the same. It is not, and we will help you understand critical differences in the ways domestic violence manifests in different families. We will also explain the various ways in which domestic violence impacts children, including introducing the counterintuitive notion that infants who are exposed to domestic violence may be at greater risk of long-term harm than older children who are exposed to such violence. We will also discuss the range of parenting plan options in family law cases that involve domestic violence issues to ensure safety of children in all of your cases.

From our experience, perhaps the most common reason judges appoint lawyers for children in family law cases is to assist in high-conflict cases. These cases are always a huge challenge because the parents seemingly hate each other more than they love their children. We will identify the problems in these families, the various ways such conflict affects children, and suggest some strategies for representation of children exposed to their parents' high conflict.

One of the most troubling types of cases is when a child resists/refuses contact with one of her parents. It is common for one parent to accuse the other parent of "alienating" the child against him. However, we will point out that many forces often contribute to a child's resistance/refusal, only one of which is the actions and emotions of the alleged alienating parent. By explaining the potential sources of this resistance/refusal, we can offer some suggestions for your representation of children in these circumstances.

Many children experience significant external and internal problems that will affect your child client. External problems can include the placement, the child's school, a history of neglect, and presence at court. Internal problems can include

Attention-Deficit Hyperactivity Disorder (ADHD) and oppositional disorders, autism and other diagnosable neuropsychological conditions, developmental delays in speech and language and other areas of child development, extreme mental health issues, or severe emotional dysregulation. In addition, cultural differences among children and children's emerging sexuality are often central to the case despite not being part of the legal issues. Although in some ways your representation of children experiencing these issues may not differ from other children, knowledge of the impact of these conditions and experiences is critical to your work with such children.

Some of you who read this book may have had some introduction to these issues, but it is likely many of you have had little to no formal education or training in any of these issues. This section will provide you with the starting point for your work. At the same time, note that this is only a starting point. We encourage you to learn all you can about these topics, and we will provide a list of additional resources online. We also encourage you to attend interdisciplinary conferences and programs that integrate psychological and legal issues. Interaction with mental health professionals at such meetings can enhance your skills and knowledge about these critical issues.

Trauma 4

Trauma is the new legal buzzword, and the way trauma affects children as clients (and therefore the lawyer-client relationship) is paramount to everything else we discuss in this book. We most commonly discuss trauma outside the legal context when discussing war veterans and post-traumatic stress disorder (PTSD). Trauma, however, comes in a variety of forms. There are also multiple definitions of trauma. Most importantly, this chapter will focus not only on what trauma is and how prevalent it is but also on the resilience research beginning to emerge.

The other way to describe trauma is toxic stress. Much of the child welfare world has historically used the phrase toxic stress, and in some ways, it is the more pertinent phrase because trauma often is used more colloquially. Here, however, we use trauma to describe toxic stress as well because the definition we decide upon is the one that exists in the nervous system, and you could even call our use of the word *trauma* a "term of art."

Definitions of Trauma

There is no single definition of trauma, but this section will try to make some sense of the varied definitions. Different definitions of trauma affect how your clients receive services but should not affect your representation of your client.

Merriam Webster provides three separate definitions:[116]

> a: an injury (such as a wound) to living tissue caused by an extrinsic agent
> b: a disordered psychic or behavioral state resulting from severe mental or emotional stress or physical injury
> c: an emotional upset

In this definition, the important piece to remember is that trauma can be physical or emotional, and often they go together. A child falling off a bicycle can be traumatic. Rebecca recently had a client who, when asked about the issues involved in the case, seemed to be uninvolved because the allegations involved her brother allegedly molesting their younger siblings, but she was also shaking. Upon further inquiry, Rebecca discovered she had been in a terrible car accident a year previously, and it was affecting her in her life and in terms of how she was responding to the case at hand. The conversation changed once that information was provided. Thus, it is important to remember that trauma in your clients is not limited to the trauma you hear about from the case in which you are involved.

The American Psychological Association website defines trauma as "an emotional response to a terrible event like an accident, rape or natural disaster."[117] Interestingly, from the psychological standpoint, trauma here is defined only as the emotional response to a traumatic event, which can include physical forms of trauma. The *Diagnostic and Statistical Manual-5* (*DSM-5*) does not really provide a definition of trauma; instead, it provides a diagnosis for PTSD. It defines the effects of trauma and, within that definition, defines the types of events that qualify as precursors to PTSD.

---

116. Merriam Webster, https://www.merriam-webster.com/dictionary/trauma (last visited Oct. 31, 2017).

117. American Psychological Association, Trauma, www.apa.org/topics/trauma/ (last visited Oct. 31, 2017).

The *DSM-5* redefined trauma from the *DSM-IV-TR*. Where PTSD used to be defined as an anxiety disorder, the *DSM-5*, which was released in 2013, now has a category called "Trauma and Stressor-Related Disorders," which "include disorders in which exposure to a traumatic or stressful event is listed explicitly as a diagnostic criterion."[118]

The *DSM-5* redefined what a traumatic or stressful event is. The *DSM-IV-TR* defined trauma as "the person experienced, witnessed, or was confronted with an event or events that involved actual or threatened death or serious injury, or a threat to the physical integrity of self or others."[119] The *DSM-5* added to the definition of a traumatic event.[120] The additions include adding sexual violence as a form of traumatic event and changing the definition of *exposure* to include learning the events happened to a close friend or family member or being exposed to repeated or extreme details of the event, as is the case with vicarious trauma.[121] The *DSM-5* requirements, therefore, limit the definition of trauma to that which the *DSM-5* writers objectively believed is traumatic. It did not consider the subjectivity of traumatic experiences. In the *DSM-5*, there must be at least a threat of harm or actual harm.

Dr. Peter Levine, who has spent the past thirty-five years studying trauma, says that defining trauma is still "a challenge."[122] But he does provide some clues. First, he says trauma is subjective, not objective. He states, "[w]e become traumatized when our ability to respond to a *perceived* threat is in some way overwhelmed."[123] The word *perceived* is the piece left out by the *DSM-5* definition. The second part of this definition states that the system is overwhelmed. The human nervous system, like all animal nervous systems, has the ingrained ability to resolve trauma. This is where the definitions for trauma and toxic stress overlap. The body is designed to deal with stress, but stress becomes problematic

118. DSM Library, https://dsm.psychiatryonline.org/doi/abs/10.1176/appi.books.9780890425596.dsm07 (last visited Oct. 31, 2017).

119. European Society for Traumatic Stress Studies, DSM IV PTSD Definition, https://www.estss.org/learn-about-trauma/dsm-iv-definition/ (last visited Oct. 31, 2017).

120. Laura K. Jones & Jenny L. Cureton, *Trauma Redefined in the DSM-5: Rationale and Implications for Counseling Practice*, The Professional Counselor, http://tpcjournal.nbcc.org/trauma-redefined-in-the-dsm-5-rationale-and-implications-for-counseling-practice/ (last visited Oct. 31, 2017).

121. *Id.* Note that we will discuss vicarious trauma in Chapter 11.

122. PETER A. LEVINE, HEALING TRAUMA: A PIONEERING PROGRAM FOR RESTORING THE WISDOM OF YOUR BODY 9 (Sounds True, Inc. 2005).

123. *Id.* (emphasis in original).

when it becomes toxic stress. When the system is overwhelmed, trauma gets stuck in the nervous system and manifests problematically.

Dr. Levine takes an even broader approach and states:[124]

> In short, trauma is about loss of connection—to ourselves, to our bodies, to our families, to others, and to the world around us. This loss of connection is often hard to recognize because it doesn't happen all at once. It can happen slowly, over time, and we adapt to these subtle changes sometimes without even noticing them. These are the hidden effects of trauma, the ones most of us keep to ourselves. We may simply sense that we do not feel quite right, without ever becoming fully aware of what is taking place; that is, the gradual undermining of our self esteem, self confidence, feelings of well-being, and connection to life.
>
> Our choices become limited as we avoid certain feelings, people, situations, and places. The result of this gradual constriction of freedom is the loss of vitality and potential for the fulfillment of our dreams.

Bessel van der Kolk states:[125]

> For human beings the best predictor of something becoming traumatic seems to be a situation in which they no longer can imagine a way out; when fighting or fleeing no longer is an option and they feel overpowered and helpless.

Neither of these last definitions requires an event. Both of them can be slow, but they are about the human loss of control and connection. Taken together, trauma is an overwhelm of the system and a loss of wholeness. Our system, when whole, functions well, but when the system fractures and breaks apart, the result is a feeling of isolation, which results similarly to all of the definable forms of trauma provided by the literature. Humans are pack animals, and they thrive in communities. That sense of community, as we will discuss later, is one of the greatest predictors

---

124. *Id.*

125. Pat Ogden, Trauma and the Body: A Sensorimotor Approach to Psychotherapy 21 (W. W. Norton & Company, Inc. 2006).

of resilience against the effects of trauma. Thus, the broadest definition of trauma can be defined as a separation from ourselves and those around us. This can happen over time and be barely noticeable at first, but it can be the most damaging.

What is interesting about this definition is how it works directly with the work you do with your child clients. Whether you are in family or dependency court, you are working with children who have been taken from a structure of normalcy in their life,[126] had that shattered, and often are disconnected from those they love the most. In family court, it can happen as a separation of their parents, where they live in a different family structure than before. In dependency, they are often removed from one or both of their parents. This lack of connection begins the case and, in some ways, is the ultimate definition of what trauma is for humans.

For our nonclinical purposes, trauma is a subjective situation, which is important for us to remember when representing children. Whether we believe our clients have experienced trauma is not the issue; the real issue is whether they are affected by their life experiences in ways that feel traumatic to them and that affect their daily lives and, by extension, their relationship to us and the legal situation.

In addition to these definitions of trauma, the National Childhood Traumatic Stress Network (NCTSN) provides a definition of "complex trauma," which "describes both children's exposure to multiple traumatic events, often of an invasive, interpersonal nature, and the wide-ranging, long-term impact of this exposure."[127] Further, the NCTSN states,

> These events are severe and pervasive, such as abuse or profound neglect. They usually begin early in life and can disrupt many aspects of the child's development and the very formation of a self. Since they often occur in the context of the child's relationship with a caregiver, they interfere with the child's ability to form a secure attachment bond. Many aspects of a child's healthy physical and mental development rely on this primary source of safety and stability.[128]

Complex trauma, therefore, is often what our clients experience. Notice this definition adds neglect as a form of complex trauma. Neglect leads to an

---

126. Or in the case of infants, what would be normal absent their abuse/neglect experiences.

127. The National Child Traumatic Stress Network, Complex Trauma, www.nctsn.org/trauma-types/complex-trauma (last visited Oct. 31, 2017).

128. *Id.*

overwhelm of the system because, as we will see in Chapter 5 regarding attach-ment, the system learns to regulate through the responsiveness of attentive car-egivers. When the infant does not have responsive and attentive caregivers, the result is traumatic for the young nervous system. Frequently, neglect as a form of trauma is one of the most difficult for lawyers to understand because without understanding its effect on brain development and its effect on attachment rela-tionships, the long-term consequences can sometimes go unnoticed.

In addition to these definable traumas in this lifetime, there is epigenetic trauma, which is trauma passed from generation to generation. Epigenetic research is new, and while indigenous cultures and Eastern religions have dis-cussed it for millennia, the scientific research into exactly what is passed down in DNA is just beginning to be discovered. But science now confirms that epigenetic trauma plays a key role in someone's ability to respond to trauma and stress in this lifetime. The specific science behind epigenetics is beyond the scope of this book, but we have provided some resources about it in the Appendix. What is important for you to know, however, particularly in family and dependency law, is that the trauma your client has experienced is not just in his lifetime. Many times, the families involved in these systems are repeat offenders over generations. Children who grow up in the dependency system have their children removed. Children of high-conflict divorce or children of domestic violence grow up and act in similar ways, thus perpetuating the cycle. What is important to know is this is not just because of learned behavior; it is because of the trauma being passed through generations through DNA.

Now that we have a working definition of trauma and what kinds of trauma your clients are likely to experience, the rest of this chapter will describe the way trauma manifests in your child clients and some of the resilience research.

Physiological Changes Resulting from Subjective Trauma

Trauma affects your clients' daily lives, and noticing the trauma when it shows up is vital to your ability to represent your clients effectively. This section out-lines the changes to the nervous system that occur with trauma and how trauma looks to the outside observer so you can notice what your clients are experienc-ing and, in turn, work with them more effectively.

Autonomic Nervous System (ANS)

Trauma, like stress, is a natural part of life. Birth itself is traumatic. Bodies and nerv-ous systems are designed to respond to trauma and to resolve it from getting stuck in the system. Everyone's nervous system has a window of tolerance for resolving trauma. As long as the trauma does not overwhelm a particular person's window of tolerance, the trauma will not get stuck in the nervous system. All mammals have this ability to resolve trauma, and in wild mammals, we see them literally shake off their trauma. They are far less likely to have PTSD-like symptoms because their nervous systems are rarely extended beyond their window of tolerance. But similarly to chronic stress, when we have chronic trauma, or even one trauma from which we never fully heal, it can begin to dominate how we act and interact in the world.

To this end, Dr. Peter Levine describes trauma not in the experience as the *DSM-5* does, but in the nervous system.[129] The nervous system stores the trauma until it is released. Trauma, like stress, shows up in the fight, flight, or freeze response, functions of the autonomic nervous system (ANS). The fight-or-flight response has become common parlance with regard to stress, but the discussion often misses a key component—freeze. The ANS activates in response to trauma similarly to how it activates in response to stress.[130]

Simply put, the fight and flight responses activate the sympathetic nervous system. Imagine you are walking down a street at night and you hear a noise behind you. What is your reaction? Most people jump and either turn toward the sound or start to run away. The heart rate increases, muscles tense, and blood flows to the limbs and away from the internal organs. Nonessential bodily functions shut down because they are not necessary to help a person fight or flee from danger.

Once the person realizes it is some children playing in the trees, the system relaxes and goes into a parasympathetic response. In this normal "window of tolerance" description, the parasympathetic response is often described as the "rest and digest" response. This parasympathetic response brings blood back to the internal organs, allows the muscles to relax and heal, slows down the heart rate, and slows down the breath. Then the nonessential bodily tasks return, and the body quite literally, can rest and digest.

The ANS can also respond to danger through parasympathetic means in the freeze response. This is when the body goes into such a "relaxed" state it shuts down. The freeze response is also a normal, healthy response to a traumatic event.

---

129. Peter Payne et al., *Somatic Experiencing: Using Interoception and Proprioception as Core Elements of Trauma Therapy*, FRONTIERS IN PSYCHOL. (2015), *available at* https://www.frontiersin.org/articles/10.3389/fpsyg.2015.00093/full.

130. We will discuss the flow between sympathetic and parasympathetic responses in Chapter 12 on vicarious trauma, but here we discuss the effects when they are outside someone's window of tolerance.

It exists in all mammals. Many people liken the freeze response to a deer in the headlights. There are videos of gazelles being chased by predators and "playing dead," going into the freeze response; as soon as the predator gives up, the gazelle stands up, shakes itself, and goes back to normal.[131] The animal shakes itself to bring its body out of that extreme freeze response and then can function normally.

Humans, like all mammals, have a freeze response, and when it works appropriately, humans can release the freeze from the system and go back to a more normal, regulated state. When coming out of freeze, the sympathetic nervous system must turn on sufficiently to bring the body out of the freeze but not so much that it becomes over activated. The system can, however, get stuck in these responses even in forms of acute, defined trauma. You see this in your clients when they tell you they feel numb, they have a very flat affect, and they seem as though they are not quite present when you are talking to them.

The fight, flight, and freeze responses are the body's survival instinct. Problems arise in two ways: (1) there has not been sufficient time to come out of one of these states, such as shock, which we describe later in this chapter, or (2) the process gets stuck. In the foreword to Peter Levine's book *Trauma and Memory*, Dr. van der Kolk explains what happens when trauma gets stuck:[132]

> Post-traumatic actions do not only consist of gross behaviors such as blowing up at anyone who offends you or becoming paralyzed when you are scared, but also in imperceptibly holding your breath, tensing your muscles, or tightening your sphincters. [Levine] showed me that the entire organism—body, mind, and spirit—becomes stuck and continues to behave as if there is a clear and present danger.

Thus, when these natural processes get stuck, the body and the nervous system believe the danger continues to exist, and they respond accordingly.

The reason trauma gets stuck in the body is because usually the incident or incidents that create the trauma are so overwhelming for the emotional system they cannot resolve in the normal course of the ANS. So, the trauma gets stuck

---

131. Gazelle's escape, https://www.youtube.com/watch?v=IlwzPIUtRPc&index=1&list=PLKt47oQNSAs5AQSZtMt5Pv5oPXTkEJll7.

132. Peter A. Levine, Trauma and Memory: Brain and Body in a Search for the Living Past: A Practical Guide for Understanding and Working with Traumatic Memory xiv (North Atlantic Books 2015) [hereinafter Trauma and Memory].

in one or more aspects of the ANS. Everyone has a limit to how much stress and trauma he can handle before it gets stuck. Up until that point of overwhelm, the system can recover. But once that point of overwhelm is reached, the system cannot recover on its own, and it needs intervention, which we will discuss below. As we will discuss later in this chapter and in Chapter 5, children need the help of a loving, caring adult to resolve the trauma in their nervous systems; unfortunately, the children with whom you work in the dependency and family court systems often live in this state of overwhelm, and one of their parents is rarely capable of being that supportive, healing presence. If they were, they would not be your clients. Thus, most of your clients are stuck in these unresolved processes. Being stuck in the sympathetic response can lead to hyperactivity, panic, rage, hypervigilance, and elation or mania. Being stuck in the freeze response can lead to disconnection, depression, deadness, and exhaustion.

Trauma does not have to get stuck in the nervous system. Wild animals that go into a state of deep freeze, or "play dead," come out of that state, shake it off, and walk away. They do not experience PTSD the way humans do. Humans attempt to resolve trauma similarly. Often human instinct is to cry or rock or tremble. The problem is that society views these actions as weakness. We prefer to believe "whatever does not kill us only makes us stronger." Instead of feeling the pain of the trauma—and therefore being able to move it through the body to move toward wholeness and wellness—we expect people just to get over it. That prohibits the body from going through the natural resolution process. Instead of experiencing the event or events, responding appropriately to them, and healing from them, society asks us to halt the process and pretend everything is okay. This works until the trauma we never resolved comes back, and we act from that traumatized place.

Noticing when people are in these extreme states is important because one of the key aspects of overly active sympathetic and parasympathetic responses is what happens in the brain. Because these instincts are survival instincts, the brain reacts in a survival response.

Trauma and the Brain
For our purposes, the brain has three levels:[133] (1) the reptilian brain, (2) the limbic brain, and (3) the neocortex. The reptilian brain is the brain stem, and it controls all the unconscious aspects of our lives—breath, heartbeat, temperature, balance,

---

133. Certainly, brain science is much more advanced than what we are going to discuss here, but we want to discuss it enough so that you understand just how natural your clients' responses are; they may not be as in control as you would like to think because of how automatic the effects of the trauma are.

and the execution of the ANS. The limbic brain controls the emotions required to connect to others, including attachment, and contains two very important parts of the brain—the amygdala, which regulates fear, and the hippocampus, which regulates memory. The limbic brain governs early affect states apparent in infants as well as emotions humans use to express and connect to others, such as compassion. Both the limbic and reptilian brain can speak through sensation and a felt sense within the body. This will become important to our discussion later in this chapter. Finally, the neocortex is the executive functioning of the brain. It is where thought intervenes and interrupts impulsive reaction; it also controls language, reasoning, and voluntary movement.

Without the impact of trauma, children's brains are already different from adult brains. The neocortex is not fully developed, and the prefrontal cortex, the reasoning center of the brain, can take until the mid-20s to develop fully. Thus, children already act more from an emotional and impulsive place than do adults. When trauma is added to the mix, and someone is stuck in a fight, flight, or freeze pattern, that chasm grows even wider. The amygdala can go into overdrive, and children can sense fear in a multitude of situations that otherwise should not induce fear.

When trauma is involved, the brain goes into survival mode. And as the saying goes, when a tiger is chasing you, there is no need for a neocortex. It shuts down. There is no time to analyze and reason as to whether you are going to run. You must act and act immediately, or you die. Remember that trauma feels to the person like a life-or-death situation; therefore, the brain goes into a life-or-death response. Because the ANS is governed by the reptilian brain and emotions are governed by the limbic brain, when the body is in fight, flight, or freeze, the neocortex shuts down. It is not necessary. There is no reason to think about multiplication tables when a tiger is chasing you. But if the body is stuck in that state, it can cause problems for your clients as well as your relationship with your clients.

If the neocortex shuts down, children act more on impulse than they would otherwise. They go into hyper- or hypo-aroused states where there is too much or too little feeling, respectively. If they are very young, the higher brain may not develop language and reasoning abilities, or those abilities will be greatly impaired. If they are older, they may struggle in school both academically and socially. And if they are teenagers, the normal risks teenagers take as they grow into adulthood can become impulsive aggression and extremely high-risk behaviors, all because the neocortex is essentially impaired or shut down.

One interesting way these brain changes affect your representation is that when the neocortex is shut off, imagination becomes more difficult. Imagination is crucial to children generally, and it is crucial to being a lawyer because part of your job is to imagine possibilities with your clients, including safety plans for children you worry are in an unsafe situation. The only person who can tell us how a situation will truly affect the child is the child, so children must be part of the process of determining what happens to them. In that sense, you must be able to brainstorm and imagine a variety of possibilities with your clients. If the higher brain is offline, imagination disappears.

If your clients are absorbed by trauma, they will be less likely to see ways out of their situation. It becomes nearly impossible to imagine that life will be different than it is today. This causes multiple problems for children, but the two most important are that (1) they can become depressed and hopeless about their future and (2) they can find it too difficult to come up with ideas to move beyond where they are today.

Memory and Trauma

Memory is one aspect of life everyone thinks they understand, but often what we believe to be true is moderately to significantly false.[134] Memory is a confusing topic for neuroscientists, and neither of us are neuroscientists. This section, therefore, is not an overview of everything science knows about memory. It is an overview of how what we think we know about memory is often incorrect and how trauma affects memory.

First, and perhaps most importantly, memory consists of more than recalling events. In his book, *Trauma and Memory*, Dr. Peter Levine discusses different types of memories. The hippocampus, where we store many explicit event memories, comes online at about 18 months of age. Therefore, it is very unlikely someone can recall events that happened prior to that age in the colloquial sense of remembering an event. But the brain is making other forms of memory from birth (and perhaps before), and those memories have a potentially greater impact on us as we grow.

The memories we hold generally in our tissues are bodily implicit memories, whereas the memories we hold in our conscious memories are explicit. Levine states, "Implicit memories appear and disappear surreptitiously, usually far outside the bounds of our conscious awareness. They are primarily organized around emotions and/or skills, or "procedures"—things the body does automatically,

---

134. In addition to what we are writing about in this chapter, in Chapter 11, we will be addressing the illusion of memory as it relates to bias.

sometimes called "action patterns."[135] You know the adage "You never forget how to ride a bicycle." This is true because it is a procedural memory; the body remembers even if you cannot consciously remember the last time you were on a bicycle. These implicit memories are the memories that cause children and adults to recoil in fear for reasons they do not consciously understand. Thus, if a young child has been exposed to trauma at the hands of someone frequently enough, that child may cry or stiffen around the perpetrator of that trauma despite there being no safety concerns in the moment.

Declarative memories, by contrast, are a form of explicit memories. These are usually the only types of memories people are referring to when discussing memory in general. "Declarative memories are relatively orderly, neat, and tidy, like the highly structured cerebral cortex that they use for their hardware and operating system."[136] No feeling or emotion is attached to them. Episodic memories are another form of procedural memory, but they "are often infused with feeling tones and vitality, whether of positive or negative valence, and richly encode our personal life experiences."[137]

What might be most interesting about episodic memories, those infused with emotion, is how they change as they are recalled.[138] This has its advantages; the memory becomes a narrative that can influence how you feel about yourself as it grows and changes with each recollection.[139] These episodic memories generally begin for people around age 3, but they can occur earlier.[140] The mutability of memory is crucial to our growth in that it allows us to learn with each new experience we have. When a memory is mutable, "our present feeling state may be the major factor determining what and how we remember a particular event."[141] This means we do not need to get fixated on the memory and it does not need to become overwhelming to us. Instead, it can grow and change and help us learn. What is important to remember is that our current emotional state influences the memory, so the memory changes with our emotional states.

---

135. Trauma and Memory, *supra* note 132, at 21.

136. *Id.* at 16

137. *Id.*

138. Mark Fischetti, *Why Do Our Memories Change*, Scientific American, Feb. 10, 2017, https://blogs.scientificamerican.com/observations/why-do-our-memories-change-video/.

139. Trauma and Memory, *supra* note 132, at 19.

140. *Id.* at 20.

141. *Id.* at 3.

Levine describes two types of implicit memories—emotional and procedural. Emotional memories help us remember emotional experiences and seek out those experiences again. If you have a wonderful experience at a party with friends and later your body feels the same way, your understanding of that new event is that it is safe like the party. There has been research on where specific emotions appear in the body, and people indicate similar experiences.[142] Procedural memories, like emotional memories, are a felt sense rather than a conscious recollection of an event. They consist of learned motor actions, emergency responses, and fundamental responses such as avoidance or approach.[143]

Even very young children can experience the effects of traumatizing events because the memory of that event is stored in the body memory even if the child has no conscious memory something bad happened. These memories can affect them later in life in how they react to the person or people who caused the trauma as well as in response to others in their lives. In addition, even when a child is not in the room when traumatic events happen, the fallout from that trauma can affect them on numerous levels. First, they can feel it happening even if they are asleep and cannot hear it in the moment.[144] Second, caregivers who experience trauma act differently, and that affects the children's relationship with the caregivers.

Trauma can also affect explicit memory recall. Instead of memories being mutable and part of a coherent narrative of someone's life, traumatic memories appear as overwhelming fragments filled with emotion and other sensory input. Levine explains:[145]

> In sharp contrast to gratifying or even troublesome memories, which can generally be formed and revisited as coherent narratives, "traumatic memories" tend to arise as fragmented splinters of inchoate and indigestible sensations, emotions, images, smells, tastes, thoughts, and so on. For example, a motorist who survived a fiery car crash is suddenly besieged by a racing heart, stark terror, and a desperate need to flee when he catches a whiff of gasoline while filling his tank

---

142. Lauri Nummenmaa et al., *Bodily Maps of Emotions*, PROCEEDINGS NAT'L ACAD. OF SCI. U.S.A (2013), *available at* www.pnas.org/content/111/2/646.full.

143. TRAUMA AND MEMORY, *supra* note 132, at 25.

144. *See, e.g.,* California Attorney General's Office, *First Impressions: Exposure to Violence and a Childs Developing Brain*, https://www.youtube.com/watch?v=O4zP50tEad0.

145. TRAUMA AND MEMORY, *supra* note 132, at 7–8.

at a service station. These jumbled fragments cannot be remembered in the narrative sense per se, but are perpetually being "replayed" and re-experienced as unbidden and incoherent intrusions or physical symptoms. The more we try to rid ourselves of these "flashbacks," the more they haunt, torment, and strangle our life force, seriously restricting our capacity to live in the here and now.

Memory is, therefore, more than the conscious recall of an event that happened in the past. It lives in the emotions and feeling states of both our past and present. In addition, if the event was overwhelming at the time, the memories can be fragmented pieces without any coherent narrative, causing someone to react to current situations in ways that make little sense in the moment. For children, who are already more emotion- and feeling-oriented than adults, these problems with memory become even more difficult parts of your job.

Think about the 3-year-old during a forensic interview who cannot recall the event of the day but squirms and curls into a ball while trying to remember the sex abuse the interviewer asks about. Then think about the 7-year-old child who can give you a very specific narrative of what happened during what should have been an incredibly traumatic experience. She can tell you where she was every minute for over an hour. The first example does not necessarily mean the abuse happened, and the second does not necessarily mean it did not. What it means is you need to ask more questions—and not necessarily questions of the child—because conscious recall of an event can have a multitude of meanings. Knowing that memory, particularly traumatic memory, is deeper than conscious awareness and often shows up as emotional states will help you better understand your clients and the words they say to you. Moreover, with preverbal, or nonverbal children, these understandings of how memory leads to instinctual actions can help you better interpret what these children are saying without words.

Long-Term Effects of Trauma

We would be remiss if we were to discuss trauma and not the Adverse Childhood Experiences Study. It helps put into perspective the importance of understanding trauma not only for your current relationship with your client but also for its long-term effects on her life. Kaiser Permanente, the largest healthcare provider in California, did a study on adverse childhood experiences (ACEs), asking participants about their adverse experiences prior to their eighteenth birthdays.

The ACE study consists of ten questions regarding specific types of childhood trauma,[146] including:[147]

1. Did a parent or other adult in the household often or very often ... Swear at you, insult you, put you down, or humiliate you? or Act in a way that made you afraid that you might be physically hurt?
2. Did a parent or other adult in the household often or very often ... Push, grab, slap, or throw something at you? or Ever hit you so hard that you had marks or were injured?
3. Did an adult person at least five years older than you ever ... Touch or fondle you or have you touch their body in a sexual way? or Attempt or actually have oral, anal, or vaginal intercourse with you?
4. Did you often or very often feel that ... No one in your family loved you or thought you were important or special? or Your family didn't look out for each other, feel close to each other, or support each other?
5. Did you often or very often feel that ... You didn't have enough to eat, had to wear dirty clothes, and had no one to protect you? or Your parents were too drunk or high to take care of you or take you to the doctor if you needed it?
6. Were your parents ever separated or divorced?
7. Was your mother or stepmother: Often or very often pushed, grabbed, slapped, or had something thrown at her? or Sometimes, often, or very often kicked, bitten, hit with a fist, or hit with something hard? or Ever repeatedly hit at least a few minutes or threatened with a gun or knife?
8. Did you live with anyone who was a problem drinker or alcoholic or who used street drugs?
9. Was a household member depressed or mentally ill, or did a household member attempt suicide?
10. Did a household member go to prison?

---

146. Centers for Disease Control and Prevention, Adverse Childhood Experiences (ACEs), https://www.cdc.gov/violenceprevention/acestudy/.

147. The Adverse Childhood Experiences Study: A Springboard to Hope, www.acestudy.org/the-ace-score.html.

Every yes answer equals 1 point. What the ACE study ultimately showed was those who had a higher ACE score were more likely to have physical illnesses and social problems later in life. Specifically, an ACE score of 6 or more leads to significantly higher risks of many physical diseases later in life, including, but not limited to, heart disease, diabetes, and chronic obstructive pulmonary disease (COPD). It further leads to an approximately twenty-year decrease in life expectancy.[148]

The idea that emotional trauma could have such lasting impacts on us physically has been the most important finding of the ACE study. It was a reminder to the medical community that we must look to emotional reasons for some, if not most, physical ailments. As Peter Levine has found, trauma exists in the nervous system just as stress does, and its effects, therefore, are just as profound on our health as having a stressful life. Therefore, we know the trauma our clients experience will likely have a lasting impact on them if we do not help them find ways to mitigate the harmful effects of the trauma. Moreover, as we will discuss in Chapter 12, these issues affect your own life and health as well.

By definition, children involved in the dependency or family court system have an ACE score of at least 1 because the ACE questions list most of the reasons a child would enter the court system. If they are provided a lawyer in a high-conflict custody case, they often have a much higher score, and certainly children involved in child welfare cases frequently have scores higher than 1. What the ACE study does not cover is the trauma of being involved in the court system itself. The ACE study does not ask about removal from primary caregivers, most likely parents, and it does not ask about being interviewed numerous times by several different strangers about preference between parents or about topics society generally tells children they should not discuss with strangers, especially when the children's caregivers have told them to keep these issues secret.

Child clients, therefore, have many more indicators of trauma than the ACE study contemplates, but the findings of the ACE study are what should interest us. It teaches us that the effects of trauma last long past the end of the case, and they manifest as more than just emotional issues. As professionals in the system, and the ones working with the children directly, you can help find ways to counteract the trauma your clients experience.

---

148. Carina Storrs, *Is Life Expectancy Reduced by a Traumatic Childhood?*, Scientific American, Oct. 7, 2009, https://www.scientificamerican.com/article/childhood-adverse-event-life-expectancy-abuse-mortality/.

Manifestations of Trauma

Now that you know what trauma is, how it affects the nervous system, body, and brain, and its long-term effects, the rest of this chapter will focus on how it manifests and why it matters to the work you do with your clients. This is in no way a complete overview of every form of trauma manifestation, but we hope to increase your awareness of what children are saying when they are speaking verbally and when they are speaking in ways you, as lawyers, are less trained to see.

In his book on stories of complex trauma in children, *The Boy Who Was Raised as a Dog*,[149] Dr. Bruce Perry provides examples of what happens when children are severely neglected or severely traumatized. These include stories of the children who were freed prior to the FBI destroying the Waco complex, a little girl who had been sexually abused and believed all adult men were sexual predators, a 3-year-old girl who watched her mother get murdered, a little boy who was adopted from a Russian orphanage, and a little boy who, quite literally, was raised in a cage like a dog because that's the only type of mammal his caregiver knew how to raise. Dr. Perry describes his work with these children and others and explains how we can begin to help children who have been severely traumatized.

Dr. Perry describes how these types of trauma manifest in children. For example, a young 7-year-old girl crawls into Dr. Perry's lap and tries to undo his zipper because, in her world, men existed only in a sexualized way. He described how a child with "intermittent care" from his parents resulted in his sociopathy and in him committing murder. Dr. Perry described this child as being left home alone for entire days while his mother was out on walks with her older son. Tragically, Dr. Perry writes, "Receiving no consistent, loving response to his fears and needs, [he] never developed the normal association between human contact and relief from stress. What he learned instead was that the only person he could rely on was himself."[150]

One story Dr. Perry recounts is a good reminder that you, as the child's lawyer, may see the trauma very differently than the children do. Dr. Perry worked with the children who were rescued from Waco, Texas, prior to the FBI raid that destroyed the Branch Davidian compound. To the children who were removed from that complex, the FBI and the ever-increasing number of well-meaning

---

149. Bruce D. Perry & Maia Szalavitz, The Boy Who Was Raised as a Dog (Basic Books 2006).

150. *Id.* 113.

professionals who entered their lives, not their parents, were the danger. When one child saw Dr. Perry arrive, she calmly asked, "Are you here to kill us?"[151] "These children did not feel as though they had just been liberated. Instead, because of what they'd been taught about outsiders and because of the violence they'd survived, they felt like hostages."[152]

This example of the children from the Davidian compound is an important reminder about the work we do. As outsiders to these children's families, we may believe they have been traumatized. We may see all forms of abuse, neglect, and problems in parenting, but to the child, that life is normal. You may believe the child has been rescued from a dangerous situation, whether it be abusive parenting or an alienating parent, but from the child's perspective, the legal system is the danger, not the abuse you see. It is important never to lose sight of the fact that the lives these children lead are their normal, that it can take time to readjust their thinking, and that sometimes you cannot. The fear of the outsider, you included, may never shift in your clients even though you know or think you know the interventions being taken are appropriate. Further, there is a long history in the United States and around the world, of the dominant culture attempting to "save" people who have a different culture. What you may view as traumatizing may be normal to the child's culture. Where you draw that line, as discussed in Chapter 1, is critical to your work with children, and it must be navigated by considering the effect your choices have on the child's nervous system functioning.

The stories in the book *The Boy Who Was Raised as a Dog* are some of the most intense trauma imaginable. And while you may not see such extensive trauma in your work, you often see children who have experienced what we would objectively define as less trauma, but that does not mean it affects children less. It cannot be overstated here that the "level" of trauma is not what matters; what matters is how the trauma affects the nervous system and, therefore, how it affects the child's daily functioning. We do not believe in relative suffering.

People may respond to traumatic experiences in ways that seem counterintuitive. In *The Body Keeps the Score*, Bessel van der Kolk stated that children who suffer abuse respond in ways that make the trauma worse and leave it within the body's system longer:[153]

---

151. *Id.* at 64.

152. *Id.*

153. BESSEL VAN DER KOLK, THE BODY KEEPS THE SCORE: BRAIN, MIND, AND BODY IN THE HEALING OF TRAUMA 13 (Viking Penguin Group 2014).

Most of them suffer from agonizing shame about the actions they took to survive and maintain a connection with the person who abused them. This was particularly true if the abuser was someone close to the child, someone the child depended on, as is so often the case. The result can be confusion about whether one was a victim or a willing participant, which in turn leads to bewilderment about the difference between love and terror; pain and pleasure.

As van der Kolk points out, the response to trauma is sometimes traumatic for the person as well, and you have the opportunity to normalize, if not condone, peoples' behaviors, including those that cause them shame. If a child believes he was a willing participant in the trauma, then he might believe it is his fault the trauma occurred. This can be exacerbated in children who have younger siblings, as they believe they need to take care of their younger siblings and prevent the abuse from harming their siblings.[154] Then the problem arises wherein the victim is less able to process the trauma because he believes he is a co-creator of the trauma.

The more common types of trauma our clients experience, such as exposure to domestic violence, neglect due to drug use or mental health issues, physical abuse, sexual abuse, and emotional abuse, are still detrimental to the development of our young clients and the behavior of our older clients. It can be too easy to believe one client's trauma is not as bad as another client's, making it more difficult to understand why a child is acting in a certain way. But all nervous systems are different, and what matters is the subjective experience of the child and how her daily life is affected. Therefore, in the rest of this section, we will discuss how you can notice these minor—and major—manifestations of trauma.

Recognizable Manifestations of Trauma

DSM-5 Manifestations

Although as children's representatives your job is not to diagnose PTSD, knowing its diagnostic criteria can help you understand how best to interview your clients about their symptoms and better understand whether their behaviors are

---

154. See Chapters 5 and 9 regarding parentified children.

a result of the trauma they experienced. As a result, you can help them receive the services they need and better understand what they are trying to express to you. As you read about the symptoms, consider clients you have met who experienced or demonstrated some of these behaviors.

First, the *DSM-5* requires the person experience trauma, as defined by the *DSM-5*.[155] As stated above, that requires exposure to "death, threatened death, actual or threatened serious injury, or actual or threatened sexual violence" through direct exposure, by witnessing the trauma, by learning that a relative or close friend was exposed to the trauma, or through "[i]ndirect exposure to aversive details of the trauma, usually in the course of professional duties (e.g., first responders, medics)."[156]

Once there has been a determination the person has experienced a traumatic event as defined by the *DSM-5*, a PTSD diagnosis requires a combination of symptoms falling within the PTSD diagnosis. First, the person must re-experience the traumatic event in one of the following ways: (1) intrusive thoughts, (2) nightmares, (3) flashbacks, (4) emotional distress after exposure to a traumatic event, or (5) physiological reactivity after exposure to the traumatic event.

"Intrusive thoughts" means the person cannot shake the repetitive thoughts about the traumatic experience. The person can be thinking about something unrelated, and then without warning, the person is thinking about the traumatic event. These are the children who continuously bring the conversation back to the trauma or tell you they cannot concentrate at school because they are constantly thinking about the trauma. Physiological reactivity means the body responds as though it is experiencing the event again even if it is not. Imagine you are walking in the woods, are bitten by a snake, and you almost die. The next time you go walking in the woods and you accidentally step on a stick. but it *feels to you* like the snake bite, your body can respond with all the fear associated with almost dying from the snake bite without any objective reality to the

---

155. In this chapter, we have taken the position that trauma can be anything that subjectively feels overwhelming to the system, but we are including the *DSM-5* requirements as a baseline. It is important to remember that the *DSM* serves a purpose for the insurance industry as much as it does for the therapeutic community. For our purposes in this book, therefore, we look at trauma in a broader perspective, but the requirements of the *DSM* are important to understand because children involved in the court system are often on Medicaid or can only receive therapy through insurance, which require diagnoses.

156. U.S. Department of Veterans Affairs, PTSD: National Center for PTSD, PTSD and DSM-5, https://www.ptsd.va.gov/professional/PTSD-overview/dsm5_criteria_ptsd.asp.

fear because stepping on a stick is not dangerous. The body, however, responds as though it was just bitten by a snake again.

Second, the person must have one form of avoidance of trauma-related stimuli after the event—either avoidance of thoughts or feelings about the event or avoidance of trauma-related reminders. Third, negative thoughts and feelings must begin or worsen in at least two ways. These can include (1) an inability to recall key features of the event, (2) overly negative assumptions about oneself or the world, (3) negative affect, (4) decreased interest in activities that used to be enjoyed, (5) feelings of isolation and detachment from friends and family, and (6) difficulty in feeling positive affect.

Affect generally refers to how emotions show up for someone. It can refer to "the conscious subjective aspect of an emotion considered apart from bodily changes" or to "a set of observable manifestations of a subjectively experienced emotion."[157] As children's representatives, you can notice a child's affect. People are often described as having a flat affect if their external emotional state does not appear to change between joy and sadness or anger and contentment. A child with a flat affect will tell a very traumatic story with the same outward appearance as telling a story about winning an award at school. A child who has difficulty feeling positive affect can go from external appearances of sadness to more of a flat affect but rarely, if ever, demonstrates external joyful emotional states.

Finally, for a PTSD diagnosis, a person must exhibit at least two forms of trauma-related arousal and reactivity that began after the traumatic event or worsened because of it. These can include (1) irritability or aggression, (2) risky or destructive behavior, (3) hypervigilance, (4) heightened startle state, (5) difficulty concentrating, or (6) difficulty sleeping. For children under the age of 6, irritability or aggression may include extreme temper tantrums.[158] Hypervigilance and a heightened startle state are slightly different, but they often go together. Hypervigilance is when a person constantly looks around to understand her surroundings. A person who is hypervigilant may walk into your office and look at every corner. A person in this state also may try to sit with his back to a wall so as not to have space behind him where he cannot see what is happening.

A heightened startle state, by contrast, is an overly excessive response to otherwise benign stimuli, e.g., a door slamming or something falling on the floor.

---

157. Merriam Webster, https://www.merriam-webster.com/dictionary/affect (last visited Oct. 31, 2017).

158. Matthew Tull, *Diagnostic Criteria for PTSD in Children*, verywell, Feb. 15, 2017, https://www.verywell.com/dsm-5-ptsd-criteria-for-children-2797288.

A person who exhibits a heightened startle response often turns toward the sound with a jerk of the head and possibly the body. This person may also have other signs of fight-or-flight manifest despite the fact there is no objective fear inducer. Babies who are raised in violent homes often have a heightened startle state. It is a great question to ask about very young children. These PTSD requirements are an interesting starting point, but they are not the complete picture of how trauma will manifest in your clients.

Broader Manifestations of Trauma in Your Clients

Because trauma is in the nervous system, talking about traumatic events can bring up that trauma in children. This section discusses what you might see children do while you are talking to them that indicates the trauma is coming to the surface.

First, you may notice your clients discussing how their bodies feel. Compared to adults, children are more kinesthetic, so they often talk about their emotions through their body sensations. Bodily sensations include feelings of lightness, heaviness, and shakiness, for example. We have included a list of sensation words in the online materials. Children in family and dependency systems rarely describe feeling light and soft. Rebecca had one 7-year-old client describe, without provocation, a feeling of swirling in her belly. She described stress as "all the feelings inside me" and motioned to her stomach in quick circles. She further stated that when she feels stress, her legs go numb. While this was an unusual conversation, it exemplifies exactly how body- and sensation-based children are. When children do not remember a specific event, bringing them to the sensation of the event might help you understand how the event feels to them.

Children can also describe images and memories. When discussing events or telling you about a dream they had, they may tell you they see colors. It is always important to ask children how well they are sleeping. Sleep disturbances can indicate traumatic distress, but children often will tell you about their dreams and even their nightmares. Children often can tell you what they heard and saw, but as we discussed earlier in this chapter, memory is not always accurate, particularly traumatic memories. Notice the fragmentation in the memory and how many other trauma manifestations appear while the child describes the memory.

Noticing how a child sits, gestures, and moves while you are talking is vitally important. Most of us do this unconsciously, and sometimes these movements are huge and obvious. For example, Rebecca has had multiple children literally turn around in a spinning chair so as not to look at her when discussing distressing events. One child got out of his chair and hid behind a couch when a person was mentioned he did not want to discuss. Those are obvious actions by children. But often these cues are subtler, and they can be just as important.

Is the child looking around the room as though he is scared? Is he looking away from you? Is he fidgeting? Is he only talking while drawing or spinning? Is he stroking his arm or pulling/stroking on his hair while telling a story? These can be signs that a child is distressed about the conversation; they also can be ways a child soothes and calms himself. If a child is holding a stuffed animal while you are discussing something distressing for the child, encourage the child to notice the stuffed animal. Sometimes children will begin to shake nervously in your presence. That is often a sign they feel overwhelmed. Other behaviors such as rubbing their hands together, stroking their arms or legs, or even drawing and spinning around in circles are often signs they are mitigating the increased stress they are feeling in themselves while telling their stories.

Another very interesting but less well understood manifestation of trauma is a child's gait. Remember the discussion of how the reptilian brain affects balance. Dr. Perry has noted that a child's "curious slanting gait" was the result of early childhood trauma "because coordinated walking relies on a well-regulated midbrain and brainstem."[159] We mention this because it is rare to think of these deep-seated physical issues as trauma manifestations. But once you understand how trauma effects development, and development affects every action humans take, you begin to see how trauma affects every aspect of your clients' lives, including potentially the way they walk.[160]

Children will also show emotions while speaking with you. These can be broader than those necessary for a PTSD diagnosis. You are probably well versed in understanding the emotions, or affect, your clients show. The most common affect not discussed above with the PTSD diagnosis is a flat affect. People with a flat affect appear disconnected from their emotions. These children do not laugh or cry and have a similar external state despite talking about issues as unrelated as sex abuse and their favorite puppy. This is generally a sign children are in a deep freeze state, as described earlier. You may, of course, see other emotions, including joy, sadness, anger, frustration, happiness, etc. One important fact about children, particularly those who are in a state of trauma, is that sometimes laughter is a nervous tick and not genuine laughter.

---

159. Perry *supra* note 149, at 135.

160. We do not mean to imply that trauma is the cause of every child with a strange gait, but we hope that these examples help you think outside the box on what causes different changes in your clients.

It can be beneficial to ask children about somatic issues. Biologically speaking, *soma* means "body." Somatic issues are different from sensations. The sensations are just that; somatic issues are the longer-term effects of what might be described as sensations. Trauma often manifests as somatic complaints, most specifically low back pain, stomach pain, and headaches. Children who report everything is going well in their lives but also report frequent, unexplained headaches are likely experiencing trauma, but it is manifesting in a way most people are not accustomed to asking about. If your client describes any of these symptoms, ask her when they happen. Can she remember what she was doing just before her most recent headache? Some children will tell you they know these symptoms occur when they think about something specific. Compared to adults, children tend to be more attuned to their bodies, so they often know what is happening. And if they do not, your inquiries can help you and the child understand how the case is affecting her.

Outside of your specific conversations with your clients, trauma manifests in many behavioral ways, including aggression, regression in development, tantrums, and loss of sleep. The NCTSN provides information on behaviors children may express indicating they are acting from a trauma response. Many of these behaviors are similar to the behaviors used to diagnose ADHD and other mental health diagnoses many of your clients in these systems receive and for which they receive a plethora of psychotropic medication. For example, the NCTSN explains these children are easily triggered and are more likely to participate in high-risk behaviors, including drugs, alcohol, and other activities that could result in their entry into the juvenile justice system.[161]

Unfortunately, it is still new for society to see these actions as trauma responses and not children being out of control. Instead, they are seen solely as problematic behaviors leading to removal from placement, removal from school, delinquent behaviors, and diagnoses that remain with children their entire lives. Further, dissociated children who do poorly in school are seen as needing tutors, not trauma therapy. As we will discuss specifically with types of trauma later in the book, these behaviors often result from traumatic events and chronic trauma in children, and it is important to recognize the *why* of these behaviors more than *what* the behaviors are.

---

161. The National Child Traumatic Stress Network, Effects of Complex Trauma, www.nctsn.org/trauma-types/complex-trauma/effects-of-complex-trauma (last visited Oct. 31, 2017).

It is very common for children to attach meaning to their experiences as well, especially believing their case is their fault. That is the meaning they have ascribed to the case or the separation of their parents. Rebecca once had a client say she was cutting herself because she felt guilty. She had ascribed meaning to her situation such that she believed the situation was her fault, and it caused her to use a cutting behavior. Children can also assign a meaning that no one loves them. This question of meaning is similar to asking your clients why they feel the way they do. It gets deeper than just the initial statements, and it can help explain what their experience is like for them. We all prescribe meaning to every event. When that meaning is tied up to trauma, however, it can be damaging to the child and how he interacts with the world around him.

Many of your clients believe no one, including you, is to be trusted or that they are completely alone in life or that all professionals in the system are against them. Often children see you as just another person paid to be there, so what is the point of engaging with you? Understanding these deeper meanings children have about life in general can help you put their specific experiences into the context of the case and your work with the child. When children have these core meanings tied around the system, it can be very difficult for you to work with them because they do not believe you are to be trusted. It takes time to repair these relationships, and you may not be able to work with that child client the first time you meet. It may take several meetings where you let the child be angry with you and you keep showing up anyway. You keep working for her anyway.

Our hope is that this section has helped you see children manifest trauma in numerous ways. The problem for your clients, however, is that most therapy systems in this country, particularly when they involve insurance (and Medicaid is insurance), ask the therapist to focus on behaviors and not the underlying cause of those behaviors. These systems are behavioral health systems, not mental health systems. This means that if your client is not expressing "negative" behaviors, she will not qualify for mental health services. Moreover, if your client is expressing negative behaviors but does not meet the *DSM-5* criteria for PTSD, she may be diagnosed with something she does not have, such as oppositional defiant disorder. This diagnosis can cause other problems later in her life. Children who do not express overt, external signs of distress may not qualify for therapeutic services despite the fact that they have somatic complaints, and you know they think the case is their fault, but no one else has asked, so they have not told anyone else.

For your client's sake, and her therapeutic process, it is important for you to know the signs of trauma. But knowing those signs also is important for your direct representation because of how trauma affects your client's ability to interact with you and the system.

Shock

Shock is a form of ANS freeze response and a manifestation of trauma, but because it is so common in your practice as a children's lawyer, we believe it needs its own explanation as one of the major trauma manifestations. Shock makes your job as a children's lawyer more difficult. Physiologically, shock is when the nervous system shuts down. Whatever is happening externally is too intense for the nervous system to process, so it becomes overwhelmed and goes into a near-complete freeze state. People in a state of emotional shock have lost the function of the neocortex, so their executive functioning is turned off. Very often the emotional center of the brain shuts down too. People in a state of shock are in a non-feeling state. When there is a physical injury, shock allows the person not to feel the pain of that injury. It quite literally shuts off the pain receptors so the pain is not so overwhelming to the person. Emotional shock works similarly, wherein all emotions shut down, and this includes "good" emotions, e.g., joy, happiness, and excitement.

This is a vital protection for humans in many ways, as it allows us to continue living despite what would otherwise be overwhelming emotional or physical pain. But when your child clients experience it and you meet with them at that time in their lives, it is very difficult to have any real conversation with them about the past, the future, or even the present. Besides numbing the emotions, shock also shuts down the higher brain functioning, making it difficult for children to remember who you are and what you tell them and often means they have forgotten you the next time you meet.

Imagine for a moment what the experience of removal is like for a child. It involves, at the very least, a social worker showing up and telling the child to take the most essential parts of his life and put them in a bag and go to someone else's home, sometimes that of a stranger. It often includes an act of violence, an interview reviewing traumatic history, or police involvement. These are situations that would shock anyone, let alone a child who has little control over his environment generally and no control in these situations. This experience by itself leads to a state of shock for many children. And it is in this space that you arrive for the first time, usually within a week of this occurring.

The other problem with the shock state, and any freeze state for that matter, is that it can appear at first glance as if everything is going well for the child, particularly for very young children. One of the red flags with infant clients is when someone says a child is a "good baby" who never cries. With a child whose needs are always being met, slight whining can be sufficient to get her needs met, so it may not be unusual that a child like that rarely cries. In your clients, however, they likely have a history of not having had their needs met, or even if their needs were being met, the fact the court system is involved means the child has had a recent trauma. Therefore, a child in that state who is not crying is a red flag. It may not mean anything bad for the child, but it generally means you need to look more closely. Thus, it is very important to ask not only about negative behaviors but also about these numb-like behaviors.

Familial Trauma Is Unique

Now that we have discussed what trauma is and how it manifests, it is important to understand what makes familial trauma unique. As we will discuss below, trauma resolves best when there is a strong, stable adult in the child's life. Thus, in war or when someone dies in a car accident, families come together to support one another. Although the external event is terrible, healing happens with this support.[162] As we will discuss in Chapter 5, children learn to self-regulate through the emotional regulation their primary caregivers express and teach. As noted elsewhere in this chapter, Dr. Levine teaches that trauma is held in the nervous system and can be released safely in situations where we can cry, shake, and move the trauma through our system. Thus, children must have (1) the implicit self-regulation knowledge and (2) a safe environment in which to move the trauma through the system in order to heal.

Familial trauma can destroy that ability to heal. When the trauma exists within the family structure, the very people who are supposed to be supporting the child through the trauma are the ones causing it. Therefore, even if the adult is capable of self-regulation, which is often not the case, the adult is not a safe person in whom to confide and release the trauma the child experiences. It is important to recognize that caregivers may be sources of ongoing trauma for children despite laws giving them rights to contact the children and even rights for visitation and placement. This can be true in both dependency and family court.

Resilience

This chapter can be a little overwhelming, but we do not want you to think that simply because someone has experienced traumatic events and that trauma has

---

162. This is not to say there is no residual trauma from war-torn countries, only that the nature of how trauma heals is different in external vs. familial trauma.

become stuck or unresolved there is no hope for him. This section will look at the beginning of the resilience research and some of the forms of therapy that work best with trauma.

The Center on the Developing Child at Harvard University created a working paper that stated:[163]

> Science shows that children who do well despite serious hardship have had *at least one stable and committed relationship with a supportive adult.* These relationships buffer children from developmental disruption and help them develop "resilience," or the set of skills needed to respond to adversity and thrive. This working paper from the National Scientific Council on the Developing Child explains how protective factors in a child's social environment and body interact to produce resilience, and discusses strategies that promote healthy development in the face of trauma.

This makes sense. Remember that Dr. Levine defined trauma as a loss of connection. Thus, coming back to a sense of connection is vital to healing trauma.

With regard to the nervous system, the polyvagal theory, as described by Stephen Porges, describes "a complex social engagement system mediated by facial gestures and vocalizations,"[164] meaning that humans' nervous systems regulate through engagement with others and we learn to regulate through viewing others' facial expressions. Thus, when someone feels safe, his defensive emotions become less intrusive.[165] In other words, social interactions that feel safe are what help the nervous system stabilize and come back into the normal ebb and flow the system can handle rather than the stuck sympathetic and parasympathetic responses you see with trauma. This is why it is so important for your clients to have someone in their life with whom they feel safe.

This is good news and difficult news for those who work with children in the family and dependency law systems. The good news is that children have the

---

163. Center on the Developing Child at Harvard University (2015), *Supportive Relationships and Active Skill-Building Strengthen the Foundations of Resilience: Working Paper No. 13* (emphasis added).

164. STEPHEN W. PORGES, THE POLYVAGAL THEORY: NEUROPHYSIOLOGICAL FOUNDATIONS OF EMOTIONS, ATTACHMENT, COMMUNICATION, AND SELF-REGULATION xiii (W. W. Norton & Company, Inc., 2011).

165. *Id.* at xiv.

potential for resilience and having a stable adult in their life can help them make it through these difficult times. The problem, as stated, is that a resilient adult is often the child's caregiver, but in family and dependency law cases, the caregivers often cause the trauma. It can be difficult because of laws, child welfare constraints; and in family law cases, the adversity between families to help children connect with these stable, resilient adults. But supportive adults can be a coach, a pastor, a band teacher, a therapist, or even a neighbor. The most important resilience question you can ask your clients is, "Who matters to you?" Helping ensure that your clients have continued contact with these people is vital. Your own ability to create a safe place for a child is important to a child's healing in this difficult process.

Peer relationships can also help in the healing process and sometimes are necessary for healing. As Dr. Perry learned with a child who spent his first three years of life in a Russian orphanage, even very young peers can provide healing for extensive trauma patterns. In one of the most incredible stories in his book, Dr. Perry went to a first-grade classroom and explained how the brain develops and how it learns from having experiences and how young Peter's brain could learn from his classmates:[166]

> [O]ver time, their (the other students') natural goodness emerged . . . They were tolerant of his developmental problems, patient in correcting his mistakes and nurturing in their interactions. These children provided many more positive therapeutic experiences than we (the clinic where Dr. Perry worked) ever could have given Peter.

And, of course, there are different forms of therapy that help children. For young children who have attachment/relationship trauma, they need a form of dyadic therapy,[167] meaning the therapy is with an adult who can be a parent or another caregiver. If the child is not living with a biological parent and is having issues, the therapy can begin with the caregiver, and if the child is eventually returned to a biological parent, the parent can begin to do the therapy with the child.

---

166. Perry, *supra* note 149, at 229.

167. Dyadic simply means two; thus, there are two people in the therapy, generally the child and any caregiver or parent.

Generally, talk therapy is not very helpful for children, particularly when there are deep trauma patterns because "the best verbal therapies can offer is to help people inhibit the automatic physical actions that their emotions provoke."[168] Thus, the trauma is still present in the nervous system, but the talk therapy helps the child to stop acting on his impulses. Over time, that will be insufficient to resolve the trauma itself. One form of therapy becoming more common, however, is trauma-focused cognitive behavioral therapy. When done in its best form, this also is a form of quasi-dyadic therapy. It involves a caregiver as someone who helps use the skills learned in therapy in the home setting. One of the benefits of talk or play therapy with traumatized children is the fact that the therapist is a stable, calm, consistent, and supportive adult in the child's life. But ultimately, we believe other forms of therapy are better suited to resolve nervous system trauma.

New trauma therapies continue to emerge. Somatic experiencing, a form of therapy created by Dr. Levine, is showing promise with PTSD[169] and has worked very well with children, even preverbal children.[170] Unfortunately, because somatic experiencing is still in the early stages of becoming "evidence-based," it is rarely available with insurance. Eye movement desensitization and reprocessing (EMDR) is another newer form of non-talk trauma therapy with good results for trauma. As EMDR has become more accepted, it is slowly making its way into the offices of therapists who take insurance. Therefore, it may be available to your clients depending on your jurisdiction. There are still other forms of emerging somatic-based therapies, and we will continue to update the online materials with them.

Interestingly, sometimes therapy is not the most therapeutic avenue, especially for children. In *The Body Keeps the Score*, Dr. van der Kolk provides a list of a variety of non-therapy therapeutic interventions specifically for trauma, including yoga and theater. Both of these are body-based and bring some structure to actions. Yoga allows the body to learn to move in new ways and release energy

---

168. Ogden, *supra* note 125, at 22.

169. Danny Brom et al., *Somatic Experiencing for Posttraumatic Stress Disorder: A Randomized Controlled Outcome Study*, 30 J. TRAUMATIC STRESS 304 (2017), *available at* https://traumahealing.org/wp-content/uploads/2017/06/Somatic-Experiencing-for-Posttraumatic-Stress-Disorder-2017.pdf.

170. PETER A. LEVINE, IN AN UNSPOKEN VOICE: HOW THE BODY RELEASES TRAUMA AND RESTORES GOODNESS (North Atlantic Books 2010).

in safe patterns. Meditation can also help calm an overactive nervous system.[171] Theater allows someone to enter the cathartic aspect of playing someone else and working through issues somewhat at distance rather than through a direct experience that may be too overwhelming. Rebecca had a client who had been sexually abused and raised by a variety of relatives; the client found her voice and her healing in her drama class in high school. Similarly, Phil had a teenage therapy client from a very high-conflict divorce who had previously been socially avoidant; he found his voice and learned to trust his peers when he started acting in college. Both of these children explained the acting itself as being therapeutic along with the community they met in the theater class.[172]

Sports are also a great way for children to begin to heal from trauma. Sports get bodies moving, and they often have a team component. For children who refuse therapy, see if they are interested in joining a sports team if you believe your client is experiencing trauma reactions. It may not be the right time to work through the trauma itself. It could be years before the child is ready for that. But getting the body and the nervous system moving in a healthy way is a big step toward allowing the healing to begin.

Finally, humans need human contact to heal. Yes, touch. This is difficult for us to write because in the work you do in family and dependency law, when you talk about touch, it is almost always unsafe touch. But supportive, loving touch is not only helpful but also crucial to a child's development. Dr. Perry describes a foster mother who would rock and hold children of all ages, and as Dr. Perry stated, "Mama P. discovered, long before we did, that many young victims of abuse and neglect need physical stimulation, like being rocked and gently held, comfort seemingly appropriate to far younger children."[173] If children were never provided that safe, loving touch, it can be necessary for them much later in life. Food and shelter matter, yes, but the care and love that comes with holding and rocking and interacting with children is just as important. Many of your clients will have missed this part of their infancy. Instead, caregivers either were too

---

171. Rebecca is a yoga teacher and still believes it is necessary to point out that there are times when yoga and meditation can be too overwhelming for someone who is in the throes of a trauma response. That stillness can set off an activation response that can overwhelm a system. That said, if that does not happen, yoga and meditation can greatly reduce the trauma responses that people hold in their bodies.

172. There are numerous examples of popular actors (male and female) who have described abusive childhoods and that acting has helped them learn to deal with those residual issues.

173. Perry, *supra* note 149, at 95.

absent to provide it or did not know how to provide it. Therapists who work with adults who have experienced significant trauma in their childhood often need to teach their clients about safe touch and how much rocking can help. Even using a phrase such as "always rocking with you," with or without the actual rocking, can help these clients learn to feel safe.

You can help foster parents and caregivers understand the importance of this in children's lives. This is one of the reasons it is important for children to be placed with people they know, if possible, because children and caregivers alike are less fearful to provide this physical closeness. But you can also encourage it in foster caregivers. This educational piece can be one of the most effective interventions in helping children heal from the trauma they have experienced because it allows the trauma to heal in a more natural course than through means that could make it worse and increase the PTSD-like symptoms.[174] We cannot overemphasize the importance of loving and comforting caregivers in a child's life to help that child heal from trauma.

Implications for Your Practice

This chapter has been focused on the science and the psychology behind trauma. This section pulls these issues together and discusses how and why these issues affect your practice and what you can do to help your clients understand themselves better and to help you understand your clients better.

Myths about Trauma

First, it is important to dispel some common myths we have experienced in the legal profession. After reading this chapter, we hope you will understand why these myths are myths. We continue to hear people say the effects of domestic violence are not as bad because the child was not in the room and did not see the violence. We continue to hear that a dirty home is only a dirty home and not a form of severe neglect. We continue to hear that if a child cannot remember the trauma, it cannot affect the child's development later in life. Why are these all false? Because trauma is in the nervous system. It is in a lack of connection. It is in the feelings of fear and not being safe. These are key components of severe

---

174. *Id.* at 71.

neglect or abuse, as described by the NCTSN, and trauma that happens around but not to the child. Remember that children are exposed to the traumas even if they are too young or are somewhat removed from the traumatizing events.

Another common myth is that if a monitor can be present during visits, a child is safe with a dangerous parent. After reading this chapter, what would you think if an infant were placed in a visit with a perpetrator of domestic violence and that perpetrator fed the child and cared for her but the child remained silent the entire time? What if after the visit the child cried for two hours? There are many ways to interpret these actions, but from a trauma-informed place, we see a child who is in a state of freeze while in the presence of the perpetrator because that is the only safe way to be around that person who has committed such acts of violence. Then after the visit is over, the child's system is so overwhelmed with having been in "freeze mode" for the visit, the child begins to cry to release all of that pent-up activation. We continue to hear people say that these visits are safe for children because "nothing bad happens during the visit, and the perpetrator appears to parent well during the visit."[175]

Remember that one of the requirements of a PTSD diagnosis is either avoidance of trauma-related thoughts or feelings or avoidance of trauma-related reminders. So someone experiencing PTSD wants to avoid reminders of the initial trauma, but if the court system places children in a room with the trauma reminder, is that not just retraumatizing the child who has no say in the matter? Obviously, this is not true of all children, but understanding how trauma affects the nervous system gives you another avenue for understanding how the decisions you make in court affect your child clients.

These examples are not to say this interpretation is the only one, but rarely have either of us heard it offered as a possibility at all. Instead, we encourage you to use the information in this chapter to make a more holistic evaluation of the circumstances. Always ask about behaviors and think about the effects of what the child experienced previously before assuming that just because you know nothing bad will happen in a situation, the child's nervous system knows that as well.

---

175. We also often hear stories that children seemingly act fine while at the home of an allegedly abusive parent, but the other parent expresses concerns that the child has meltdowns not long after the exchange. Such discrepancies can be a function of that trauma experience.

Speaking with Your Client

One aspect we discuss less often as lawyers for children is that part of your job is to have distressing conversations with your client and then often leave them in that distressed state. Unlike therapists who have an opportunity to mitigate the increased distressing responses in their clients, your job is to get information, discuss issues relevant to the case, and move on. This causes two main problems. First, when children are distressed, they are less able to have a meaningful conversation, *particularly* if they are young children; remember that the neorcortex shuts down when in a trauma response. Second, you likely do this work because you care about children, and seeing children in that distressed state and sending them on their way can be draining on you as their lawyer. We will discuss that issue more in Chapter 12, but here we will discuss how to notice what is happening in your client and some simple tools to help you manage it.

To be clear, this is not a section on how to be a therapist. But there are simple techniques you can use to help your client (and potentially yourself, but that will be discussed in Chapter 12) regulate some of the extreme emotions and nervous system states that exist during conversations with you. This is important for another reason; if your client is so activated or frozen by your discussion, the conversation you have will not benefit the case in any way. Your client's memory will be shot, and her ability to tell you what she wants will be nearly gone. We call this trauma sensitive interviewing.

Perhaps the most important aspect of trauma-sensitive interviewing is ensuring you are as regulated as possible. Your own state of dysregulation can cause dysregulation in a child. Thus, it is important to self-regulate before entering a conversation with the child client. We will discuss ways to do this in Chapter 12, but your self-regulation helps in two main ways. First, it models self-regulation for children, and second, if you are self-regulated, your client can feel safe in your presence. In contrast, if you are dysregulated, your client will likely feel less safe. Every person has days when they are more and less regulated, but being conscious of your own dysregulation and regulation when entering conversations will begin to help create that safer space for children. Being self-regulated can also help you monitor your child client's traumatic symptoms.

First, it is vital to notice what trauma a child has experienced, including the trauma that is specific to the case as well as the trauma that is not. Second, one of the best ways to help a child regulate the trauma in the moment is to take a break when you notice something is becoming overwhelming. The easiest way to do this is to intersperse asking the child a question about something he likes to do for fun or a movie he recently watched. That simple question can bring a child out of a trauma response and into a more functional and coherent place.

We cannot state this enough; let children cry. We have both seen countless well-meaning caregivers and professionals who tell children not to cry because everything will turn out all right in the end. Rebecca also sees this frequently with judges in the courtroom. But these cases deal with very difficult situations that would overwhelm most well-adjusted adults, not to mention children with underdeveloped coping skills. Crying is going to happen. And it is perfectly natural and very healthy for children to release some of that grief through tears. Phil was in the middle of a relocation evaluation with a school-aged girl who loved both of her parents and needed to cry as a way of managing her distress that her parents were likely to live a plane-ride apart. This is normal. Crying is one of the releases Dr. Levine mentions for resolving an overactive ANS response. It can be very difficult to learn just to sit with someone who is crying, but it can also be the greatest gift you give your clients. Let them know it is okay to be sad, to be upset, and to cry. You can still let them know you will do everything in your power to help them through this difficult process as their legal representative.

That said, try not to let them stay there too long. The nervous system is designed to move, not get stuck, and you can help by bringing the conversation to a topic unrelated to the trauma. After a short time, ask about movies, fun, school, animals, anything that is not connected to the trauma. Help these children's nervous systems, and eventually their higher cognitive functioning, understand that nothing lasts forever, knowing that while it is appropriate to be sad in the moment and going forward, there is a place in them that still feels joy and can laugh and can play with puppies. After letting the crying continue for a while, one of Phil's favorite expressions is to tell the child, "I know this is how you feel now, but let's also talk about other feelings you have and will continue to have as things improve." This process of simultaneously supporting and acknowledging the current emotion and then providing a temporal structure to it can be very comforting.

Because of the memory issues and cognitive issues involved with trauma, it is often important to provide the same information to children multiple times. Make sure you reintroduce yourself and explain your role each time you speak with children. Do not just ask if they remember you. No one feels comfortable saying they do not remember someone, and children are no different. Let them know it is okay not to remember you and, even if they do, you just want to give them a reminder in case they forgot anything else.

Children who are experiencing trauma responses can be easily overwhelmed. Thus, it is important to slow down—a lot. This can be a very difficult task for lawyers. The law moves quickly. You have hundreds of tasks to finish. You are never done. You just want to get information and move on. The judge is telling you to hurry up if you are interviewing your clients at court. But that rushing can overwhelm the child, and you are unlikely to get any beneficial information from the conversation. If you catch yourself rushing and talking faster than you can think, stop, slow down, and tell the child you want to start over, but slower. Phil routinely slows down when the children with whom he is talking speed up in their talking. Sometimes he takes a deep breath and encourages his clients to do the same.

Finally, have a little fun. Sometimes children enjoy being goofy. Sometimes they like to play. Sometimes they like to draw. Sometimes they want to ask you a million questions. Let them be themselves and guide the conversation. You have a job to do, but part of that job is helping these children navigate the legal system, and part of that is letting them have a little fun in the process. This will not work for every client, but it can be very beneficial when it does.

Conclusions

Most of this book connects strongly to the concepts identified in this chapter. There is so much to learn about trauma, and some court systems are doing an incredible job of becoming trauma-informed and trauma-responsive. We hope this chapter has helped reshape how you think about your clients, from birth through adolescence. We hope you can engage with your clients a little differently and be the imaginary friend they need to navigate this court process.

Child Development 5

We suspect that when you went to law school, you were not provided much, if any, training in child development. When you decided to represent children in family or dependency cases, you might have received some training in interviewing children or on the impact of abuse, neglect, high conflict, or domestic violence on children. Although these trainings are likely to be very important in your professional growth, they often lack specific differentiation among children of different ages. This chapter will provide an overview of critical development information that will help you better understand your child clients based on their age and developmental needs.

This chapter will cover physical, emotional, and social child development as well as key issues to consider at specific developmental ages and aspects to consider when interviewing your clients or their caregivers. Knowing where your clients should be developmentally helps you understand whether your clients are being neglected or if something else is happening in the home that is affecting your client's development and may affect your representation.

Birth–3 Years of Age

In many ways, this is the most critical developmental stage because so much growth takes place in just these three short years. The brain develops neuropathways that allow for growth in many aspects of development, including both physical and language development.

Physical development includes learning gross motor skills such as crawling, walking, and climbing and fine motor skills such as grasping, drawing, and using scissors. By age 3, many infants have begun the process of toilet training, gaining even greater physical control over their body. The Centers for Disease Control and Prevention (CDC) has a list of milestones for multiple developmental stages up to age 5.[176] By age 3, children should be able to walk up the stairs using opposite legs and balance briefly on one foot. They should also be able to run easily. As their lawyer, that is the easiest one for you to notice. Using the developmental checklists provided in the online resources will also help you with ages before age 3.

Language development includes receptive skills in which children begin to understand what others are saying and the meaning of different words. It also includes expressive skills, going from one-word "sentences" such as "mama" and "dada" to two-word sentences such as "pick up" or "want bottle" to more complex sentences of three or more words. Even more incredibly, children at this age are able to learn more than one language, and some learn sign language. Most importantly, by age 3, children should be understandable to most strangers. Because of neglect, many of your clients will have poor speech skills. So knowing that you, as a stranger, should understand children by age 3 is vital to your work as a lawyer.

For example, "in the first few years of life, more than 1 million new neural connections are formed every second."[177] As children grow, the plasticity of the brain decreases, and the ability to learn and change and adapt begins to slow. By the time children are 18 years old, the effects of language begin to appear in that

---

176. Centers for Disease Control and Prevention, Developmental Milestones, https://www.cdc.gov/ncbddd/actearly/milestones/index.html (last visited Oct. 31, 2017).

177. Center on the Developing Child, Harvard University, *Five Numbers to Remember about Early Childhood Development*, https://developingchild.harvard.edu/resources/five-numbers-to-remember-about-early-childhood-development/#note (last visited Oct. 31, 2017).

children with college-educated parents have two to three times the vocabulary of those whose parents have not completed high school.[178]

At the same time these physical and verbal skills are forming, infants are beginning the reciprocal process known as attachment. Tomes have been written on attachment, and considerable research is being done and often changes what we think we as a society know about the topic. This section provides the most basic information necessary for you to do your work as a children's lawyer.

Attachment occurs when the parent is responsive to the infant's needs while the infant simultaneously engages with the parent. Attachment serves two main functions. First, attachment serves to support the child's relationship with her caregivers. Second, attachment serves to support the child's neuropsychological reduction of stress, the beginnings of the nervous system's ability to handle stress and trauma as described in Chapter 4.

In other words, when the infant is stressed (e.g., hungry, dirty, or otherwise stressed) and the parent provides calm, soothing touch and voice, the infant feels safe and secure. Healthy parenting leads to a secure attachment, one in which the infant recognizes the world is a safe place and one in which the infant is soothed and begins learning to self-soothe, a skill that will continue to grow well into adulthood. The attachment process increases over the first several months, but during the first six months of life, an infant is comfortable being soothed by any warm caregiver. Around age seven months, however, the infant begins to experience a phenomenon known as stranger anxiety, in which the infant feels anxious if someone other than the primary caregivers (usually the mother or father but possibly a full-time caregiver) attempt to soothe the infant. However, usually within a month after the start of stranger anxiety, the infant can again be soothed by warm caregivers as long as she feels safe in the caregiver's care. One way the infant can learn to trust strangers is to look at the primary caregiver; if the caregiver is not stressed by the stranger, the infant can feel safe. An infant with a secure attachment can tolerate the stress typically associated with short-term absence from one of the primary caregivers.

On the other hand, some infants experience trauma or other experiences that are likely to interrupt any of these processes. Physical and language skills may become delayed, and more importantly, attachment is harmed. The brain is harmed when the infant is exposed to trauma, and the infant senses that the world is unsafe. For such infants, attachment is often insecure or disorganized. Children with insecure attachments become clingy and are unable to self-soothe

---

178. *Id.*

when stressed. They often fail to develop language or physical skills, and if those skills were developing, they may begin to regress. Insecure attachments are further distinguished in that some children experience avoidant attachments. In this case, the child generally avoids getting close to caregivers, whereas others experience ambivalent attachments in which the child is generally ambivalent and passive in the presence of her caregiver.

Children with either insecure or disorganized attachment are often hard to understand, in part because all of this is occurring at a preverbal level. All of this is taking place without language skills that would otherwise help them understand what is going on around them. Instead, without language, they simply feel insecure and overwhelmed emotionally. Although it takes more work, children with insecure attachments can be soothed and can learn to self-soothe, although many will need therapeutic assistance from ever-increasing infant mental health services.

Even worse, some children develop what is known as disorganized attachments. Children who develop disorganized attachments alternate between clinging and withdrawing and are extremely difficult to soothe. For them, the world is a very scary place, and they have no one they can trust. Usually, these infants have been exposed to severe trauma, domestic violence, or caregivers with severe mental health or personality disorders. You will note the disorganized attachment in children under age 3 who indiscriminately come to you, a stranger, for a hug while simultaneously crumbling to the ground when overwhelmed.

As a lawyer representing these children and not a clinician, perhaps it is best to look at attachment from a nervous system perspective. The goal of a healthy attachment figure is for a child to learn to self-regulate when he encounters a stressor in life. If you notice that the caregiver is unable to help the infant regulate or that your young client has tantrums that are more extreme than usual, you would likely want your client evaluated by a clinician. Further—and this is more difficult to notice—ask about whether children cry. Some caregivers like to tell you, "He is such a good baby; he never cries." That is a red flag that a child might have attachment issues and should be evaluated. Rebecca always asks the follow-up question "Does he cry when he needs something?" If the answer is no or not really, it is generally helpful to have your client evaluated.

Given the types of cases in which you will likely be involved, your client is likely to experience an insecure or disorganized attachment. As noted earlier, this can make it very difficult for your client to be soothed no matter how hard you or temporary caregivers (e.g., foster parents and relatives) try.

By the time infants are about 18 months old, they are likely to be developing some language and, with sufficient warmth from caregivers, may begin to learn to understand, at a very basic level, words for some of their feelings. At this age, toddlers typically begin the process of separation-individuation, during which they develop some increased separation from their caregivers. Their physical skills improve, and they become more mobile. Toddlers become more oppositional, test limits, and develop their own identity. They no longer need caregivers to meet every need, as they can begin to feed themselves and toddle around. They engage with their peers in parallel play, often playing side by side with their peers rather than interacting in shared or symbolic play.

From an attachment perspective, toddlers of this age who have a secure attachment will use their caregivers as a base for safety while wandering off and trying new things. If you watch children of this age who have a secure attachment, when they fall down, they look to their caregiver before crying and if the caregiver looks unstressed, the child often does not cry (unless, of course, the child is hurt more than a slight fall would elicit). Toddlers with insecure or disorganized attachments often do not know how to act when something bad happens to them. As infants, they rarely had their needs met in a safe, warm, and loving manner, so as toddlers beginning to explore the world on their own, they often cry or retreat into themselves for no apparent reason. Some have learned it is unsafe to cry; others have learned that if they cry, their needs will not be met, so there is no point. Some children simply crumble when they fall (e.g., those with ambivalent-insecure attachment) even when there is no physical evidence of being hurt, largely because they cannot manage any hurts. Others never show pain (e.g., those with avoidant-insecure attachment), again almost being in a freeze-like state. Those with disorganized attachments show no patterns to how they might act when having fallen, sometimes seemingly overreacting in hysterics and other times freezing and seeming emotionally flat.

By the age of 3, children are usually able to understand and express concrete emotions such as happy, sad, scared, and excited. If the toddler has a secure attachment with his caregivers, he is ready for moving onto the next stage of development, i.e., the preschool stage.

However, if the toddler has an insecure or disorganized attachment, she is likely to be extremely clingy or to push the caregiver aside, delayed in language or physical development, socially awkward and either fearful or bullying, and unable to have a secure separation and differentiation. She is unlikely to understand and be able to express her feelings in healthy and concrete ways. She is likely to be overwhelmed easily, have meltdowns for no apparent reason, and be difficult to soothe when anxious and overwhelmed. She is likely to be a challenge for you and her caregivers. This child is likely at high risk for functioning successfully in an early preschool setting. Infant/toddler mental health services, combined with predictable and warm nurturing, will be needed to assist her in healing from her challenges.

Preschool Stage (Ages 3–5)

Well-functioning preschoolers, i.e., those who have had a secure attachment with their caregivers, are fun, engaging, and full of life. Some may be wary of strangers initially, and remember, you are a stranger the first time you meet such a child or even the second and third times if a significant amount of time occurs between visits, but within minutes, they are likely to start talking and playing without fear. They have a difficult time expressing complex feelings and often cannot recount specific experiences; other times they can talk specifically about their experiences, including both good and bad. However, their memory can be affected by many internal and external circumstances. These memory issues will be addressed later in the chapter.

Preschoolers begin to develop friendships, engage in interactive and symbolic play with their same-aged peers, begin to understand more complex emotions, and widen their circle of adults in whom they trust. They begin to learn academic tasks and start to feel a sense of competence in skills they enjoy. They also begin to differentiate their parents' respective strengths and weaknesses and recognize the differences in what they like and don't like about each of them. Over time, preschoolers who have secure attachments grow into confident and secure children who are ready for kindergarten.

Of course, those preschoolers who have experienced trauma without the requisite nurturing to reduce the impact of that trauma will have very different experiences. As noted, their attachments will be insecure or disorganized, and as a result, they will have significant difficulty developing and maintaining relationships with the peers and adult figures in their lives. This will make it very difficult for your significantly traumatized or neglected preschool-aged clients to form a relationship with you. They are at risk of being the preschoolers who are aggressive with their peers, easily emotionally upset, and difficult to soothe when they become upset. Their behaviors and emotions are often dysregulated, meaning there is no predictability or apparent connection between what they are experiencing and the symptoms they are showing. Often these children will be expelled from day cares and preschools.

They also are likely to struggle at learning because their energy is spent trying to manage their traumatic experiences and emotional responses. Some children become depressed and withdrawn. Nightmares may become more pronounced.

Self-confidence may suffer, and there can be increases in aggressive and anxious behaviors. Many of the children in this age group worry about their parents and may try to act "perfect." They may do this out of fear or they unconsciously may be taking care of their parents or siblings. We may be seeing the early signs of parentified behavior, in which they care emotionally for their parents and younger siblings, ignoring their own needs.

Like the infants/toddlers who need therapeutic assistance to learn to manage their emotions and heal from their traumas, these preschoolers will likely need therapeutic assistance with play therapy or newer evidence-based models such as Parent-Child Interaction Therapy or Child Parent Psychotherapy, as well as the consistency and stability of a therapist trained in helping these children heal from their experiences. These forms of therapy are dyadic, meaning the toddler and a caregiver participate because, as we discussed about attachment, the way children of this age heal is through relationships. Thus, at this age, therapy should help to improve relationships and not be a form of individual therapy where the child has not fully individuated yet. It is important to understand whether the therapy your client receives focuses on helping her learn to regulate toxic stress and trauma.

Representing children from birth to 5 years requires a different type of interaction than representing older verbal children. While many people say you cannot represent the wishes of a nonverbal child, children can tell you what they want in more ways than words, and children under the age of 5 are master communicators without words. While we will discuss how children may respond differently in specific situations, from a development perspective, it is important to see how your client interacts with all of the caregivers in his life and how your client interacts with you, a stranger. Knowing these developmental milestones and the risk factors of insecure and disorganized attachments in these young children will help you better understand what your young, nonverbal, or barely verbal clients are telling you through their actions.

School-Aged Stage (Ages 6–11)

This is an age at which children thrive on structure and routine. Children with secure attachments can continue growing in their peer relationships, and they are learning to master social rules. Creativity continues to grow, and these children are adept at making up games with unique rules. Rules are important because these children focus on fairness in their lives. Socialization and being part of a group are important to children of this age. They are learning to understand and express their feelings even better and to master cognitive and academic skills. They continue to feel confident in certain areas, even while feeling insecure in others. They still can be silly and prefer to play much of the time. They are learning skills in areas such as academics, sports, music, dance, and art. Self-esteem grows when they function well in school, on the playground, and in the family. It is not uncommon for children of this age to have different relationships with each parent, preferring mom for some things and dad for others. They continue to differentiate between their parents and each parent's respective skills, and unless they become alienated or estranged from one of their parents (see Chapter 8), they enjoy healthy and unique relationships with each of their parents.

Children of this age who have experienced significant trauma often feel directly responsible for those experiences. They may exhibit multiple symptoms, including tantrums, regression, sleep problems, acting out, behavioral and academic problems in school, withdrawal or aggression with peers, and depression. This is a population that believes in fairness, and these children usually want to please their parents and other adults in their lives, including you. Children in high-conflict divorces feel overwhelmed by their parents' conflict and usually try to fix it, yet they are ill-equipped to do so. Children who have experienced trauma are often hypervigilant and worry about family members and their well-being. When a parent is depressed, these children are at risk for parentified behavior in which they attempt to take emotional care of that parent and their siblings.

Some traumatized children may present as asymptomatic on the surface but feel overwhelmed and vulnerable underneath. These children are at risk for boundary issues, in which they lose their childhood in unhealthy ways. Some children engage in emotional splitting, in which they begin to see one parent as "all-good" and the other as "all-bad," resulting in the child becoming alienated and rejecting one parent, for no apparent reasons. Others simply feel stuck due to loyalty conflicts and may become emotionally constricted (the freeze response), worrying about both of their parents and being afraid to learn, to engage with peers, or to take on typical extracurricular activities. Some of these children have difficulty maintaining a strong internalized self-image because of the trauma, instead becoming overwhelmed and disorganized, struggling with multiple emotions at the same time. Still others are at risk of becoming parentified, in which children take care of their parents or siblings emotionally or physically.

A group of these children are at risk of becoming infantilized, in which they do not develop age-appropriate maturation skills. Many of these children cling to and/or sleep with one or both parents and have difficulty differentiating their own feelings and needs from those of others.

As with younger traumatized children, these school-aged children will benefit from therapy designed to help them learn to understand their feelings and express them in healthy ways. Teaching school-aged children to develop healthy coping skills rather than isolating, avoiding, and splitting, will also be helpful to them. Finally, these children need to learn to heal emotionally and develop some understanding they are not responsible for the trauma they have experienced.

As a children's representative, it is important to remember these children are in an "in-between" stage where in some moments they will appear to act much older than they are and in other moments they will appear to act much younger than they are. Rebecca first noticed this while working as a day camp director. The fifth-grade boys would act tough, but if something happened that upset them, they would break down in tears for what appeared to be fairly insignificant issues. At times, it was difficult to know how to act around this age group because they needed something different so often.

If you have the opportunity to see these children over time, you may notice how their stated position on the issues of the case can change, and they are usually fiercely loyal to their parents despite years of trauma. If they are not loyal, they often feel guilty about it. So, if they are telling you something they think will harm their parent, they often get very quiet about it. Sometimes they do the opposite and tell you everything is fine, but their entire demeanor shifts from when they are talking about issues unrelated to the case. It is important to get to know these children by talking about issues unrelated to the case so you understand their baseline before attempting to discuss the case issues. Then if you notice something shift, even if you never fully understand why it shifted, you at least have the information that something did shift and you need to keep your eyes open for other information.

With children this age, it is important to ask about peer relationships. This is the time when friendships begin to form in a way that makes them the primary component of their lives. Often children will not tell you about problems at home, but they might tell you they have no friends at school or that they are getting into fights with their friends at school. These are often indicators that something is bothering them elsewhere. Asking children about their extracurricular activities and school is vital to understanding what is happening in the home.

Finally, children of this age tend to believe the case is their fault regardless of the underlying reason for the case being in the court system. Children from situations as varied as domestic violence and sexual abuse have tendencies to feel as though the case is their fault. Remember, children of this age want to believe their parents are good and want life to be fair, so it makes sense for them to believe this is their fault. It is important not only to try to help them understand how this case is not their fault but also to do it in such a way as not to blame their parents. It can help to say that no one thinks their parents (or whoever is the cause of the case being in the system) are bad people, that everyone makes mistakes, that and our job is to help solve those mistakes and bring the family back together in whatever way works for the new family dynamics. Remember these children come from their parents, so if you blame the parents, it may sound to the child as though he is bad as well.

Because these children are in an in-between stage, from a legal perspective, they can be some of the most difficult children to represent. With younger children, who are less able to care for themselves and have less of a sense of individuation, it is often easier to determine a course of action from a developmental perspective. Older children, as you will see below, tend to be very emphatic about their desires. This age group tends to provide less guidance because of their fierce ambivalence or loyalty; their needs grow and change; and the fact that they are not at risk of brain development issues, like younger children are, sometimes make this age group the most difficult to represent. It is much easier to be sure of yourself as a lawyer with other age groups, and these younger school-aged children can be incredibly difficult clients from a legal perspective.

Tween Stage (Ages 12–14)

As anyone who has spent time at a middle school can tell you, children in this stage of development are, by their very nature, emotionally turbulent. Hormones are raging; their brains are going through the second major development stage, causing them to become more impulsive; and they are beginning a process in which they are more connected to peers than to the adults around them. Healthy tweens engage in activities that suit their personalities, and they gain confidence and feelings of self-worth when they succeed in school and their interests. They still rely on parents to guide them while simultaneously becoming more independent in their lives. Most importantly, although they make mistakes, those mistakes tend to be relatively harmless, and tweens are open to learning adaptive ways of engaging with others. All tweens begin to take risks, but healthy tweens tend to take safer risks.

In contrast, the tweens who have experienced trauma are significantly more likely than their same-aged peers to engage in riskier, perhaps harmful behaviors, including cutting, suicidal ideation and attempts, and use and abuse of alcohol and drugs. With ever-increasing societal pressures and cyberbullying, the more vulnerable of these children are at severe risk of suicide, the second-largest cause of death in children of this age. Traumatized children of this age typically do not feel confident academically and tend to avoid healthy extracurricular activities like their more successful peers. Some, by contrast, absorb themselves in school in an attempt to hide from what is happening in the home.

Lacking emotional maturity, they are more impulsive and more likely to withdraw and be depressed and/or more likely to act out behaviorally. They can be bullies, can challenge authority, and are at risk of engaging in petty criminal behaviors. They may become diagnosed with oppositional defiant disorder or aggressive disorders. They shut down emotionally and avoid letting anyone, least of all themselves, know how they are feeling. In fact, much of their acting out behavior serves the unconscious purpose of avoiding their feelings, usually because they are afraid of how they feel. Like their younger selves, they are disconnected from their feelings and develop internalizing or externalizing symptoms (or both) to remain in that disconnected state. They too can benefit from therapy designed to help them understand and feel safe with their feelings, while simultaneously developing active coping skills that are not harmful to themselves or others.

Adolescent Stage (Ages 15–18)

The major task for the adolescent is developing greater independence and autonomy from the family. Their separation-individuation process is like that of the 2-year-old. There can be a tendency to act with oppositional and negative behaviors, which do not rise to the level of diagnosable personality problems. Like toddlers, adolescents express some resistance and rebelliousness while forming their identity. Healthy adolescents function well in school, are self-confident, and have strong and supportive peer relationships. They learn to talk with their parents about life goals, and they begin to plan for driving, working, and attending college or vocational school. As a group, adolescents tend to be somewhat moody and reactive in their emotions. They may feel overwhelmed by pressure from their peers, use poor judgment, and be socially insecure. Their ideas, values, and goals are in a state of turmoil and may change considerably over their high school years. However, these years can be exciting ones as psychologically healthy teens grow into productive and idealistic individuals.

However, with this considerable internal turmoil, the adolescent stage is at potential risk. This is true for adolescents of intact families as well as for adolescents who have experienced trauma. When a major family trauma occurs to children at this age, such as experiencing parental separation or entering the dependency system, they worry about the loss of their family life. They tend to feel a blend of responsibility and guilt and/or blame or anger for the way it has affected them. Children of this age tend to be self-centered naturally, and the divorce becomes a disruption to them. If they experienced trauma earlier in their life, it tends to reinforce negative self-feelings and self-blame. They may avoid parents and authority figures, especially parents who burden them with loyalty conflicts and adult problems. When they have experienced parents who are in a high-conflict relationship, children in this age group are at increased risk for persistent academic failure, depression, suicide, delinquency, promiscuity, or substance abuse. Again, this is worsened if the adolescent has also experienced some form of trauma, especially sexual abuse. Lacking positive coping skills, many adolescents withdraw and avoid expressing their feelings and often lack an understanding of why they feel the way they do. Therapeutic intervention is critical for adolescents who are experiencing this array of symptoms, lest those symptoms spiral downward and out of control. As discussed in Chapter 4, therapeutic intervention can also include extracurricular activities the child enjoys.

Tweens and teens are similar to school-age children in their often-changing verbal positions, but more frequently than their younger counterparts, they have a tendency just to want to be over the situation at hand. Often this is a defense mechanism. Despite the fact tweens and teens act as if they need nobody in their lives, they still require parental or caregiver involvement. Thus, if parents or caregivers give up on difficult tweens and teens, it can cause them even more emotional damage and turmoil. This can make it difficult for you to represent them. Unlike nonverbal children who you recognize must communicate in other ways, it is easy to think that you can rely only on what a tween or teen is saying verbally about specific questions asked. As children get older, it becomes even more important to understand what matters to them in life and, more importantly, who matters to them.

As mentioned above, this is a period when children are transitioning from one form of relationship to another—from family oriented to peer oriented. The biggest concern in this age group is when children state they have no one in life upon whom they can rely. Many of them believe their families have failed them, the system has failed them, and even their friends have failed them. So why should they bother trusting anyone but themselves? These children often partake in exceedingly dangerous behaviors because they come from a place of believing no one cares and no one matters. Helping these children find positive peer groups or finding a strong support person is vital to helping them begin the healing process. Social media, while potentially dangerous, can be helpful, particularly where children have been removed from their school or neighborhood by a parent or the system. Tweens and teens can continue to communicate with friends across social media, and you can get court orders stating they may remain in contact with their friends in person as well. This is a crucial aspect to teens' lives and one that is often overlooked in the court system.

Children's Memory and the Question of Suggestibility

The final point to understand in some detail is how children develop memories and how what they tell us may be influenced by both real memories and memories that are not quite accurate. This section will outline the various ways in which children's memories may be affected by various internal and external influences. As we discussed in Chapter 4, these issues with memory exist because of development and not necessarily because of trauma.

Memory is a process that includes encoding, i.e., the process in which some experience is registered in memory, storage, i.e., the process in which those registered memories are stored in short-term memory, and retrieval, i.e., the process in which a memory is recalled and talked about. Long before we meet them, children are at risk of getting any of these processes confused and distorted. In this section, we will discuss the ways in which children's memories are at risk of becoming distorted over time.

First, recall the discussion about memory from Chapter 4 on trauma. While the rest of this chapter will focus on how memories may be influenced by external sources, particularly for younger children, it is important to remember that traumatic memories are different from other memories. It may be that someone can tell you only how they feel about something but not exactly why because the explicit memory of the event does not exist. Emotional memories are more disjointed than explicit memories. Procedural memories are deeper still and may be the only memory a child has of an event even if she cannot remember the facts surrounding why she feels the way she does. With that in mind, it is important to understand how explicit memories can change and be manipulated.

Let us discuss the progress of a typical case using an example of a sexual abuse allegation in a high-conflict divorce matter, although this process would be the same in any other type of allegation in either dependency or family court. In this case, the 3-year-old daughter came home, and when her mother changed her diaper, the daughter started to cry. When her mother asked what happened, the little girl said that her daddy had hurt her. Her mother then called her daughter's pediatrician to have her checked. When the pediatrician asked what happened, the mother, in front of the child, said that the child's father had touched the child's vagina. The pediatrician then asked the child if her father had touched her vagina, and the child said "yes." When the pediatrician asked the child if her father had hurt her, the child said "yes." Being a mandated reporter, the pediatrician contacted the local social services office and filed a suspected child abuse report. Over the next few weeks, the child was interviewed by a social worker, a forensic psychologist, a police officer, and the forensically trained sexual abuse expert. These interviews took place over the span of four weeks. Some of the interviews had a blend of open-ended and forced-choice questions, whereas others were more open-ended. The results of these interviews were inconclusive. Father also was interviewed, and he is adamant that he never touched his daughter inappropriately and that Mother is making up these allegations as a way of interfering with his parenting time.

In the meantime, Mother filed a motion in family court to halt Father's parenting time, and in an abundance of caution, the child is unable to see her father until all the evaluations are completed. Even after the inconclusive interviews of the daughter, Father was allowed only supervised visitation because the court wanted to be sure the child was safe. You were appointed to represent the child. When you saw your client, she told you that her daddy hurt her "peepee" and that she is afraid of him. You are unsure what to do.

According to Kathryn Kuehnle,[179] there are multiple hypotheses about what is happening in this situation. One is that the child has been molested and specific allegations are accurate and that she has accurately named her father as the perpetrator. However, other possible hypotheses include the following:

- The child has been sexually abused, but due to her young age and limited language and cognitive skills, she is unable to provide sufficient details about what happened.
- The child has been sexually abused, but due to fear or misguided loyalty, she is unwilling to disclose the abuse.
- The child is not a victim of sexual abuse but has misperceived an ambiguous or innocent touch.
- The child is not a victim of sexual abuse but has been influenced in some way by a concerned or hypervigilant caretaker.
- The child is not a victim of sexual abuse but has been intentionally manipulated in some way to allege sexual abuse.

---

179. KATHRYN KUEHNLE, ASSESSING ALLEGATIONS OF CHILD SEXUAL ABUSE (Professional Resource Press 2011).

- The child is not a victim of sexual abuse but has knowingly made a false allegation because of pressure from caretakers or others or for some personal reasons.

In other words, when an allegation is made, there are potentially many different "truths" about what has happened, and the investigators must be thorough in their efforts to understand which of those hypotheses has the greatest likelihood of "truth." Under the circumstances of this case, it is more likely than not that no abuse occurred, even if the child experienced some pain due to an irritation, and the child and/or mother misperceived some innocent or ambiguous touch as abuse. Then given the amount of questioning she experienced, the child perceived that her father had harmed her. This, of course, is the most innocent of explanations, whereas an explanation of abuse or an explanation of the mother manipulating the child are the most devious of explanations. Understanding the concept of base rates, in other words, the likelihood of one event or another, the most likely explanation is like one just described, with much lower base rates for abuse by a parent and active manipulation of the child and the circumstance by the mother.

Let us examine the potential events that could have influenced this child to keep making an allegation if there was no basis for it. The leading book on the subject, *Investigative Interviewing of Children: A Guide for Helping Professionals*,[180] provides guidance on this subject.

Source Monitoring

Source monitoring refers to developing an understanding of how a child knows what the child thinks she knows. For example, some children can remember being touched or hurt by someone, whereas other children have been told about being hurt or abused. The fact is that younger children, such as this 3-year-old, have more difficulty discriminating between what they have been told as compared with what they have experienced. Sometimes they will say something bad happened to them just because they have been told that something bad happened to them.

Question Type

Another potential source of difficulty in these situations lies in the types of questions the child has been asked. The most neutral, and useful, type of question is

---

180. Debra A. Poole & Michael E. Lamb, Investigative Interviews of Children: A Guide for Helping Professionals (American Psychological Association 1998).

the open-ended question such as, "Tell me what happened?" "What makes you afraid?" or "Tell me about your dad?" Of course, young children often omit the kinds of information that help adults understand what may have occurred, for example, on a particular weekend at their father's house. Also, although some young children can provide considerable information with open-ended questions, other children may give very short, limited answers, especially if they feel afraid for any reason.

Although open-ended questions may not result in quality answers, especially with very young children, other types of questions have potential problems and can lead to incorrect information. The second type of question that can be asked, and is common to lawyers, is the leading question. Similar to good cross-examination, leading questions in this scenario might be "What did your daddy do to hurt you?" It seems like it is open-ended, but it leads the child directly to the ultimate question and conclusion. Those are perhaps the most damaging types of questions one can ask. It assumes the answer in the question and essentially forces the child to say she was hurt even if she was not.

A third type of question attempts to get the child to explain a specific event by mentioning it more specifically. For example, asking a child "What caused your peepee to hurt" presupposes she was hurt and will remember it. Even more specific questions might include the phrase "when daddy hurt you," which assumes the fact her daddy hurt her. These suppositional questions are quite challenging, as they may cause the child to assume the fact that is embedded in the question, i.e., that daddy hurt her or that her peepee was hurt.

A fourth type of potentially challenging question is the forced-choice type of question, in which children are asked questions with only yes-no answers or other questions that can be answered only in a binary way. An example of such a question might be "Were you in the bathroom or the bedroom when you were hurt?" An example of a suppositional, forced-choice question might be "Were you in the bedroom or the bathroom when your daddy hurt you?"

Although open-ended questions are best, it is important to note that children's memories may not be influenced by timely or appropriate use of forced-choice or suppositional questions. If after appropriate open-ended questions and the child's limited answers you still have more questions for the child and after you've exhausted further open-ended questions such as "Tell me more about this" or "Please explain," you might want to take the child's actual words and ask a further question that might otherwise appear forced-choice. For example, in the above scenario, you might, after considerable open-ended questioning ask, "I'm a bit confused. Were you in the bedroom or bathroom when you were hurt?" By this stage of the questioning, it is unlikely that such a question will cause harm; instead, it may jog some memory that you can then use to ask further open-ended questions.

Too Many Questioners

Another potential problem is that when children are interviewed multiple times, they begin to think that what they said in previous interviews might not be accurate. As noted earlier in this chapter, young children try to please adults, and if they keep getting asked the same question, they will tell adults what they think the adult wants to hear. This may lead the child to change her story across different sets of questions. Then when the questions stop, the child assumes the most recent response was the correct one, reinforcing this desire to please. This may lead to an inconclusive finding, solely because the child's story changes over time because of many questioners.

This is why Children's Advocacy Centers were created to conduct forensic interviews of children who allegedly experienced abuse. Too often children have been interviewed by a neutral party (perhaps a teacher or day care provider), a caregiver, other family members, the police, and social services even in family law cases where they do not take the case to court. By the time a child gets to you, she may have had multiple interviews, and your own interview can be tainted as a result. We suggest asking that no one except a trained forensic interviewer in a properly recorded interview be allowed to interview a child after the case goes to court. If there already has been a proper forensic interview, everyone in the case (social services included) should be ordered not to interview the child about the underlying allegations. Rebecca has had multiple children tell her they are tired of being interviewed so many times about the same facts. It is unfair to the child, and multiple interviews only decrease their efficacy.

High Emotionality

Another source of influence comes from the emotions surrounding the event. If people respond to the child and her statements with a calm demeanor, the child is more likely to answer questions calmly. On the other hand, if the child senses that the adults around her are experiencing intense emotions, she is more likely to respond to those emotions and retrieval of memory might suffer. It is not uncommon for caregivers to respond to abuse allegations with high emotionality, particularly in a situation where parents or caregivers do not get along. Keeping an eye out for these issues in your cases can help you determine whether there might have been undue although not conscious influence.

Other Internal/External Influences

As noted in the possible hypotheses above, some children are influenced by pressures from caretakers or even therapists to make false accusations. Some children are angry, are revengeful, or want to hurt a parent and will make false allegations against that parent or stepparent. Still other children have significant emotional problems, including delusions and other psychotic experiences. Each of these types of children is at risk of having memory affected by such external or internal factors.

Always Maintain a Perspective of Disconfirmation

Given the possible variations associated with children's memory, it is important to maintain an attitude of disconfirmation when assessing or interviewing children about historical events, especially when there have been multiple interviews of the child over a span of time.[181] It is easy to assume abuse when a child expresses fear or says she was "hurt" at daddy's house. Recognizing that children's memories can be influenced requires you to look for evidence supporting the fact that abuse has taken place, as well as evidence that abuse has not taken place. Of course, if the child continues to confirm abuse, it is also important to accept that abuse has happened, despite efforts to seek information to discount it. In other words, after maintaining an attitude of disconfirmation, if the data supports confirmation, follow that path.

These considerations have been in the context of a high-conflict family law matter. Nothing is different in a dependency matter in which there are similar allegations of abuse or possible allegations of neglect. One of the reasons you will want to talk with your client about her life outside of the allegations is that it may help in building rapport and reducing the risk that you are contributing to the suggestibility or distorted memories. It also serves as a baseline for understanding children's demeanor and recall ability for non-traumatic events. If you keep these issues in mind and maintain an attitude of disconfirmation, looking for evidence that does and does not support the multiple hypotheses of your case, you can reduce the likelihood that your actions will add to your client's suggestibility.

---

181. The attitude of disconfirmation is to guard against confirmatory bias, a type of cognitive bias that will be discussed in detail in Chapter 11.

Some children are highly suggestible, and their memory retrieval might be faulty; others are less likely to be influenced by either internal or external factors, and their memory retrieval is likely to be accurate. Those who are most suggestible are younger than age 5, have been interviewed multiple times over a span of weeks/months, and have been asked many leading or suppositional or forced-choice questions rather than open-ended ones. In addition, if there are internal influences such as fear, anger, loyalty, or embarrassment or external influences such as being pressured or influenced by adults whom the children trust, that will increase the risk of suggestibility as well.

Putting This into Practice

Children's representatives are appointed in one of three ways: (1) client-directed, (2) best interests, or (3) some combination of the two. It is important to know your task when representing children. Regardless of your task, however, you must understand and consider the child's voice and what it represents. In this section, we will outline considerations to keep in mind when you talk with children about their voice.

First, let us consider the types of cases in which the child's voice comes into play. In all dependency court cases, children are supposed to have representatives who will listen to them and can understand their wishes. In high-conflict family law cases, children's representatives can also be appointed to understand the children's thoughts about the family and their wishes. In some family law jurisdictions, children might also be seen by the judge. In international child abduction cases, when a Hague matter is brought to the court, children are often seen by a child's representative to understand their wishes as well. Although their voice does not always lead to them getting their choice, in nearly all jurisdictions, a child's mature, well-articulated wishes are a factor when the ultimate decision is considered in front of the court. As the child's advocate, how you come to understand those wishes and the process used to understand your client are critical.

The important question is how to develop an understanding of your client's wishes. As described elsewhere in this book, interviewing children is an art. It requires a combination of getting down to the child's level, knowing when and when not to talk, building rapport with the child, explaining your role, and learning about the multitude of things your client cares about. Children's representatives need to get to know their client in as many areas as possible. This includes but is not limited to the child's favorite music, foods, TV shows, games, and activities; her feelings about each of her parents and, if in dependency court, feelings about being removed from her home; things she likes, things she doesn't like; things that make her scared, sad, angry, and happy; who she goes to when she is scared; and what makes her laugh and cry. Expect one- or two-word answers to many of your questions and do not forget that open-ended questions are best. We typically start our questions with "Tell me about . . ." and follow up with "Tell me more about . . ." or "Help me understand. . . ."

Only after getting to know your client in other areas of her life do we suggest talking about the ultimate issue. Regardless of whether you are in family court and your client is addressing her wishes about a parenting plan or you are in dependency court and your client is addressing whether or not to return home, you need to understand all relevant aspects to that voice. There are essentially four parts to this discussion:

1. Explaining your role and ensuring that your client understands the differences between her wishes, her best interests, and what you are advocating for;
2. Giving your client permission *not* to state a wish even while exploring her feelings about the critical and ultimate issues in front of the court;
3. If your client identifies a wish, explore it in depth. As best as possible, understand all of the nuances around your client's wishes, the reasons for the wishes, your client's ability to understand multiple perspectives and think through various options and why your client is picking a particular option, and both the risks and benefits to your client of making that particular choice; and
4. Exploring the risks and benefits of other options and all of the reasons your client is not choosing any of them.

Obviously, you cannot engage a child in such a discussion until you have developed rapport with your client and you have explored other less emotionally charged issues in some depth. The depth and breadth of this discussion will enable you to understand your client's maturity level and her ability to differentiate her feelings from those of other players in the system, including what your client thinks you want to hear. It will also test her ability to think through the ramifications of different options, which helps you understand and gauge your client's ability to see various outcomes through various perspectives, not just her own. All of this will assist you when you are advocating a particular position with the court.

A couple of final notes about children's voices in the court. First, recognize that younger children, especially those school-aged children identified above, often just want to please their parents, their therapist, or you. They have a tendency to say "yes" to anything we propose, and they often believe, just because we are adults, they need to go along with what we think. This is one of the critical reasons for asking open-ended questions that do not lend themselves to "yes" or "no" answers.

In a similar vein, older children, especially tweens and adolescents, are often somewhat oppositional and say "no" to similar questions. They often believe no one is to be trusted and are sensitive to what you think is best for them. In fact, many child representatives often tell children what they think is best and are surprised when the young client supports that decision or the older client rejects it. Sometimes it is a mere reflex reaction to whatever the child thinks you want to hear.

To counter that, Phil suggests reminding child clients that this decision is about "their life, not ours," there are "no right or wrong answers" to anything we discuss, and we are just "brainstorming" options in their lives. Then if they have a particular option they like and they want us to know, this is the time to tell us and explain why. In other words, the child should never feel pressured into expressing a wish, and no matter how forcefully the child does so, we need to know more about why she feels the way she does than what she feels. Again, curiosity is the key.

Finally, Rebecca suggests never asking a child to choose between parents or to choose between two people the child loves. Despite the law requiring children's wishes regarding custody to be considered, asking children to choose, as one question, is rarely appropriate. We will discuss resistant children later, but unless a child has expressed resistance to a parent, asking about custody and visitation specifically can be damaging to children.

Conclusions

Understanding children requires a developmental perspective not only when speaking with children but also when understanding their developmental and unique needs, wishes, and best interests. If you notice your client is delayed, you can ask yourself why that might be, knowing how development can be thwarted by neglect and trauma. If your client informs you he has changed since the case began, in school, with friends, or with other important life issues, that can help you help your client. Knowing how many times children have been interviewed, and possibly knowing the questions asked, can help you determine what may be true in the case.

We believe this is fundamental to anyone serving as children's representatives in family or dependency court. The developmental perspective is important, but so is understanding the children's language, their voice and perspective, and the risk that they are influenced both internally and externally to say things that may not be accurate or that may not reflect their beliefs. You may never be able to fully grasp what has happened to your clients, but knowing the key issues to consider should help you better evaluate the facts being provided to you from all sources, including your client's statements and actions.

Introduction to Domestic Violence and Its Impact on Children | 6

Domestic violence continues to be a serious issue for families in both juvenile and family court. Since the 1980s, there has been an increased focus on understanding domestic violence and how it affects families, particularly children. Domestic violence is a serious issue, as in any given year, there are many cases in which fathers murder their ex-spouse, commit murder-suicide, or kill other relatives. These cases receive considerable publicity, and judges and attorneys are blamed when such tragedies occur.

These cases are tragic, and we should worry about them, but they are not the only form of domestic violence. It is troublesome when a broad brush is used to deal with allegations of violence, and relationships between children and a parent can be affected because of unnecessary limitations placed upon those relationships by the courts. It is important to ensure the protection of children and victims, and it is important to ensure that in the absence of significant risk, children and parents maintain healthy and secure relationships. This chapter will focus on addressing the relevant research on domestic violence to help in your child representation in such cases.

Domestic violence advocates, who have continued to try and protect victims and children and end the cycles of violence in families, have continued to endorse research focusing on the power and control dynamics that are consistent with domestic violence. They cite research that suggests the majority of domestic violence is perpetrated by men against women and that there is significant risk to women and children around the time of separation. At the same time, others have endorsed community research that suggests domestic violence is perpetrated equally by both men and women and that, although the dangerous violence that gains the publicity is real, it is much less frequent than the typical violence that occurs in families. The tension between these two groups has increased, as they cite different research and reach different conclusions about violence in families and the ways in which violence affects women and children.

In 2007, two organizations, the Association of Family and Conciliation Courts (AFCC) and the National Council of Juvenile and Family Court Judges (NCJFCJ) convened a conference of researchers, mental health professionals, domestic violence advocates, attorneys, judges, and others to address these issues.[182] One result of the Wingspread Conference on Domestic Violence, so called because it took place at the Wingspread Conference Center in Racine, Wisconsin, was a special issue of *Family Court Review*, published in the summer of 2008. In this chapter, we will focus on the research and publications associated with the Wingspread Conference and others that followed and integrate that knowledge with guidance on representing children when there are allegations of domestic violence.

The research is varied, and if you look for research to support any position, you are likely to find it. Thus, it becomes even more important to ask deep questions in these cases to try to get a full picture of what is happening. Further, because there is still a prevalent belief in society that the only form of domestic violence is physical, it is imperative you look deeper than others might have because you may be the only person in the case asking those questions. We hope this chapter helps you ask those questions based upon the research we believe is

---

182. Peter Salem & Billie Lee Dunford-Jackson, *Beyond Politics and Positions: A Call for Collaboration Between Family Court and Domestic Violence Professionals*, 46 Fam. Ct. Rev. 437 (2008); Nancy Ver Steegh & Clare Dalton, *Report from the Wingspread Conference on Domestic Violence and Family Courts*, 46 Fam. Ct. Rev. 454 (2008).

best able to support protecting your child clients and ensuring they have as good a relationship as possible with each parent.

The Concept of Differentiation

One of the key results of the Wingspread Conference was an agreement that the concept of one-size-fits-all is not appropriate in domestic violence cases. While the cases that gain publicity are terrible and tragic and are likely the result of a long-standing pattern of power and control, not all families with domestic violence behaviors fit this pattern. As the research has shown for years, all violence is harmful and for some it is potentially lethal, but the majority of violence in families is less severe. That also makes it more difficult to recognize. Participants at Wingspread recognized there was some tension in dealing with these issues. On the one hand, family relationships can be compromised if all domestic violence is viewed as the type that needs strict interventions and should result in limited or supervised access between the violent parent and child. On the other hand, safety can be compromised if we allow open and unrestricted access in those cases where there is legitimate risk. The only way to manage these tensions is to ensure that judges and those who present evidence to the court consider lethality, the risk of future violence, and the presence of other forms of intimidation when looking at these families. We would add, particularly in cases of young children who are nonverbal or barely verbal, there could be potential nervous system risks if the appropriate measures are not taken and the child is exhibiting trauma pattern responses. The key task for those working with families of violence is to understand the various risks involved with all families.

Another key task highlighted by the Wingspread participants was to identify a language upon which all could agree. They recognized that the research identified many different types of violence and that there was considerable overlap in the terms being used. They reached agreement that domestic violence must be differentiated along various dimensions. We will focus on the different types of domestic violence identified in the literature, using the language agreed upon by the participants at the Wingspread Conference. We will identify each group in order based upon the apparent frequency in families.

Separation Instigated Violence (SIV)

In terms of base rates, the most frequent type of family violence is referred to as separation instigated violence. As its name suggests, this type of violence occurs when a couple has problems at the time of separation but has no prior history of any type of violence. In these families, in addition to there having been no prior violence, neither partner describes coercive, controlling, or intimidating behaviors.[183] SIV couples seem to have problems with short-term impulse control and anger, as the stress of separating seems to lead to the violent behaviors. The most unique feature of SIV families is how the violence represents an atypical loss of self-control. Another key trait is that the perpetrators of this violence (both male and female) not only acknowledge the violence but also are often embarrassed, bewildered, and ashamed by their uncharacteristic actions. The SIV couple typically complies with court orders, and neither partner is fearful of the other. Finally, SIV parents tend to have fewer parenting problems than other parents who exhibit problems with domestic violence. In fact, in addition to the parents being ashamed of their actions, their children are often bewildered by the actions of their parents and may exhibit signs of PTSD due to exposure to the shock of their parents' uncharacteristically violent behavior.

Situational Couples Violence (SCV)

For situational couples violence (SCV) families, in which the violence is usually initiated by both genders without any evidence of power and control being a central dynamic of the relationship, it is common for the partners to be angry with each another, and over time, the anger flares up into some type of violence. As with the SIV parents, neither partner is fearful of the other, except perhaps during the flare-up of anger. For the most part, injuries are rare when a couple engages in SCV, and serious injuries very rarely occur.[184] In this population, minor forms of violence such as pushing, shoving, and grabbing are most common. Frequency can vary among families, but generally, this type of violence decreases over time. Unlike those families who engage in coercive-controlling violence (CCV) (see below), partners who engage in SCV are quick to acknowledge their actions and recognize that it was unhealthy for the couple. It generally stops after separation.

Although the instigation of SCV is generally considered to be gender-neutral, in some families, one partner initiates SCV most of the time. When this occurs,

---

183. Joan B. Kelly & Michael P. Johnson, *Differentiation Among Types of Intimate Partner Violence: Research Update and Implications for Interventions*, 46 FAM. CT. REV. 476 (2008).

184. *Id.*

women are likely to initiate SCV more frequently than men.[185] Common forms of emotional violence in this group include cursing, yelling, and name calling; jealousy may also be a part of this type of violence, but not isolation, stalking, or other controlling types of behavior, as will be described with CCV below.

Coercive-Controlling Violence (CCV)

In this type of violence, which has often been referred to as battering or intimate partner violence (IPV), intimidation, power, coercion, control, and severe psychological/emotional abuse are central dynamics. CCV is primarily male-initiated, with only a small number of heterosexual females initiating this type of violence.[186] Despite the publicity these families receive and the seriousness of the violence, the incidence of CCV in the general population is lower than the incidence of SIV and SCV. Another difference is that injuries to the victim are more common in CCV than in the other groups, and these injuries are often more severe. In addition, perpetrators, and often the victims, of CCV are more likely to engage in denial, blame, and minimizing than are the perpetrators of SIV and SCV. Unlike the other couples, the victims in CCV families live in fear and often walk on eggshells when interacting with their partners. Finally, unlike the other two groups, in which partners disengage and tend to follow court orders after separation, at the time of separation for CCV couples, there is an increased, rather than decreased, risk of violence. Therefore, we are likely to see serious incidents after separation, including stalking and homicide, with CCV compared to any other type of domestic violence.

A hypothesis about the above data lies in the reasons for the violence. In SCV, the violence is largely the result of anger and impulsiveness that has escalated in one or both partners intermittently over time; in SIV, the violence erupts in one or two incidents because of the stress that is a function of the pending separation. In contrast, the violence in CCV is largely the result of a need to control the victim. Different reasons have been hypothesized for this need to control, including the use of male privilege, strong jealousy, and strong feelings of dependency.[187] Regardless of etiology, all perpetrators of CCV con-

---

185. *Id.*

186. *Id.*

187. *See, e.g.*, Robert F. Bornstein, *The Complex Relationship Between Dependency and Domestic Violence: Converging Psychological Factors and Social Forces*, 61 Am. Psychologist 595 (2006); Amy Holtzworth-Monroe & Gregory L. Stuart, *Typologies of Male Batterers: Three Subtypes and the Differences Among Them*, 116 Psychological Bulletin 476 (1994).

trol their partner and use a combination of emotional, psychological, verbal, physical, economic, and sexual violence to maintain the control. Typical emotional abuse includes cursing, humiliating, screaming, isolation of the victim partner from family and friends, checking up on the whereabouts of the victim partner, monitoring phone calls and mail, threatening to harm children and pets, and controlling all of the money. After separation, stalking is a significant threat. It also is hypothesized that many, although not all, perpetrators of CCV are psychopathic.

Again, as noted above, this type of violence is the most severe and is most likely to result in serious injuries, with a higher level of risk after separation. When confronted with this type of violence, it is critical that someone, more than likely a mental health professional, in the system do a risk assessment that includes determining the risk of ongoing violence and lethality.

It is critical when faced with dynamics of domestic violence, especially dynamics of CCV, to assess for lethality and continued risk. Gathering data about these risk factors may help in determining which families are more likely than others to erupt into more serious and harmful violence. While the absence of these risk factors does not mean there is no risk, the presence of one or more of these factors significantly increases the risk of ongoing violence within a family. It is not your job to do the lethality assessment, but as a part of your job, you can work to ensure that such an assessment is done.

In order to help you, as the child's representative, determine what kind of violence exists in this family, it is important to have as much information as possible. One difficulty is knowing what information to believe. It is not uncommon for stories to change, for there to be deception, and for there to be significant secrecy when domestic violence is involved. While the child's representative is not the fact finder, your role is to help the court have the information necessary to help your clients, the children.

The first step is knowing the history of the violence. For example, try to determine whether this was SIV, SCV, or CCV. What kind of violence is being perpetrated? Is it physical, emotional, controlling, economic, sexual, or something else? To determine this, it helps to have access to police reports and medical reports of all family members. Speaking to other family members can also be helpful because isolating someone is often a form of abuse.

Unfortunately for the legal system, some of the most damaging forms of abuse are not physical violence. What appears benign in one family can be emotionally traumatic when it exists in a family with CCV. For example, couples often have phone apps that show them where their family members are. Some would argue this is good parenting and a good way to know whether your partner is somewhere you can call, especially in an emergency. But in a CCV a relationship, this can be a form of abusive and controlling behavior. A victim may not be able to live a free life without the perpetrator knowing every move the victim makes. And that means the victim is unable to take appropriate steps to leave the relationship or even go to the grocery store without being questioned. Thus, it is important to know a family's entire story as much as possible because these seemingly benign situations are potential red flags when there is violence. Phil was involved in a case recently where the parents had several cameras in the house and had agreed to them for security; they also had the "Where's My Phone" app on their phones, reportedly by mutual agreement. However, after separation, Father continued to monitor Mother's whereabouts by accessing the camera in Mother's bedroom and occasionally frightened Mother by showing up at places she was at, allegedly by accident. Although the court did not make a finding of stalking in that case, the court did order those behaviors to stop.

The most robust predictor of violence is past behavior, which is much more useful than personality traits. Look for a history of restraining orders, arrest, probation, or parole. Often by the time the family or juvenile court system is involved and the child has a lawyer, there is a history of these types of legal interventions. There can also be a history of violating restraining orders because the perpetrator promises to change, and the couple reunites. That allows the cycle to begin again. Further, past arrests do little to deter future violence because too often perpetrators are released from jail without convictions and without the need to participate in any form of batterers' intervention programs. Prior jail time can backfire, leading the perpetrator to believe there are no legal ramifications for the violence and therefore enable to perpetrator to act more violently going forward.

With CCV families, there is greater risk of future violence when violence has been long term, there has been no treatment or interventions, the perpetrator externalizes blame and/or denies problems, and the perpetrator focuses on the victim. There is a lower risk of renewed violence in CCV families when there is acknowledgment of the violence, guilt and remorse that focus on the impact on the victim and/or children, responsibility for violent behavior, empathy for the effect of the violence on the children, awareness of children's needs, an understanding that the abuse has served to maintain control in the relationship, and a motivation to change.

While lawyers are not fully trained to make these assessments, it can help to know the lethality risks to better understand the potential analysis for assessing your clients' safety when you believe CCV exists. Although as the child's lawyer you may not be asking the following questions, know that the following lethality factors are critical to understand:

- Is there access to a gun?
- Has the perpetrator ever used a weapon against you?
- Has the perpetrator threatened to kill your children?
- Do you have a child living with you who is not the perpetrator's biological child?
- Do you think the perpetrator will kill you? (Not surprisingly, the victim's own feelings on this are one of the highest predictors of homicide threat.)
- Has the perpetrator ever tried to strangle you?
- Is the perpetrator jealous or controlling most of your daily activities?
- Does the perpetrator spy on you or leave threatening messages?
- Have you left or separated from the perpetrator after living together or being married?
- Is the perpetrator unemployed?
- Has the perpetrator ever tried to commit suicide?
- Has the perpetrator ever avoided arrest for domestic violence?
- Is there a substance abuse issue? (Alcohol and stimulants such as cocaine, methamphetamines, and crack are highly problematic.)
- Are you an immigrant to this country?

Other factors to consider when assessing the domestic violence in a family are the first, the most recent, and the worst incidents of violence between the parents. This serves several functions. At times, the victim will provide a history full of incidents, perhaps starting early in the relationship or during pregnancy of a child, and provide graphic descriptions of each. You can learn about the multiple types of IPV, including the emotional, verbal, physical, or other types abuse. As you begin to hear about a history of possible CCV, explore for all types of abuse, including sexual, economic, isolation, and stalking. This history helps provide detail to the CCV experiences of the victim. On the other hand, there are times when the first, more recent, and worst incidents were all the same and are explained as having been associated with the stress of the separation and divorce—clearly an indicator of SIV. Or perhaps you will hear about many incidents over a period of time, each developing out of an angry or impulsive outburst but without descriptions of fear, with both partners alternating as the perpetrator, and all of generally mild form. This might sound more like SCV. The key here is having sufficient curiosity to explore the issue, explore what led up to each event, what followed each event, and where the children were during each event. All of this will help in your understanding of the type of violence between the parties.

It is important as well to understand the parents' relationship with the child. Do the parents have empathy for the impact their relationship has on the child, or is there a mentality that it is between the parents and therefore none of the child's business? How do the parents manage their anger at the child? How do they discipline the child? Those are two separate questions. It can also be helpful to know what the child does when she gets angry. Again, the answers to some of these questions might help in understanding the type of violence as well as the potential for the child struggling with her traumatic responses. Parents who are sensitive to the impact of any family turmoil and violence on children are positive parents who are likely to buffer the negative traumatic experiences associated with their child's exposure to the violence.

The Child's Responses to the Violence

Another important question to ask children is what they do when the violence occurs and when it is over, at least the violence they can see or hear, e.g., yelling/screaming, name calling, and physical violence. While children can be harmed by violence regardless of whether they are present for it, what our clients do when it occurs is useful information for us in terms of providing a history of what type of violence there is and in terms of determining future parenting plans and necessary therapeutic intervention for our clients.

The first question is how the child reacts to the violence as it occurs. Has the child had to intervene by pulling the parents apart, standing between them, or calling the police? Does the child find a hiding place such as a closet or a room with music turned up loudly? Does the child sit somewhere out of the way and listen to the violence but not intervene? Has the child ever been told a treasured pet or object will be taken away or harmed because of what the child has seen? Has either parent abducted the child? It is important to ask children about specific incidents of violence, and if they are willing to discuss them, this is a way to gain additional information. If they do want to talk, ask what the violence looks like. How does it show up? What do they see? What do they hear? What do the parents tell them about the violence? What does one parent tell them about the other parent?

The next question to ask is what the child does when there is violence in her family. Does the child leave the house? Does the child get involved in school and activities as a distraction? Does the child refuse to leave the house for fear the violence will be worse if she is not in the home? Does she try to protect her parents? Often the answers to these questions help give you, as professionals, insight into what is really happening in the home. Children often feel as though they cannot speak about the violence specifically, but asking questions along these lines can sometimes be another avenue into understanding what is happening in the home. It is also vital to understand the child's functioning. Whether an infant or an older teenager, the child's functioning can provide information about the effect of the violence on her.

Children can also help you understand whether the violence includes coercive, controlling behavior. For example, some children have been told they are not allowed to discuss the physical violence, or they choose not to discuss it to protect their family. To get around that, you can ask other questions that provide information they may not know helps you understand the violence. You can ask if both parents work. If one does not, ask why. Ask whether the child has a good relationship with both maternal and paternal family. If not, might it be because the perpetrator is isolating the victim? Do both parents have friends? Do both parents drive? What do the parents call each other both when feeling loving and feeling angry toward the other? Some children have never experienced parents feeling loving toward each other. Even asking about who does chores in the house can help you understand the depth of the violence without ever asking about the physical acts.

Once we understand the history of the violence and what form of violence we think exists in the home, the next big question is, "Now what?" What do we do about it for this particular family? And to answer those questions, we must understand how these forms of violence affect the children and the parents' ability to parent and co-parent effectively.

As children's representatives, it can be difficult to know where in the process someone is. In family law cases where you are the only lawyer on the case, you are not trained to assess these issues. Further, in child welfare cases, it depends on the training of the child welfare social worker and the jurisdiction in which you practice whether you will receive this information from the people ostensibly trained to provide it to you.

Parenting Problems of CCV Domestic Violence Parents

Children need good parenting. In contrast, significant parenting problems typically are associated with parents in CCV relationships.[188] While there are different issues between perpetrators and victims, one of the key issues in CCV

---

188. R. Lundy Bancroft et al., The Batterer as Parent: Addressing the Impact of Domestic Violence on Family Dynamics (Sage 2002).

relationships, as opposed to other forms of violent relationships, is the fact they are not relationship-specific. As mentioned above, these relationships tend to be pattern driven, so the fact that someone is out of the parenting relationship does not mean the person is out of the pattern of violent behavior, and the risk for exposure to the child of another domestically violent relationship is strong. There are also specific parenting issues associated with both perpetrators and victims.

For perpetrators, the following are typical risks:

- Uses coercive discipline tactics, including physical abuse of child;
- Is alternately overly permissive and rigidly authoritarian;
- Reverses roles with child erratically;
- Violates child's emotional boundaries and may perpetrate sexual abuse;
- Abuses child emotionally with mind games, put-downs, and social isolation;
- May encourage immoral and criminal behaviors in child;
- May abduct or threaten to abduct child;
- Shows lack of empathy for the impact on child of exposure to the violence;
- Is intolerant of developmentally appropriate behavior or "special needs";
- Demands that child demonstrate affection and loyalty;
- Uses access to coerce or harass other parent;
- Rewards child for rejecting/punishing the other parent;
- Is unable to focus on child's needs;
- Has limited awareness of child's personality, preferred activities, achievements, and the like;
- Displays angry outbursts, flies into rages, especially when discussing child's situation;
- Denies child's expression of ideas, feelings, in favor of own;
- Is convinced that all child's feelings/needs are identical to own or manipulated by other parent; and
- Displays impulsive responses, with occasionally odd or bizarre remarks about child.

Similarly, victims of CCV violence are at risk of experiencing potential parenting problems,[189] including:

- Display anxiety, depression, PTSD symptoms;
- May use drugs/alcohol to numb pain;

---

189. Peter Jaffe et al., *Custody Disputes Involving Allegations of Domestic Violence: The Need for Differentiated Approaches to Parenting Plans*, 46 FAM. CT. REV. 46, 500 (2008).

- Is preoccupied with demands of the abuser;
- Is physically and emotionally exhausted and unavailable;
- Is less warm, more permissive or coercive and power assertive;
- Adopts role reversal with child;
- Is unable to protect child from abusive partner;
- Is brainwashed by abuser to accept that child is abused;
- Lacks confidence in parenting/poor self-esteem;
- Has difficulty managing children (especially boys); and
- Acts irrationally or with seemingly poor judgment.

Thus, the potential problems with perpetrators of CCV are that the parent is unwilling to learn proper parenting techniques because the parent wants to control everything about the child, including controlling what the parent thinks is appropriate development. By contrast, the victim parent has more of a potential risk of being unable to be a proper parent because of the trauma associated with being victimized.

Many of these parenting risks in the perpetrator indicate controlling behavior, either trying to control the adult ex-partner through the child or controlling the child through direct controlling behaviors. Attempting to control the child can be through physical or emotional abuse or a failure to understand the child's developmental level and abilities. This can show up for the child as mild or severe emotional abuse.

Impact of Domestic Violence on Children

When we talk about family violence, it is important to understand the child's exposure to the violence. But perhaps most importantly, the severity of the violence is not directly connected to the child's experience of trauma. As we discussed previously, the experience of trauma is subjective, and it affects different children differently. Children are not affected only by witnessing violence directly; it also includes hearing the violence, seeing the effects of the violence, e.g., broken dishes, a hole in the wall, and bruises, and even noticing the tension after the violent outbursts. As stated in Chapter 4, trauma shows up in the nervous system, so if children feel the violence occurring around them, including the emotional violence, they can, and likely will, respond with forms of traumatic responses. In addition, if the victim parent is unable to be present and responsive emotionally for the child, particularly a very young child, the child's development and attachment can be negatively impacted as discussed in Chapters 4 and 5.

Therefore, even when children are not direct witnesses of violence, they may experience symptoms of post-traumatic stress, regression, vulnerability, and other forms of psychological injury. If abused themselves, they are likely to exhibit many of the signs commonly seen in abused children. Many of these children are in love/hate relationships with both parents because they love their parents, as most children do, but they are also afraid of the perpetrator parent and upset by the victim parent for not leaving or for not protecting them from the violence.

Older children are typically able to modulate their emotional responses. Modulation occurs when children can use language to understand what they have been exposed to, can understand their feelings and their parents' feelings, can engage in other activities (such as playing with friends, playing a musical instrument, or doing homework), and can participate in activities that help them self soothe. This lessens the impact of their stress and softens their emotional reactions. It is as important to ask children in these moments what they do for fun as it is to ask them what they do when they experience the violence in their families as discussed in the trauma chapter.

Just because older children are more able to modulate their emotional responses does not mean they are not affected by the violence in the home. Many older children either act out or shut down. Older children often act out aggressively because that is the learned behavior in their home. They may also do poorly in school because they are unable to concentrate due to the violence in the home. They may shut down and dissociate because of the violence. It can be easier for children to hide from the violence than to have to feel it, so they retreat from family and even friends. Older children, although increasingly younger children too, may begin to participate in self-destructive behaviors, including substance abuse.

Younger children, especially children under the age of 3, have little ability to self-soothe and, of course, cannot use language or an understanding of their feelings to modulate their emotional responses. For those in the first eighteen months of life, emotional reactions are typically a mirror of what they experience. If they experience screaming, emotional chaos, and violence, their emotional reactions will be chaotic and overwhelming. Their only outlet is behavioral, and as such, they often experience nightmares, temper tantrums, and difficulty being soothed. They often act aggressively both at home and in day care settings. They can begin to show signs of a disorganized attachment because often when they are most scared, their caregivers act in a way that is not supportive.

Violence also affects brain development most specifically in children under the age of 3. This includes children who are not yet born. Maternal stress hormones affect the fetus's development, so domestic violence during pregnancy can affect the child upon birth. Domestic violence during pregnancy is also a noticeable sign of CCV, often because the perpetrator cannot tolerate the mother's normal withdrawal from the spouse and his needs to care for her and the unborn child. Children exposed to violence while the brain is developing have been shown to have less developed brains, resulting in developmental issues, including speech delays. Similarly, as the brain is developing, it is developing its patterns for the future, and if a child learns to be fearful and hypervigilant because of violence in the home, the child retains that learning later in life.

This can lead to an overactive fight, flight, or freeze response as described in Chapter 4. This can happen because of an insecure or disorganized attachment. When children live primarily with victim parents, even if the perpetrator is out of the home, the parent may not have the emotional capacity to help the child grow emotionally or have a secure attachment. Victims often suffer from their own PTSD, and as we discussed in Chapter 4, trauma is in the nervous system. Attachment, from a baby's nervous system perspective, needs another nervous system to help it grow and learn. If the nervous system from which it is supposed to be learning and growing is insufficiently capable of meeting the child's needs, the result can be attachment problems for your young client, which could lead to developmental issues as well. It can also lead to medical problems as serious as Failure to Thrive.[190]

Another element of the fight, flight, or freeze response is to become a fighter. Some children respond to family violence by becoming violent themselves. Identifying with the aggressor, these children start to act out in a variety of places, typically school classrooms and other places with their peers. They may become bullies or act with hostility toward authority figures. For the most part, however, their aggressive actions are likely to be covering up intense feelings of insecurity associated with the acting-out behavior. In other words, we can consider the aggressive behavior to be covering up the insecurity the child feels. If you believe your child client is experiencing such aggressive behavior, you will want to guide him to counseling that can help him become more aware of his insecurities and learn healthier ways of dealing with his feelings.

Other common childhood responses can be internalizing responses such as depression, learning problems, or anxiety or externalizing responses, such as ADHD or peer problems without aggression. Phil has long believed children

---

190. Nadine Burke Harris, The Deepest Well: Healing the Long-Term Effects of Childhood Adversity (Houghton Mifflin Harcourt 2018).

experiencing ADHD symptoms should have their families screened for family violence since ADHD symptoms are commonplace among children exposed to family violence. Research is beginning to back this up.[191] To the extent ADHD symptoms are associated with the family violence, it is likely a trauma response. The same would be true for depression, isolation, or withdrawal. Note these symptoms and consider their potential association with the family violence.

In families with more than one child, it is common for each child to have a different reaction to the violence, especially CCV. One sibling may take care of the others, another sibling may take care of the victim parent, and another sibling might start acting like the perpetrator of the violence. Some siblings may become abusive with one another; others may soothe one another. Knowing the relationship between the siblings can help, especially when working with them in a dependency court environment because children may be removed from their parents' custody; if the children act violently toward one another, it may be important to separate them until they are able to work on their own relationships. Similarly, if teenage children have had to protect younger children from violence, even if we as a court system do not want children to be parentified, it can be significantly more traumatic to separate those children. It is painful for both the protected child and the protector child because even if we know children should not have to take care of their siblings, if that is the way the home has been, older children can spend all their time worrying about younger siblings if they are separated.

Your clients are likely to need a differential assessment that helps in understanding their vulnerabilities and future needs. They typically exhibit a range of responses, some internalizing responses such as hopelessness and guilt, low self-esteem, depression, vulnerability, hypervigilance, school problems, and fear and some externalizing responses such as bullying, temper outbursts, and problems responding to authority.

Considerations for Parenting Plan Options

Regardless of whether you are representing a child in juvenile or family court, you are likely concerned with your client's relationship with her parents. Should she be reunited with an abusive parent? Should she have an opportunity to spend equal time with both parents? Should she have little or no time with an abuser? Research helps us understand an approach to these and similar questions. The next section will outline parenting plan considerations for your client and her family.

---

191. *Id.*

The Alphabet Soup Used to Formulate Outcomes

Multiple factors are critical to understanding whether there should be a primary parent or shared physical or legal custody in family court and whether there should be limited, supervised, or no contact between children and an abusive parent in dependency court. The critical factors include "5 Ps" and "3 Rs."[192] They are as follows:

Pattern

The first "P" factor to consider is the pattern. As described above, CCV families have significantly greater risk after separation than do SIV and SCV families. If the pattern involves controlling and emotionally damaging behaviors, the patterns are more difficult to break. If the patterns are more about the stress because of the separation, dealing with that stress can alleviate much of the problem. In an SCV family, it is important to know the structure and frequency of the violence in the home. Knowing the patterns, including knowing which parent was more frequently the perpetrator, or whether both parents perpetrated similarly, will affect how the parents can co-parent and what the risk factors are for the children's development and safety in each home.

Potency

Potency refers to lethality. The lethality risks were described above. The higher the potency, the higher the danger to the child.

Primary Perpetrator

If there is a primary perpetrator, you are likely dealing with a CCV dynamic, which, as described above, increases the risks to your client, including, or especially, your very young client.

Parenting Problems

The fourth "P" factor is the quality of parenting by each of the parents. As described above, SIV parents are often "good-enough" parents who can be responsive to and soothing with your client. SCV parents may need parenting help, especially learning to be more aware of how their anger and impulse control problems have affected your client. The list of parenting risks in both perpetrators and victims in CCV families previously identified in this chapter is critical.

---

192. *Id.*

Perspective of the Child

The fifth "P" factor is the perspective of the child. How your client feels is quite important, i.e., is he afraid, is he refusing access, is he estranged from a parent due to the history of exposure to the violence, or is he in need of protection. Some children are immature and inconsistent in their stories, and other children are reasonably mature and able to focus on their observations and feelings. Some children want to spend time with both parents, and other children express concern about spending time with one of the parents. Understanding your client's feeling and fears is critical to creating an appropriate parenting plan for him.

Within the Perspective of the Child are three more factors. These "R" factors are discussed next.

Reflective Functioning This is related to empathy by the parent. It is important to understand how much each parent truly understands your client and what she has been exposed to and experienced? Higher reflective functioning is consistent with lower risk of harm if parenting time is granted because the parent is better able to make changes to reduce the risk of harm to his child.

Responsibility Does a parent take responsibility for what has happened or blame the victim and your client for the family violence? Parents who take responsibility are less likely to put children in harm's way. On the other hand, when parents do not take responsibility for their behavior, they cannot apologize to their child and are likely to continue engaging in behaviors that are harmful to your client.

Repair Abused and traumatized children need to heal. The repair function is consistent with helping children heal. Parents who can express empathy and take responsibility for their behavior are likely to help your client repair the insecurities and vulnerabilities that were caused by the family violence.

Using the PPPPP Analysis with the RRR Concepts to Guide Your Advocacy

Jaffe et al. suggested using these eight factors when considering optimal parenting plans for children exposed to family violence. The various options are along a continuum, ranging from limited or no access to open and complete access. At one end of the continuum, they suggest that a pattern of CCV, continued high potency, one primary perpetrator, significant parenting problems, and a child who is afraid to be alone with that parent would lead to supervised or limited contact with the perpetrating parent. There might be no contact if the child is extremely afraid and the parent takes no responsibility, cannot help the child heal, and lacks empathy for the impact of this violence and his behaviors on the child.

In the middle of the continuum, families engaged in SCV, where there is low potency, both parents are equally involved in initiating the violence, each parent has different parenting problems, and children want contact with both parents, might have a plan in which the child spends quality time with each parent, but more time with the parent with fewer parenting problems. In addition, in order to continue reducing any risk of anger problems surfacing in front of the children, it may be necessary to have the exchanges take place with some monitoring or in a public place, thus reducing the risk that conflict will erupt at the exchange of your client. Also, CCV parents who have gone through and learned from quality intervention programs and are prepared to help with the repair and healing of the children and there is now a low risk of potency might also lie somewhere in the middle of the continuum.

At the other end of the continuum, parents who were both very involved with a history of healthy parenting, who had one incident of SIV, where there is little to no concern about risk of future violence, and where children want quality time with both parents might have a parenting plan with relatively equal parenting time.

Therapeutic and Structural Interventions

In addition to the parenting plan options, on behalf of your client, you will want to understand the intervention options most suited to your client and the family. Starting with the children, it is important for children exposed to violence to heal. Typically, children will benefit from a range of interventions based on their developmental functioning. Very young children, such as under age 3, are likely to benefit from dyadic therapy with the abused parent regardless of whether they are exhibiting symptoms. A key task of this therapy is to help the child and parent develop their bond in safer and healthier ways. Dyadic therapies are designed to work to heal the relationship between caregiver and child. If children are exhibiting toxic stress symptoms, dyadic therapy with the victim parent can help the child heal and give the victim parent useful tools to use in engaging with the developing child. These therapies can be helpful as a form of therapy to the parent as well if she was previously emotionally unavailable to the child due to the ongoing domestic violence.

Older children can benefit from a range of interventions that include but are not limited to group counseling to help children learn to normalize and understand their feelings, play therapy to learn how to express and manage their feelings, art therapy, and family therapy with either parent depending on the needs of the family and other family dynamics. Older children may also benefit from a variety of nontherapeutic activities such as sports, music, and drama. In addition, any form of mindfulness practice, such as martial arts and yoga, in which children move and heal their bodies, may be helpful. Of course, the trauma therapies discussed in the chapter on trauma, particularly somatic therapies, can help children of all ages.

In general, most laws and literature suggests that for primary perpetrators who engage in CCV, an intervention program (BIP) lasting forty to fifty-two weeks is currently seen as the best available strategy. While some research suggests this model is effective for only about a third of participants,[193] such a cognitive-behavioral intervention is designed to help perpetrators raise their awareness of precursors to their battering behaviors, recognize that violence is a choice they do not have to make, learn new ways of dealing with their impulses, and raise empathy for their victims and the children in these families. Completion of a BIP is often a requirement for abusive parents before relationships are reunified or access with their child is moved from supervised to unsupervised. Finally, some newer interventions are being explored that focus on improved parenting as well as BIP concepts. Although some argue that BIP should be done separately from parenting programs, others have argued that implementing both together may be most helpful for SCV perpetrators.

When both parents engage in SCV, especially when the violence was caused by anger problems and impulsive behaviors, a shorter anger management program may be the intervention of choice. Such a program will focus mostly on stress reduction techniques and teaching skills to help impulsive parents learn more appropriate outlets for their anger. Note, however, that anger management and BIP are not interchangeable. CCV parents should never be considered for anger management because CCV is not an anger issue; it is a control issue. If there is also an underlying anger issue, and it is not uncommon for there to be both, then it is beneficial to do both a BIP and anger management or have the perpetrator enroll in a BIP that includes some elements of anger management into the

---

193. Edward Gondolf, *Evaluating Batterer Counseling Programs: A Difficult Task Showing Some Effects*, 9 AGGRESSION & VIOLENT BEHAVIOR 605 (2004).

curriculum. What is important is to understand they are not the same program and they cannot be used interchangeably to solve the very different problems.

When impulse control problems and violence are secondary to a psychiatric problem or substance abuse, medication and/or treatment for the substance abuse or psychiatric problem would be indicated in addition to the other therapies being used. Because many parents who become violent experience strong feelings of inadequacy, dependency, and vulnerability, psychotherapy may also be a useful adjunct, but only when addressing the violence first. Again, therapy alone is not sufficient for primary perpetrators of CCV; instead BIP is the intervention of choice.

For adult victims of CCV, treatment is often needed to build ego functioning, help raise awareness around issues of domestic violence, reduce dependency, and improve self-esteem. Many abused parents do not know how to recognize when they are in danger. Therapy that focuses on the risks of violence is important to preclude or prevent involvement in future violent relationships. Just as the perpetrators of CCV might benefit from individual psychotherapy in conjunction with BIP, victims may need insight into how their own personal issues contribute to their victimization. Individual therapy can also help victims regain the ability to engage emotionally with their children when such help is necessary.

Both perpetrators and abused parents may benefit from group therapy. BIPs are usually in group sessions, and there are victim support groups as well. Both are beneficial in addition to individual therapy for each group. For perpetrators of abuse, being in a group setting helps hold them accountable for their actions. For abused parties, it helps people recognize they are not alone. While individual psychotherapy has its advantages for getting to the heart of the issues and working on individual trauma patterns, group dynamics are important in helping perpetrators prevent future abuse and healing abused parents.

Parenting classes may also be necessary for those parents who have identified parenting problems. These classes increase the overall understanding of child development and the impact parents' emotional states may have on a child.

Conclusions

Domestic violence is bad for children and victims in any form, but it is imperative to differentiate the form of domestic violence your client is experiencing because it affects not only his development and functioning but also the interventions for the family and the future parenting plans.

High-Conflict Separated and Divorced Parents 7

Rarely do we see children of high-conflict parents, without co-occurring abuse of some kind, in the dependency courts. Sometimes, however, the conflict reaches a level of such extremes that the child welfare agency gets involved. Similarly, in some jurisdictions, there is a growing tendency to appoint a representative for the child in a very high-conflict family law matter. One piece of information to remember as a children's representative is that often the dependency case itself is the catalyst for the parents' separation and that sometimes there is a history of conflict but sometimes the high conflict begins with the separation instigated by the dependency case. Although we will refer to conflict between parents, it is often true in dependency cases that the high conflict can be between caregivers and parents, including between foster parents and parents. While that type of conflict changes the legal analysis, from the child's perspective, it can feel similar to conflict between parents. It is important to understand that the psychological dynamics that often contribute to parents being in very high conflict may also affect the children.

High-conflict parents are not all the same, but for many, they tend to have personality traits that contribute to exacerbating conflicts. They might have a relationship disorder, in which they interact in ways that contribute equally to disliking and not trusting each other. Others have individual personality dynamics that mimic personality disorders, or they actually have personality disorders. But we are not talking about diagnosis in this chapter. Instead, we are going to identify various personality traits that increase the risk that one or both parents will act in ways that contribute to the very high conflict. Your job as a child's representative is not to diagnose; it is to notice whether certain traits existing in the family are damaging or mitigating damage to your client.

High-conflict couples often look at judicial orders as merely suggestions.[194] These parents are called "Angry Associates" or "Fiery Foes"[195] depending on the extent of their conflict. These types of parents have extreme difficulty following orders or resolving their parenting plan or financial issues. They often let one set of problems interfere with another set of problems. Many of these parents seem to hate each other more than they love their children. These parents make allegations of parental alienation (see Chapter 8), substance abuse, domestic violence (see Chapter 6), and other serious problems. Many of these parents have court orders that limit their ability to be together in the same place at the same time, even at their children's events. Such parents have extremely derogatory attitudes toward each other. Some of these parents merge their own feelings with those of their children and have very poor boundaries with their children. In many of these families, there is additional conflict instigated by extended family members and friends. Sometimes even therapists and attorneys get drawn into the conflicts. Many family law judges refer to these families as "frequent fliers," the 10%–15% of the families who take up 85%–90% of the court's time.

In many ways, it appears as though the life of the child stops while the arguments between the parents continue. For many of these families, every issue becomes a potential source of conflict. Sometimes this is related to the history of the relationship and the power dynamics between the parents. Sometimes one parent will not let go of the conflict because it keeps them "together" in their relationship (albeit a destructive one). Ultimately, both

---

194. Terence Bruniers, Contra Costa County Superior Court Judge, Address at View From the Bench: Luncheon speech to the Contra Costa Bar Association, Walnut Creek, CA (Jan. 12, 2000).

195. Constance Ahrons, We're Still Family: What Grown Children Have to Say about Their Parents' Divorce (HarperCollins 2004).

parents and children are significantly affected in a negative way because of this unresolved conflict.

Contribution of Personality Features

Over the past thirty years, a growing body of literature has developed on personality styles, in particular, narcissistic and borderline styles.[196] Theodore Millon is a psychologist who researched personality disorders as well as personality traits and features that impact relationships rather than the individual. He has grouped personality disorders into types, one of which he refers to as Cluster B disorders: disorders that are conflict-inducing. Many family court professionals observe that in most high-conflict families, one or both parents exhibit either narcissistic, obsessive-compulsive, histrionic, paranoid, or borderline traits or features. Millon stated that personality disorders are caused not only by the internal personality structures but also by the social system in which these people interact. The court system, with its litigation and conflict, is an external system that may cause people who have such personality traits to act as if they have personality disorders. This is consistent with the commonly expressed phrase that "those in criminal court are bad people on their best behavior, but those in family court are good people on their worst behavior."

Such parents may become rigid in their perception of each other and tend to deal with situations in their extremes. Many parents are polarized, viewing themselves as all good and the other as all bad, and they externalize those thoughts and feelings onto their children, such that the children are at risk of becoming polarized. These parents focus on the traits in the other parent that reinforce this perception, and they approach each new conflict as verification of just how difficult the other parent is. These parents experience chronic externalization of blame, possessing little insight into their own role in the conflicts. They usually have little empathy for the impact of this conflict on their children. They routinely feel self-justified, believing their actions are best for their children. No matter how much helping professionals try to keep the focus on the child, these parents remain focused on the conflict.

---

196. *See, e.g.,* THEODORE MILLON, DISORDERS OF PERSONALITY: DSM-IV AND BEYOND (Wiley-Interscience 1996); WILLIAM EDDY, HIGH CONFLICT PEOPLE IN LEGAL DISPUTES (Unhooked Books 2016).

Generally, those with personality disorders or traits that are similar to such disorders have many of the following characteristics:

- These people have an enduring pattern of thinking and behaviors that may be pervasive in many aspects of their life;
- They create problems for others and are generally disruptive, and they do not adapt well;
- They externalize issues, blame others, and have poor or limited insight into their own contribution to the problems;
- They may also show signs of depression, self-destructive behavior, aggressiveness, or brief psychotic episodes (or behaviors that appear psychotic);
- These parents tend to use emotional persuasion when in conflict, escalating their emotions, often becoming louder, blaming, and increasing the seriousness of their allegations;
- Many confuse emotional facts with actual facts. Such parents generate facts to support how they feel, and their emotions are often triggered by cognitive distortions. They believe "facts" that are not true, even though they feel as if they are true. This often leads to cognitive distortions, exaggerations, and overt fears. They tend toward poorly modulated or over-controlled emotional and behavioral responses;
- Parents with severe narcissistic personality disorders, or who act as if they have such disorders, lack empathy for their children and their ex-partner and have a strong sense of entitlement in court proceedings.

While these parents tend to be motivated by a diverse set of emotions, we believe most of them take such rather rigid positions out of fear, often the overwhelming fear that if they let down their defenses, the other parent will take advantage of them. Many parents say, "If I give in just this one time, she will always take advantage of me" or, "If I give him an inch, he'll take a mile." Sometimes this is accurate, and sometimes this is based on fear. Many parents fear losing a relationship with their child or fear being controlled by the other parent. For the more disturbed of these parents, giving in may represent a fear of loss of self. This rigidity ensures conflict. Because these families routinely go back to court, they are also afraid that any relaxing of their position might give the other parent an advantage in court. What is lost in the conflict are the children's needs.

Another source of the fear is that winning or losing is so integrally tied to self-esteem. Parents with narcissistic traits fear losing custody and control lest they feel abandoned and depressed. Those with borderline traits must win in order to contain their internal chaos and rage. While losing might mean different things to each parent, e.g., shame, loss, abandonment, rage, etc., the key ingredient is how *unbearable* such a loss will feel to the parent. Just as trauma is a subjective feeling, this feeling of loss is subjective to the parent who feels fearful of that loss. Judges and attorneys express their extreme frustration over these "frequent flyer" families. Many of these parents come back to court several times a year, and for some of these parents, a new issue arises just before a settlement is reached. Lacking a reasonable dispute resolution mechanism, these parents feel justified in taking each other to court and letting "the judge settle it," despite their frustration and blame when the outcome is not acceptable to them.

Let us also remember that some parents are just deeply hurt or shamed by their family experiences, including the behaviors that have led to the separation and divorce. For example, a parent who discovers years of infidelity is likely to be deeply wounded, and all trust is shattered. On the other hand, some parents are ashamed by their own actions or by the divorce itself, and that shame may lead some parents to externalize blame in order to avoid experiencing these emotions.[197]

Regardless of the dynamics contributing to the conflict, for many of these parents, each issue is perceived as a new opportunity for victory and feared as a potential loss. These characterological personality dynamics, along with each parent's righteous self-justification and fear, create this high level of conflict and perpetuation of the court battle. At the same time, away from the conflict, many of these parents appear concerned for their children's needs and feelings and are capable of good parenting skills. They may be nurturing and set reasonable limits with their children. They are frequently involved in their child's day-to-day activities, participate in schoolwork, and provide encouragement and support to their children. Even when they are cold, rigid, angry, and fearful toward the other parent, many of these parents can be loving, spontaneous, and supportive to their children. In the abstract, they understand the value of the child's relationship with the other parent, and they may even recognize that the conflict is problematic for their children. Despite this acknowledgment, it is difficult for them to relax their rigid positions and attitudes toward the other parent and extricate their child (and themselves) from the conflict.

For many high-conflict families, it seems that the parents' characterological personality dynamics manifest only in a relationship disorder with the other

---

197. Bruce Smyth & Lawrence Moloney, *Entrenched Postseparation Parenting Disputes: The Role of Interparental Hatred?* 55 Fam. Ct. Rev. 404 (2017).

parent. They may be able to manage some of their chronic traits, including their narcissism, overreaction, rigidity, or anger, in their other relationships. They may be pleasant to coworkers, showing few pathological traits in their work environment. With their children, they may not personalize experiences or show signs of narcissistic injury. When seeing such parents, it is important to understand how (and whether) the vulnerabilities that exist in the parent-parent relationship manifest as well in the parent-child relationship. As a children's representative, it is important, therefore, to notice how the conflict affects the child as well as how the parent parents the child when not specifically involved in the conflict with the other parent. These can be difficult issues to parse out, but being curious and understanding how they may be different helps you ask the correct questions.

In contrast, the history of the conflict, the emotions of the divorce, and the fear of letting go bring out the worst in these parents in interactions with each other. It appears the couple's relationship has been unable to withstand the previous love, the loss of that love, and the rejection and hurt that followed. Most people believe love and hate are opposites, but in reality, love and apathy are opposites. Love and hate contain energy, so when the love is lost in a relationship, it often can turn to a feeling of hate. In the newly formed divorce relationship, dysfunctional personality traits flourish, while in other relationships, including those with the children, healthier personality traits may abound. For those parents who are less disturbed, the pathological personality traits may surface only in the context of the conflicted relationship between the parents. Each parent's negative individual traits clash, and the conflicts continue. Left unchecked, these families return to court year after year to solve what might appear to the neutral observer to be the most minor issues. These families require strategies and interventions that assist them in taking care of their children and reducing their conflict. This will be discussed later in the chapter.

Contributions from Other Sources

In addition to the personality features of the parents, several other potential sources contribute to the high-conflict nature of some parents. One potential source is the nature of litigation itself. The court system typically focuses on polarization and blame, which reinforces the polarization and blame that many parents feel in these situations. Unless judges are sensitive to these issues, they may reinforce some of the problems by criticizing both parents when only one is exacerbating most of the problems. Within that context, there is often limited encouragement of problem-solving skills, although more recently some jurisdictions are encouraging parents to participate in specialized high-conflict programs designed to teach problem-solving skills,[198] as well as focusing these parents on the needs of the child.

At other times, some lawyers seem to hate each other as much or more than the parents do. They may personalize their client's feelings and needs. They ratchet up the conflict, sometimes for a variety of reasons. While we do not want to criticize the work done by good lawyers, even they know when they are faced with a lawyer who instigates and stirs up trouble between parents. We both have known many lawyers who will not take cases that involve a more difficult lawyer from their community. It is almost as if the lawyer has a personality disorder—or acts like he or she has one. As a children's representative, therefore, it is necessary to recognize when you believe the lawyer is pushing an agenda the client may not have. Both authors have witnessed situations where lawyers argue for something because that is what "the law" allows, but where the parents may want, and the children need, something different from the case.

Although therapists are important for your clients, they may contribute in a way that exacerbates problems because courts and parties often ask them to act in ways that are not within their scope of practice.[199] Sometimes a child's therapist who has never met one of the parents will send a letter to the judge regarding the alleged abuse that child has suffered and make recommendations for custody, particularly in situations where only one parent takes a child to a therapist. In many jurisdictions, that would be an ethical violation because the therapist is making such a recommendation without seeing one of the parents. Of course, this is different from the situation where a dependency court is seeking recommendations from the child's therapist about reunification, which will be discussed below.

Similarly, adult therapists often provide "supportive" therapy without any knowledge about how the supportive therapy allows their client to avoid taking personal responsibility for the client's contributions to the problem. In supportive

---

198. For example, in Los Angeles County, various private practitioners provide parent education programs geared specifically toward high-conflict parents. Co-parent Solutions, https://www.coparentsolutions.com/parents-together-for-children (last visited Oct. 31, 2017).

199. Lyn R. Greenberg et al., *Is the Child's Therapist Part of the Problem? What Judges, Attorneys, and Mental Health Professionals Need to Know About Court-related Treatment for Children*, 37 FAM. L.Q. 241 (2003), *available at* www.lyngreenbergphd.com/wp-content/uploads/2008/04/child-therapist2.pdf.

therapy, when the client talks to the therapist, the therapist accepts and agrees with what the client says, without challenging the client about his behaviors and attitudes that may be exacerbating the problems. This problem can be exacerbated in dependency court where parents are ordered to participate in therapy and the therapists are not sufficiently trained to deal with these situations.

Another potential problem with parents involved in therapy is that therapists often do not receive information from the court and other parties, including child protection agencies. Therapists can work only with the information they have, and if the parents are the only ones providing information to the therapist, the therapist may be unable to provide anything other than a form of supportive therapy. Many therapists want nothing to do with the court process, which includes not wanting to receive or provide information. While we do not mean to say therapy should not be supportive,[200] we have found that supportive therapy alone, without some level of focus on the client's maladaptive behavior, can be counterproductive. This is especially true when the adult client has significant personality disorder traits.

The final source of conflict comes from friends and extended family who support and encourage the "tribal warfare."[201] Again, while it is appropriate to support a loved family member or friend, it is not helpful to do so in a way that exacerbates the family conflict. In some families, the conflict is quite entrenched and extends beyond just the divorcing parents. Like the Shakespearean Montague and Capulet families, these parents get armies of support for their battle against the other parent. In such families, relationships become increasingly fragmented, as children are not able to see some family members because of their role in the conflict. As a children's representative, it can be helpful to ask about extended family members the child would like to see. Often this can provide information about the tribal warfare between the extended families, especially if your child client wants to see only family members on one side of the family.

Thus, in addition to the way in which personality traits and disorders often contribute to high conflict, the court system, attorneys, therapists, and family members and friends may all contribute to the level of conflict that may occur.

---

200. Supportive therapy can be very beneficial in certain cases, but in cases of high conflict with underlying personality disorder traits, it can be counterproductive.

201. JANET R. JOHNSTON & LINDA E.G. CAMPBELL, IMPASSES OF DIVORCE: THE DYNAMICS AND RESOLUTION OF FAMILY CONFLICT (Free Press 1998).

Impact of This Conflict on Children

Essentially, the very big risks to children's well-being when their parents separate lie in three primary areas: (1) poor parenting, (2) abandonment or absence of a parent, and (3) exposure to their parents' high conflict. The emotional risks to children in a high-conflict family experience are many and include problems such as being confused, having loyalty conflicts, and potentially experiencing boundary problems in their relationships, becoming parentified, adultified, or alienated. All the issues associated with toxic stress and trauma continue to exist here, but we also discuss issues more specific to, although not isolated from, high conflict between parents.

Parentified children take care of their parents and siblings and lose track of their own feelings. In high-conflict families, this happens because parents lose track of the need to care for their children and instead focus on the conflict. The word *parentified* gets used in more appropriate and less appropriate ways. For example, there is no question that it is inappropriate for a 5-year-old child to be caring for a younger sibling and being constantly worried about how that sibling is doing. It is a different issue, however, when an older adolescent is concerned about an infant sibling. While at no time should a child be the full-time caretaker for another child, it is not necessarily a problem when older teens worry about their younger siblings in high-conflict situations. Often these situations require you, as the children's representative, to walk a thin line between helping your older clients understand it is not their job to care for their younger siblings while also recognizing it is completely natural and you are honoring their care for their younger siblings. There is a different problem when very young children are parentified, and that must be dealt with in therapy.

Adultified children serve as confidants and "best friends" to the parent with whom they are merging. Adultified children are more common in high-conflict families because the parents want their children to take their side, thereby treating them more as friends than as children. Alienated children take sides and have polarized feelings in their relationships with their parents. Alienated children will be discussed in the next chapter.

None of these reactions are healthy for the child. Children of high-conflict parents often experience strong loyalty conflicts. This can manifest where children sometimes tell each parent what they think the parent wants to hear. This will make it difficult to know if what your client tells you is objectively truthful or more of a reaction to this conflict. It also means children's statements can change throughout the case. This can be one of the most difficult aspects of representing children—they can change positions, and sometimes it appears it is not done for a genuine reason, particularly in high-conflict cases. This can be difficult because children always have a reason for telling you what they tell you. Thus, the child's statements appear truthful even when they tell you information that appears to be opposing. This is why asking "why" is so important. Sometimes you can read between the lines, and sometimes you cannot.

Loyalty conflicts also manifest when children are confused and struggle to differentiate their own feelings and experiences from those of their parents, both of which can lead to increased risks of anxiety and low self-esteem. When children honestly do not understand what they are feeling, it can be beneficial as a children's representative to ask different questions, exploring various aspects of the child's life and experiences. While many people think it is appropriate, and even required, that the children's representative ask the child with whom they want to live, in high-conflict cases especially, this question can be damaging to children. Instead, you can ask questions about each home, about friends at each home, and about which parent supports or lives closer to children's extracurricular activities, for example. Asking these questions instead of putting the child directly in the middle of the conflict can help ease some, although likely not all, of these loyalty and anxiety issues. Later in the chapter we will address therapeutic interventions designed to help such children deal with their high-conflict parents.

Finally, it is imperative to help the child understand it is the court who makes the decisions. Neither you, the child, nor the parents, make the final decision in a case unless parents reach a stipulated agreement before the conclusion of a hearing or trial. Only the judge can do that, and the judge has multiple factors she must consider in making her decision. Reminding children of this can help alleviate some of their concern about being stuck in the middle of their parents' (or caregivers') conflict, although as noted above, it is unlikely to reduce all the conflict they feel. While many children still will take on that responsibility, your reminder to them of what the judge's role is and what your role is can help alleviate some of their anxiety.

Recommended Interventions for High-Conflict Families

Recognizing that high-conflict families are by themselves a unique category of cases and recognizing that the impact of high conflict can be quite problematic for children, you can make a difference by advocating for interventions that might reduce the impact of this conflict on your client. There are typically four main goals for these families: (1) therapeutic healing and problem solving; (2)

structured parenting time arrangements; (3) the use of a neutral decision maker, often referred to as a parenting coordinator; and (4) having the parents engage in parallel parenting rather than attempting to force cooperative co-parenting. This section addresses these issues.

Therapy

In those jurisdictions where it is legally authorized, courts commonly make orders for therapy at the conclusion of litigation in family law cases. In dependency cases, of course, therapy is often a requirement of the case plan. With high-conflict families, these orders must relate to the psychological and personality issues identified in the case. For high-conflict parents, this might include something like the following:[202]

- Providing therapy or counseling that encourages parents to develop empathy and understanding of their children's feelings and needs;
- Teaching parents to differentiate between their own thoughts, feelings, and needs and those of their children;
- Teaching parents to take personal responsibility;
- Teaching parents to consider alternative solutions and improving problem-solving skills; and
- Teaching parents communication skills.

Although it is always important for a therapist to be supportive with his client, supportive therapy does not work with high-conflict parents. It is critical to confront these parents therapeutically to focus them on the issues that are contributing to the conflicts with their ex-partner and negatively affecting your client.

For your client, therapy or counseling is likely needed to help him learn to cope. Children cope best when they learn active skills for coping, such as understanding their feelings, learning to express their feelings in a healthy way, and learning to separate their feelings from the loyalty conflicts and the conflicts of their parents.[203] To the extent children feel caught in the middle, or are used as

---

202. Of course, the specifics of the order will vary depending on the nature of each parent's critical issues and amenability for interventions.

203. *See, e.g.,* Laurie Fields & Ronald J. Prinz, *Coping and Adjustment During Childhood and Adolescence,* 17 CLINICAL PSYCHOL. REV. 937 (1997); Katherine H. Shelton & Gordon T. Harold, *Marital Conflict and Children's Adjustment: The Mediating and Moderating Role of Children's Coping Strategies,* 16 SOCIAL DEVELOPMENT 497 (2007).

spies or messengers of communication, such therapy can help them learn to get out of the middle and cope more successfully with the tension of their parents' divorce. Note that these goals are very different from those specific to trauma. These goals are specific to resolving the feeling of being in the middle of a high-conflict situation, particularly when the child recognizes he is a by-product of the two parents. The trauma resulting from exposure to the high conflict must also be considered and addressed, but the issues we address here, different from the issues identified in Chapter 4, are necessary in addition to those related specifically to the trauma of the high conflict.

Structured Recommendations

Another important intervention for these families is providing structured recommendations. It is not uncommon for parents to have litigated their residential schedule, often arguing about as little as fifteen minutes between what each parent wants. Many parents cannot agree on what a court order states, and some resort to calling the police regularly to resolving their disputes. Still others can manage the regular routines of caring for the children during the school year but cannot resolve requests for vacations, for example, and cannot manage the start and end times of holidays. Whatever the issues in the high-conflict family with whom you are working, and regardless of how much stress it might be causing you, the parents' attorneys and the judge note that its toll is highest in the children.

Structured recommendations may help reduce the stress on everyone. The more specific the court order, the more parents know the rules and help the neutral decision maker (next section) enforce the rules. This is just as true in dependency as in family law. If one of the reasons the case is before the dependency judge is because of high conflict between the parents, it is imperative the dependency court provide the same structure for the family as a family court would.

Some families have a rather vague schedule outlined in their parenting plan order stating, for example, "The children are to be with [one parent] every Wednesday overnight and every other weekend. Each parent has the opportunity for a summer vacation in each calendar year." Some are even vaguer and state that "[one parent] has reasonable rights of access." Some even say, "Visitation to be agreed upon by the parties." While such phrases may be acceptable for many low-conflict and medium-conflict families that are flexible and manage their conflicts, they will not work for high-conflict parents. High-conflict parents argue about the start and end times of the overnight, how to define the times of the weekend, the length and times of vacations, and how to resolve the likely occurrence that each parent wants the same vacation dates. Court orders that address these and other issues might look like the following:[204]

- The children are to be with [one parent] from his pickup of the children at school at the end of their school day each Wednesday until returning them to school the following Thursday morning. [That parent] will have the children every other weekend (with the start date noted so that an observer can easily determine whose weekend is whose) beginning at [that parent's] pickup at school on Friday afternoon until return of the children to school on Monday morning.
- In the event of a three-day holiday weekend in which the children are off school either Friday or Monday, [that parent's] time with the children will extend to include that additional day; for example, [that parent] will return the children to school on Tuesday morning following a Monday holiday.
- In the event there is no school on an exchange day, [that parent] will pick up the children from [the other parent's] home at 3:00 p.m., and will drop the children off at [other parent's] home at 8:30 a.m.
- In addition, it is recommended that each parent have the children for up to fourteen consecutive days for a vacation in each calendar year. Such vacations can occur only during the summer school break, except as outlined in the holiday schedule below.
- Requests for vacation must be made by February 28 of each calendar year for the following summer, and in the event there is a dispute over requested dates, Father has first choice in even-numbered years and Mother has first choice in odd-numbered years.

Another way to maintain a structured schedule is to develop a clear holiday plan. Certainly, it will depend on the age of the children and the family expectations. Schools in different parts of the country are on different schedules as well. An example of a structured holiday and vacation schedule is as follows:

---

204. Although this schedule provides one parent with parenting time only on Wednesdays and every other weekend, we are not suggesting that is an appropriate parenting plan in any particular case. This is simply a way to outline effective strategies for writing parenting plans, and we chose one that is not overly simple or overly complicated to make a point about the need for specificity, not the appropriateness of this specific parenting arrangement.

For holidays, birthdays, and school vacations, the following is ordered:

- Thanksgiving break to be with Father in all odd-numbered years and Mother in all even-numbered years.
- An equal split of the Christmas breaks from school, switching at 1:00 p.m. Christmas Day.
- In all odd-numbered years, Mother to have the first half of the Christmas vacation. In all even-numbered years, Mother to have the second half of the Christmas vacation. The intent of this order is that each parent will have one-half of the break. In the event the vacation does not split evenly, the parenting coordinator will have the authority to make adjustments to the holiday schedule in a given year.
- Spring break to be treated as a whole, including the weekend days, with Father having the children in all odd-numbered years and Mother having the children in all even-numbered years.
- The children to be with Father on his birthday from 4:00 p.m.–8:00 p.m. (unless it naturally falls on his time) and for the entire Father's Day weekend and Mother on her birthday from 4:00 p.m.–8:00 p.m. (unless it naturally falls on her time) and the entire Mother's Day weekend. In addition, the children's birthdays should be alternated in the same fashion.

As shown in this lengthy and detailed order, less room exists for each parent to manipulate or feel manipulated by the other. The rules are clear. If there is no parenting coordinator, as is often the case because of a lack of finances, the parents know exactly what the parenting plan should be, and if either of them tries to go to court or keep the children at a time the children are not supposed to be with that parent, the court will find it easier to resolve the dispute. Thus, it helps keep these families out of court, although it does not preclude them from going to court.

In the event of a dispute when there is a parenting coordinator, it will be relatively easy for the parenting coordinator to resolve. The order should also include a provision that the parenting coordinator can adjust or modify the parenting schedule in the event of certain situations, such as a family emergency, a special longer vacation, the children's summer schedule, or the needs of one or more family members. Typically, such adjustments are put in writing so that there is no dispute about how or why the adjustment was made.

Flexibility does not work for these high-conflict families unless a dispute resolution mechanism such as a parenting coordinator is in place because flexibility is a breeding ground for new conflict. If there are insufficient finances for a parenting coordinator, then orders must be even more specific than when a parenting coordinator is involved. Parents can feel more comfortable with a structured order if it can be adjusted in the event a specific need arises. The above is only one example of the areas in which concrete and specific orders can be made, and to the extent you can assist the parents' attorneys and the court in reaching a structured order, you help reduce conflict and thus assist your client. It is also important to add issues that are important to your child client. If your client plays football, include information about who can attend games and practices. If your client is on a traveling team of some variety, make sure there are provisions for those trips. These parenting plans are designed to help the child have the best possible life, not for the parents to get a certain amount of time with a child.

As noted above, it is just as important to have these specific orders in a dependency case as it is in a family law case. This is often where the chasm between family and dependency law arises; dependency lawyers say specific parenting plans are the purview of the family court, and if the parents have a dispute, they can solve it in family court. Unfortunately, that neither solves the issue for your client nor provides a basis for minimizing the disagreement between the parties. Ultimately, the court will resolve these issues with clear and carefully written orders.

Neutral Decision Making (Parenting Coordinator)[205]

In many jurisdictions, courts use attorneys or mental health practitioners as neutral decision makers to assist families in such day-to-day disputes. These "frequent flyers" strain the resources of the courts, and the court system is incapable of handling the types or frequency of problems these families bring. In recent years, courts have used the assistance of a decision maker who acts on behalf of the best interests of the children. This person is empowered by the family and the court to act on behalf of the children to resolve conflicts in an expeditious manner. If neither parent has control, both can relax their fear of being taken advantage of by the other. While each parent may become frustrated periodically with the decisions of the neutral decision maker, each parent usually trusts that person more than the other parent.

An example of an order for neutral decision making might be the following:

- The parents have agreed, and this court orders by stipulation of the parties, the appointment of a parenting coordinator to assist the parties in resolving

---

205. Parenting coordinators also may be called parenting plan coordinators and special masters. We use the more general term of *parenting coordinator*.

their disputes. This parenting coordinator has decision-making authority in all day-to-day areas except for significant changes in the parenting time.

- The parenting coordinator has the authority to settle disputes in the areas of child care, after-school activities, times and locations of exchanges, disputes about vacations, therapy for the child, and each parent's participation in the child's events.

- Both parents are discouraged from engaging in conflict within earshot of their child and are directed to use the parenting coordinator to resolve their disputes. Both parents should refrain from calling the police except in an emergency without first discussing their concern with the parenting coordinator.

- The parenting coordinator has the authority to alter the basic parenting time if he or she deems that one parent is causing significant problems for the child, although the parents have the right to request this court reject the parenting coordinator's recommendation. Also, at a minimum, the parents should meet with the parenting coordinator once per month to discuss their child and the child's needs and to work toward preventing future problems from occurring.

There are three primary benefits of this role: (1) helping families more quickly resolve their differences, (2) relieving the courts of some of their most difficult cases, and (3) helping families with very young children manage the nuances of integrating changing developmental needs of the child into their parenting plan. Also, note that the use of a parenting coordinator is often less expensive than the use of two attorneys and the time and costs of going to court.

The major task of the parenting coordinator is to make decisions that help a family stay out of court and keep their children out of the middle of the conflict. Parenting coordinators need to be decisive. Just as young children often have difficulty sharing, divorced parents often have difficulty sharing their children. While the parenting coordinator needs to understand the parents' position and feelings, it is more important for the parenting coordinator to make decisions that are in the child's best interests, without taking a lot of time.[206] A good

---

206. *See, e.g.,* Matthew J. Sullivan, *Ethical, Legal, and Professional Practice Issues Involved in Acting as a Psychologist Parent Coordinator in Child Custody Cases,* 42 Fam. Ct. Rev. 576 (2004); Susan Boyan & Ann Marie Termini, The Psychotherapist as Parent Coordinator in High-Conflict Divorce: Strategies and Techniques (Haworth Clinical Practice Press 2005); Philip M. Stahl, *The Use of Special Masters in High conflict Divorce,* 28 Cal. Psychologist 29 (1995).

resource regarding parenting coordination is *Guidelines for Parenting Coordination,* which is published by the AFCC.[207]

A parenting coordinator must make major decisions on a regular and consistent basis. For most mental health practitioners, quick decision making is the most difficult task of being a parenting coordinator, which is why it may be helpful to have an attorney serve as a parenting coordinator. Someone who accepts this task must recognize that the child relies on the parenting coordinator to make decisions on the child's behalf. When the parenting coordinator keeps the focus on meeting the needs of the child, it becomes easier to make quick decisions that support and promote the child's healthy adjustment.

The role of the parenting coordinator is a multifaceted one[208] in which he is part detective (as parents describe their different stories, the parenting coordinator tries to understand the "whole truth"), part educator (the parenting coordinator helps parents learn to share their children, understand each child's developmental needs, resolve problems, and move on with their lives following the divorce), part mental health professional (the parenting coordinator understands the parents' and child's feelings and attitudes), part judge (the parenting coordinator makes timely decisions), and part advocate for the children (children's needs are the parenting coordinator's first priority). Parenting coordinators may talk with other professionals and may need to meet with the children to carry out their work. The task is complex because of the ongoing conflict between the parents.

The scope of the parenting coordinator must be defined by court order. In most jurisdictions, parenting coordinators cannot be ordered by the court.[209] Instead, this court-appointed role is stipulated by the parents and grants the parenting coordinator very specific and usually limited roles because courts cannot delegate judicial tasks to nonjudicial officers. With that in mind, parenting coordinators generally are granted the authority to make limited decisions about schedules, overnight access, choice of schools, extracurricular activities, troubles at transfers, holiday scheduling, parenting differences, health issues, children's therapy, and problematic behaviors on the part of one or both parents. The

---

207. Association of Family and Conciliation Courts, AFCC Task Force on Parenting Coordination, *Guidelines for Parenting Coordination* (2005), *available at* https://www.afccnet.org/portals/0/afccguidelinesforparentingcoordinationnew.pdf.

208. Stahl, *supra* note 206.

209. *Ruisi v. Thieriot,* 53 CAL. APP. 4th 1197 (1997).

parenting coordinator needs to understand the impact on the children before making decisions in any of these areas.

The work of parenting coordinators is very challenging. Parents who require parenting coordinators are engaged in destructive conflict, tend to have limited psychological resources and coping skills, and tend to thrive on chaos in their lives. The parenting coordinator requires time management skills that some mental health professionals may find difficult to do. Phil has heard fewer concerns with time management when an attorney is the parenting coordinator. However, being a parenting coordinator requires training in child development and conflict resolution, and attorneys sometimes have more problems with those aspects of the job.

Because many of these parents are highly litigious and vehemently express their displeasure over decisions, the job requires the mental toughness of a judge and the empathy of a psychologist to withstand the pressures that some parents apply. While this might be difficult for some, we know many parenting coordinators who find gratification in being able to support children in these families while helping parents reduce the intensity of their conflict.

It is important to note that you might be asked to serve as a parenting coordinator in some of these cases (not one in which you are the child's representative, of course) to help parents in their conflict resolution. The issues in this book about representing children are similar to the issues you would have to address as a parenting coordinator.

Parallel Parenting

A fourth intervention involves parallel parenting. Psychologists describe young children who play next to each other but interact in limited ways with each other to be in "parallel play." In the same way, parents who parent their children at different times, but who have little or no direct interaction, are engaged in parallel parenting. Although much of the separated parenting literature focuses on the goal of cooperative co-parenting, in which parents learn to communicate and work with each other to raise their children in a cooperative fashion, high-conflict families usually fail at this task. Each parent usually thinks his or her style is the only way to parent and is often quite critical of the other. Interactions stimulate conflict that harms children.

The goal of parallel parenting is to reduce the level of conflict and ensure the tasks of parenting are accomplished by one or both parents. It is important for parents, in conjunction with a neutral decision maker, to specify which parent is responsible for various parenting tasks. Parents develop a parenting plan that identifies how each parent will participate in the child's extracurricular activities, help with schoolwork, and take care of medical needs, for example. Plans are developed to ensure that parents communicate as little as possible with the expectation of less conflict. E-mails and texts may be used when conflict is high and are usually monitored by the parenting coordinator to ensure civility.[210] Each parent is encouraged to develop his or her separate routine and structure. With such a plan, for example, the child will not be exposed to both parents attending the same field trip and making things miserable with their conflict. Although some high-conflict parents cannot share parenting,[211] parallel parenting may facilitate its success.

Parallel parenting allows high-conflict parents the freedom to parent separately. Working with the neutral decision maker allows them to develop the skills to co-parent and use them later in raising their children, after the conflicts have diminished. To help these parents disengage and then learn to work together, it can be helpful for the neutral decision maker to meet with the parents periodically to develop a schedule of the child's activities and each parent's participation in those activities. The parenting coordinator can focus on the process of parallel parenting and help parents to disengage from conflict. Together they can develop routines for the child and help coordinate a similar routine in each household, schedule times for phone calls between children and the other parent, and assist each parent in doing those tasks that each parent does best. With this process, neither parent is a winner or loser, and the child benefits from separate and parallel interaction with both parents and the reduced level of conflict to which she is exposed. Once a neutral decision maker is in place and the process of parallel parenting is ensured, parents can detach from each other and reduce the intensity of their conflict. Sometimes this task of parallel parenting can be very difficult, and not all families can afford a parenting coordinator. Perhaps the parents can work with a co-parent counselor who in such cases is considered a parallel parent counselor. Others will work periodically with a mediator to keep them focused on parallel parenting. Still others may use you, as the child's representative, to facilitate the parallel parenting. Phil has known courts to order that

---

210. our family wizard, https://www.ourfamilywizard.com/ (last visited Nov. 5, 2017).

211. *See, e.g.,* Janet R. Johnston, *High-Conflict Divorce*, 4 Future of Child. 165 (1994); Philip M. Stahl, Parenting after Divorce: Resolving Conflicts and Meeting Your Children's Needs (Impact Publishers 2007) (2000).

parents read his book[212] so that they have an agreed-upon foundation for how to parallel parent. Of course, like so many issues in high-conflict divorces, parents with better financial resources have the opportunity for assistance compared with those who have fewer financial resources.

For parallel parenting to work, certain skills are required by the parents in families.[213] The first step of parallel parenting is "disengagement." These parents need to avoid communication about minor things in the child's life. They need to avoid telling each other how to parent or criticizing each other. Instead, only limited and basic information is provided, and all of it is done via e-mail, text, or letter. Parents engaged in parallel parenting communicate orally or leave voice messages only in emergencies when no other method of communication is sufficient to deal with the emergency. In their written communication, parents need to be encouraged to be factual and concise and businesslike, avoid sarcasm and impulsive emotions, and not share the communications with the children. Parents who parallel parent must support different styles of parenting and accept more than one "right way" to parent in order to avoid conflict.

When engaged in parallel parenting, each parent needs to be less rigid and more accepting of the child's other parent. It is important to note that many children of separated parents adjust well to two very different homes. Ultimately, parents who parallel parent can learn to parent differently and continue to raise their children in a healthy way.

The Use of a Parent Communication Notebook

Parents who are engaged in parallel parenting do not communicate very well with each other, but they still need to communicate about the day-to-day issues with their children, especially when children are under age 5. The parent communication notebook should include highlights of the very young child's emotions and behaviors during the time the child is with each parent.

The notebook is transitioned between parents during the exchange of the child. When children are under age 2, the notebook should have information about the child's health, feeding, sleeping patterns, and soothing. It should include information about the child's emerging language and the child's mood,

---

212. *Id.* The appendix from PAD titled Cooperative Co-Parenting vs. Parallel Parenting is on the website.

213. *Id.*

including what upsets the child and what helps soothe the child. Ultimately, the notebook should include all relevant information about the child's day-to-day functioning and needs. In order to ensure that such communication goes well, it may need to be monitored by the parenting coordinator, just like other written communication between high-conflict parents. It can also be electronic and use one of the resources in the online resource guide specifically designed to help parents communicate appropriately.

Conclusion

High-conflict families, whether in family or dependency cases, often result in having children's representatives appointed. In family law cases, as previously mentioned, children's representatives can be the only professionals on the case. This requires you to understand these issues and know what services you can request for parents as part of their dependency case plan or as part of their parenting plan.

You can ask that parents engage in parallel parenting, that they create a notebook (whether digital or paper), and that they have very specific parenting plans. For example, as a children's representative, having this knowledge about parallel parenting, you can suggest it as part of the case plans for parents in dependency cases. Parents can be encouraged to work in individual counseling on parallel parenting and even take co-parenting classes when there is high conflict in a dependency case. Not all cases can have a parenting coordinator, so having the children's representative available to provide this information to parents and to ask for these orders as part of the parenting plan is necessary for the children.

With respect to children's needs, reminding your child client multiple times about the roles of everyone involved can help alleviate, although perhaps not eradicate, her anxiety. And it is important to understand her position may change (and it may change frequently) as she feels caught in the issues between her parents. If you are the only legal representative in the case, you may also become caught up in the conflict between the parents. It is important in these cases to remember to take a step back and work with the court to create a structured parenting plan that protects the child and the parents from their own conflict, to ensure parents receive the appropriate education, and to ensure children receive age-appropriate education and therapy to deal with the issues they face in the high-conflict situation.

Alienated-Resistant Children 8

As noted in Chapter 7, one potential outcome for children in high-conflict families is that they will become alienated. But alienation and resistance can exist even without high conflict, which is why it has its own chapter. These issues arise frequently in both family and dependency cases, so you are likely to encounter them regardless of your practice area.

Alienation allegations are used as a sword and a shield by parents, who generally do not understand the dynamics of alienation and use the term when making the allegation. Children become alienated as a result of multiple factors, and this chapter will identify the various factors associated with alienation and how it manifests. We will discuss differences between an alienated child and a child who is estranged from one parent, and we will discuss the harmful effects of "true" alienation. At the end of the chapter, we will discuss a range of interventions that may, but may not, help change the dynamics.

For purposes of this book, parental alienation is defined as a child's *unreasonable* rejection of one parent due to the influence of the other parent combined with the child's own contributions. We will also discuss resistant children as the children who, for whatever reason, resist contact with one parent. The term *rejected parent* is what it appears to be—the parent with whom the resistant child resists interaction. The "aligned parent" is the parent with whom the child aligns, whether for an objectively valid reason or not. These terms, by themselves, connote no judgment; they are only words used to express the actions of the parties involved. If we discuss the alienating parent, it assumes the parent is the main cause of the child's resistance.

In these cases, the children's attorney has a very important role, for both the court and the child. Children express their rejection of a parent in a multitude of ways, so taking the time to get to the heart of the matter as best you can is imperative. And when you cannot, it is important to remember your presence—a person willing to listen to the child from a place of nonjudgment is healing for that child even if she may not realize it at the time. But because of how alienation/rejection cases play out, you can also become part of the back-and-forth, and it is important to take a step back, examine what is happening, and ensure you are not inadvertently causing some of the conflict despite your good intentions.

Early writing on the subject[214] identified the alienating parent's emotions and behaviors as the cause of the child becoming alienated and coined the phrase "parental alienation syndrome" to identify what happens to children. Scholars have argued whether there is such a syndrome,[215] but regardless of what it is called, there is strong evidence suggesting that children in high-conflict families can become alienated against one parent. Rather than blaming a parent for the child's unreasonable alienation and resistance to spend time with a parent, others[216] have

---

214. RICHARD A. GARDNER, THE PARENTAL ALIENATION SYNDROME: A GUIDE FOR MENTAL HEALTH AND LEGAL PROFESSIONALS (Creative Therapeutics 1998) (1992).

215. *See, e.g.,* Mary Lund, *A Therapist's View of Parental Alienation Syndrome*, 33 FAM. & CONCILIATION CTS. REV. 308 (1995); Deirdre C. Rand, *The Spectrum of Parental Alienation Syndrome* (Parts I and II), 15 AM. J. FORENSIC PSYCH. 23 (1997); Richard Warshak, *Parental Alienation Syndrome in Court*. Dallas, TX: Clinical Psychology Associates, 1999 (supporting the concept of PAS); Cheri Wood, *The Parental Alienation Syndrome: A Dangerous Aura of Reliability*, 27 LOY. L.A. L. REV. 1367 (1994); Carol Bruch, *Parental Alienation Syndrome and Parental Alienation: Getting It Wrong in Child Custody Cases*, 35 FAM. LAW Q. 527 (2001) (against the concept of PAS).

216. *See, e.g.,* Joan Kelly & Janet Johnston, *The Alienated Child: A Reformulation of Parental Alienation Syndrome*, 39 FAM. CT. REV. 249 (2001); Philip M. Stahl, *Understanding and Evaluating Alienation in High-Conflict Custody Cases*, 24 WIS. J. FAM. L. 20 (2003).

focused on the child herself, identifying the various factors that contribute to a child's unreasonable rejection of a parent.

In contrast to the alienated child who is unreasonably rejecting a parent, some children are estranged, having a legitimate reason for the rejection.[217] In our experience, it is not uncommon for rejected parents to have limited parenting skills and a tenuous relationship with their child prior to separation or to your involvement in the case and to claim alienation when the child's reaction is more consistent with the alignment noted above. These rejected parents also have limited awareness of the ways their behavior has contributed to the child's rejection. For example, a child may reject a parent who is violent to the other parent and emotionally abusive to the child when a child welfare agency gets involved for the domestic violence in the family. This is called realistic estrangement rather than alienation. Parents rejected for these valid reasons will accuse the other parent of alienating the child in the same way rejected parents will accuse the other parent of alienation when there is an unreasonable basis.

The third type of alienation, and perhaps the one that is most likely to occur, is called a "hybrid" case.[218] As Fidler and Bala described,[219]

> With more research and experience, legal and mental health practitioners have noted that pure or "clean" cases of child alienation and realistic estrangement (those that *only* include alienating behavior on the part of the favored parent or abuse/neglect on the part of the rejected parent, respectively) are less common than the mixed or "hybrid" cases, which have varying degrees of enmeshment and boundary diffusion between the aligned parent and the child and some degree of ineptness by the rejected parent, making proper "diagnosis" and intervention planning extremely challenging. [In addition,] [i]n some instances of realistic estrangement the aligned

---

217. Leslie Drozd & Nancy Olesen, *Is It Abuse, Alienation, and/or Estrangement? A Decision Tree*, 1 J. CHILD CUST. 65 (2004).

218. *See, e.g.,* JANET R. JOHNSTON ET AL., IN THE NAME OF THE CHILD: A DEVELOPMENTAL APPROACH TO UNDERSTANDING AND HELPING CHILDREN OF CONFLICTED AND VIOLENCE DIVORCE (Springer 2nd ed. 2009); Barbara J. Fidler & Nicholas Bala, *Children Resisting Postseparation Contact with a Parent: Concepts, Controversies, and Conundrums*, 48 FAM. CT. REV. 10 (2010); Steven Friedlander & Marjorie G. Walters, *When a Child Rejects a Parent: Tailoring the Intervention to Fit the Problem*, 48 FAM. CT. REV. 97 (2010).

219. Fidler & Bala, *supra* note 218, 15–16 (internal citations omitted).

parent's reactions may be disproportionate to the circumstances and even emotionally harmful to the child. The protective response of the aligned parent in *both* child alienation and realistic estrangement can look like alienating behavior.

Thus, in these hybrid cases, your client may give you very valid reasons for being upset with a parent, but you may find it difficult to understand the magnitude of that upset. Sometimes the aligned parent will, in an attempt to be supportive to the child, cause more friction with the rejected parent than there might have been otherwise.

As the child's representative, it can be difficult to sort out exactly what is happening in these cases, but they require getting to know your client very well and beginning to understand the *why* of what he is saying. Asking about the history of the relationships with each parent can also be helpful to begin to sort out what is happening and why a child is resisting the relationship with one parent. It can be helpful to ask about fun times with the rejected parent, what the child used to do with the rejected parent, and what the rejected parent does for the child on special occasions, for example, in order to better understand if there was a point in time when something shifted or if the rejection has been a long time coming.

Contributions to the Child's Unrealistic Alienated Response

There are multiple reasons and multiple issues that contribute to a child's response of unrealistic alienation.[220] These can include the following:

- The personality of the aligned parent and that parent's negative beliefs and behaviors that reinforce the child's aligned response. This is consistent with the view of Gardner, who hypothesized that when there is a hostile parent, the child is likely to respond in an alienated fashion;
- The personality and responses of the rejected parent, both historically in the relationship as well as in response to the child's initial alienation;

---

220. *See, e.g.*, Joan Kelly & Janet R. Johnston, *The Alienated Child: A Reformulation of Parental Alienation Syndrome*, 39 FAM. CT. REV. 249 (2001); Philip Stahl, *Understanding and Evaluating Alienation in High-Conflict Custody Cases*, 24 WIS. J. FAM. L. 1 (2004).

- Because alienation most often occurs within the context of parental separation, a more conflicted separation and intense litigation can also contribute to the child's response, especially when the child is exposed to the litigation by one or both parents;
- Marital history, especially when there has been intense marital conflict, or when there are intense emotions around the separation (such as shame or humiliation);
- The myriad of aligned professionals and/or extended family and friends who contribute their own pressures on the parents and/or the child to resist contact with one parent;
- Siblings can also be a factor, especially when an older sibling refuses contact with a parent, as this can contribute to a younger sibling becoming afraid or resistant;
- The child herself, including her age, cognitive capacity, temperament, and vulnerability. It is hypothesized that children under age 7 are less likely to become alienated because they are less able to "hold onto" the resistance when they are with the otherwise-rejected parent, but that older children can easily become alienated and often take a strong position.[221] In fact, children over age 7 are most likely to become unreasonably alienated, adultified, or parentified;
- At times, other people in the family's life, such as family and friends, and even children's therapists can join in the "tribal warfare" and contribute to the child's resistance.[222]

It is important to recognize how you, as the child's representative, can get drawn into this as well. As noted, one of the factors that can lead to an unreasonable resistance is participation in the court process, particularly when one parent has involved the child more than the other parent. But it is in these cases where you are most likely appointed, and therefore, your involvement in the case can become a piece of the resistance if you are not careful, and sometimes even if you are. This is not to say you should stay out of these cases, although as we will discuss in Chapter 12, there are times you wish you could, but instead, you find a way to be careful.

As lawyers, you are trained in the adversarial method, and there is nothing families with resistant children like more than the adversarial process. It is cases like these where it becomes even more necessary to step away, examine your

---

221. Kelly & Johnston, *supra* note 220.

222. *See, e.g.,* JOHNSTON & CAMPBELL, *supra* note 201; Greenberg, *supra* note 199.

own potential for bias (discussed in Chapter 11), and try to sort out the multiple reasons for the child's alienation and resistance to spend time with one of her parents. Everyone on these cases will try to convince you that he is correct, and despite being the child's representative, your own client's feelings and statements can get lost in the process even to you. Consider all the factors and all the corroborative evidence you can while doing whatever else you can to stay out of the ping-pong effect these cases can have.

In contrast, the child's realistic estrangement is usually caused solely, or mostly, by the behaviors of the rejected parent. When a child and parent have a toxic relationship, when a parent engages in authoritarian and harsh parenting, or when a parent is abusive, the estrangement makes sense. When there is overt abuse, it can be easy to understand why a child rejects a parent, but perhaps one of the more common reasons, particularly for teenagers rejecting parents, is when the parent simply has ignored the child her entire life. Children have told us, "He just does not know me," "She was never there for me," and "I have lost a piece of my heart because she does not know how to be a mother." Sometimes this emotional neglect and apathy by a parent is just as painful, or more so, than overt abuse by that parent. One client told Rebecca, "I don't think he even knows my birthday."

These situations are much simpler to understand for you as the children's representative. There is an objectively valid reason for the child's resistance, and for the most part, the other parent is not involved. Sometimes the resistance to contact is because of how the rejected parent treated the aligned parent, and the aligned parent, particularly with teenagers, is honest about the relationship but there is no overt attempt to stop the child from seeing the rejected parent. The rejected parent's actions are what cause the child to reject that parent.

In those hybrid families in which the rejection is caused by a blend of estrangement and unrealistic alienation, the child's response is typically not commensurate with the behaviors of the rejected parent. Consider the example in which children are very reluctant to see their mother, their father has significant anger and hatred toward the mother that the children witness, the mother has poor parenting skills, and one of the children has significant emotional problems in which she overexaggerates her mother's behaviors and equates being bored when with her mother to being treated badly by her mother. This example has multiple contributions to the children's resistance and would likely be considered a "hybrid" example. When each parent blames the other, unfortunately each parent is failing to look inward to see his or her own contributions to the child's unrealistic resistance and failing to see the child's contribution to that unrealistic resistance.

It can be difficult to make sense of these cases, and in our experience, determining which factors play the strongest roles is key. You may want to help resolve the problems, but the first step is being an advocate for the child regardless of whether you agree the rejection is for a "valid" reason.

Typical Behavioral Responses in Children Who Are Unrealistically Alienated

While the child's feelings and attitudes are important in understanding a child's alienation, the child's behaviors are critical. In children who are alienated as opposed to estranged, we tend to see some or all of the following behaviors:

- A near or complete rejection of one parent in favor of the other. While there may be some ambivalence in this, as the alienation becomes more extreme, the child becomes more absolute in her refusal to see the other parent;
- A fusion of thinking in which the child and the aligned parent think alike. They might even use the terms *us* or *we* rather than *I* to define attitudes and beliefs;
- Superficial and trumped-up or exaggerated complaints about the rejected parent with little or no substance or specificity;
- Inconsistent and contradictory statements and behaviors. For example, at times, especially when in the presence of the aligned parent, the child may be vehement in his rejection of the other parent. At other times, especially when in the presence of the rejected parent, the child may be ambivalent and act in friendly and positive ways;
- A strong tendency to become overinvolved in the adult issues of the separation and parental conflict. At times, this is parent-driven, e.g., when parents tell their child about issues like child support and discuss who has caused the divorce. At other times, this is child-driven, as, for example, some children go out of their way to look at court papers and listen in on phone conversations between adults;
- When confronted about why they are rejecting a parent, many of these children are vague in their reasons, and some just say the parent is mean. They tend to refuse to answer specific questions about the history of the relationship and stay focused on the exaggerated or vague complaints;
- When interviewed, many alienated children use the same phrases or expressions as the aligned parent even if they are not consistent with the child's

development or how they otherwise speak. This is consistent with the merged thinking often found between such parents and children;

- As indicated above, many of these children, and their aligned parent, see the world in rigid and all-or-nothing ways. Thus, one parent becomes all good and the other becomes all bad.

Some children are unlikely to succumb to the forces that cause other children to become unreasonably alienated or to resist being with one of their parents. Those children may want the relationship with the otherwise-rejected parent, have enough contact with that parent, are not too vulnerable emotionally, likely have a healthy temperament, or have a healthy self-esteem that makes them less susceptible to becoming alienated.

Siblings

Although we will discuss siblings more extensively in Chapter 10, it is important to note here how much siblings can affect a resistant child. Sometimes, as mentioned, younger siblings blindly follow their older siblings' statements about a parent. It can be difficult, especially in hybrid cases, to understand the other children's position and feelings. And sometimes younger siblings align with older siblings because the sibling relationship is stronger than the parent-child relationship. Often in these cases of extremely high conflict where there are estrangement or alienation issues, the older siblings become the only safety the younger siblings have from the conflict. So regardless of their own feelings about a parent, they may want to stay with their protector older sibling. Similarly, because they want to protect their younger siblings, older siblings who do not want contact with one parent may be willing to have that contact if their younger siblings are forced to go.

In contrast, sometimes siblings take opposite positions about a case and about their parents. Imagine a case with twins where each twin has a different emotional temperament. Mother has chronic pain and, therefore, is in need of some help. She and her second husband recently separated. Father is remarried, and his second wife does not understand the emotional temperament of the more sensitive child, so she makes statements and acts in ways the child does not like. In addition, Father takes stepmother's side in disagreements between the stepmother and the child. Mother dislikes Father and makes inappropriate statements about him to both of the children.

The case comes to you after extensive family law interventions, but the more sensitive child has just been hospitalized, so child welfare gets involved and files a dependency case. By this point, the sensitive child has fully aligned with Mother, and the other twin realizes that Father is not that bad to her. So she asks to be there instead because she can no longer deal with Mother's negativity and even her sister's negativity about Father. And they are twins, so they still love and care about each other and have codependency issues, but they have opposite positions.

As a children's representative in cases of estrangement involving siblings, if your jurisdiction allows, it can be beneficial to have separate counsel appointed for each child. If that is not possible, it is very important to try to understand each child's position despite the fact you might be having confidential communication with each child. Psycho-education can be helpful here for both the older and younger siblings about the need for them to protect or feel protected by each other. In addition, in cases where children take opposite positions, it can fall on you to explain to the court why and how different children can have such different experiences in the same family and why that might require different court orders. Having a mental health professional explain why different children react differently to the same stimuli would be beneficial in a case where you have siblings with opposing positions.

While alienation/estrangement cases tend to put you in the middle more than any other case, those with siblings, especially siblings who take opposite positions in the case, can be even more extreme.

Interventions

Perhaps the greatest challenge is knowing what to do to help solve these relationship problems. The first step is trying to understand the dynamics of the family. Although costly and time-consuming, the best first step may be to have a trained forensic expert who understands the dynamics of alienation/resistance conduct a comprehensive evaluation of the family. The best-case scenario is that this evaluation will provide a baseline understanding of the family dynamics. If you are an attorney representing a child in a family with these dynamics, seek such an expert evaluation of the family. If that is not available due to limited resources or a lack of time, gather as much evidence as possible to try and understand whether your case is likely one of unreasonable alienation or realistic estrangement or is a hybrid case.

As we have stated throughout this book, it is important to understand these issues. If your client can only tell you she is bored when with Mother but cannot explain any other reason for the estrangement, you may be seeing a form of overreaction to a parent's actions. It is also important to notice *how* children speak about their dislike of a parent. Notice the words and the way children speak when discussing school, their friends, and other ordinary activities; then notice the words and mannerisms they use when discussing the rejected parent. Often you will see a shift in their language and emotion if there are influencing sources for their rejecting behaviors.

Another sometimes effective, although less obvious and less reliable, observation is a lack of change in affect. Remember that trauma is stored in the nervous system, so if a child is discussing something that is traumatic to him, his affect will usually change as a result. If the child is telling wild tales of abuse and his affect remains the same (not dissociated, but the same as other forms of communication), it can be telling, with other corroborative information, that other forces are at play.

Once you think you have an idea of what is happening, and it might be only an idea, working with a variety of interventions is important. We will break down suggested interventions into four different kinds of cases, which are discussed next.

When the Dynamic Is Primarily One of Estrangement

The primary task in such a case is to try and get the rejected parent help in deficient areas. Abusive parents need to take responsibility for their abuse, help the child heal, and gradually show the child that they can be trusted. Parents who lack parenting skills need to take parenting classes or get a parenting coach and help the child understand that the rejected parent takes responsibility and is working to improve their relationship. When parents and children have a toxic relationship, they may benefit from joint counseling to help them work through their differences. Often a legitimately estranged child will refuse this contact, but courts in some jurisdictions must at least attempt it; some judges believe it is important as well. If a child continues to refuse, Rebecca often objects to this therapy until the rejected parent takes responsibility for the child's rejection. At that point, the healing process might have begun enough to have a conversation with the child about the potential benefits of therapy. When legitimate estrangement is clearly identified, Phil will encourage the same in his testimony and reports. Most importantly, the rejected parent needs to avoid blaming the other parent or the child, develop skills of self-reflection, take responsibility for resolving the problems, support healing in the child, and demonstrate to the child that he is working to improve the relationship.

You can be helpful in being a conduit between the parent's actions and the child. For example, Rebecca often tells clients that in their confidential communications, her job is not to blindly follow what they want, but to have a dialogue. In court, you may act differently and fight to keep the child from having contact with a parent, but in those confidential communications, you can tell a child, for example, what, if anything, a parent is doing to improve and whether the parent has taken responsibility. Further, it is important to remind a child that eventually he may want contact with the estranged parent, and while your job is to make sure contact does not happen too soon, you may also have to nudge the child along. State laws can speed up this process or slow it down, and it is important to tell children what aspect of what the court does is governed by state law and what aspect can be governed by their emotional needs.

When the Dynamic Appears to Be a Hybrid Case

As the dynamics become more complicated, it is important to consider multi-pronged interventions that address all the dysfunctional family elements. Examples include having the aligned parent deal with her emotions and support her children's relationships with their father despite the flaws in their relationships, help the rejected parent take responsibility for resolving legitimate problems in the parent-child relationships, and encourage the children to be in therapy to manage their emotions and ensure more realistic and balanced views of each parent. If necessary, a combination of psychological and educational interventions with the children might be necessary.

When the Dynamic Is Primarily One of Unrealistic Alienation and the Resistance Is Mild to Moderate

This is a dynamic in which co-parenting-related parent education is often considered helpful, especially soon after the separation. When medium-conflict parents understand the potential negative impact of the conflict on the children, they can begin to take steps to prevent such problems. Children can also benefit early from therapy that helps them learn to separate their feelings from those of the parents, as well as learn to cope with the stress of the conflict. These two tasks can help reduce the risks of these children becoming more severely entrenched in the conflicts.

When the Dynamic Is Primarily One of Unrealistic Alienation and the Resistance Is Severe

The combined severity of resistance and entrenched positions of each parent makes these dynamics the most difficult problem to solve. Traditional weekly therapy does not work very well. When children are totally resistant and refuse contact, the choice faced by the courts is either the child having no contact with one of the parents or the child being forced to have a relationship she does not want. In a celebrated Michigan case in 2015, the family court judge had been so exasperated by the conflict of the parents and the entrenched positions of the children that she "sentenced" the children to seventeen days in juvenile hall before ultimately allowing them to go to summer camp before the end of the summer.[223] They still refused to see their father, and initially the Judicial Tenure Commission reprimanded the judge for her actions in the case.[224] In 2017, the Michigan Supreme Court reduced the Judicial Tenure Commission's recommended "unpaid, 30-day suspension" and left only the "public censure." The Court cited that the circuit judge in the case displayed "poor judgment" and that the judge had no prior record of misconduct, who "in an isolated instance exercised poor judgment and displayed a lack of appropriate judicial temperament and demeanor during a highly acrimonious and protracted divorce and custody proceeding."[225] In other words, even the Michigan Supreme Court recognized that good judges may act inappropriately due to the pressures of such difficult cases.

The general belief in family courts is that absent realistic harm, children benefit from healthy relationships with both parents. The challenge is how to make that happen. It is impossible to force children to have a relationship they do not want to have. Phil had a case several years ago in which the rejected parent continued to force contact with a resistant adolescent, and the court supported many efforts to make this happen. Suffice to say the efforts failed. Moreover, several years later on the child's eighteenth birthday, the child sent Phil (and presumably others in the system) a card explicitly stating that she would never see the rejected parent again. Instead of the efforts and time helping to soften the rejection, they worked to harden this rejection over time.

When young adolescents in particular take a position, they tend to stick to that position rigidly, increasing the family tension and making resolution difficult. Children are very good at voting with their feet, and there is potential

---

223. Bill Laitner, *Judge Jails Kids for Refusing Lunch with Dad*, Det. Free Press (July 9, 2015), http://www.freep.com/story/news/local/michigan/oakland/2015/07/09/divorce-custody-refuse-parenting-time-juvenile-home-charles-manson/29905867/.

224. Brian Dickerson, *The Short, Unhappy Tenure of Judge Gorcyca*, Det. Free Press (Dec. 16, 2015), http://www.freep.com/story/opinion/columnists/brian-dickerson/2015/12/16/judge-gorcyca-accused/77365840/.

225. Ben Solis, *Michigan Supreme Court Declines to Suspend Judge Who Jailed 3 Kids*, MLive (Jul. 28, 2017), www.mlive.com/news/detroit/index.ssf/2017/07/supreme_court_rejects_suspensi.html.

harm in forcing them to do something against their will. Besides becoming more entrenched, they can suffer physical harm if the rejected parent chooses to involve the police and children wind up handcuffed in the back of a police car for refusing contact with a parent. Remember from Chapter 5 that it is normal for adolescents to assert their autonomy, so we must be careful in these cases with adolescents attempting to do just that.

As these cases become more entrenched, you are more likely to get appointed to represent a child in such a case. If that happens, you are probably going to feel pulled in two directions—listening to your client to understand all the reasons for his resistance and encouraging your client to try having a relationship with the nontoxic parent he is refusing to see. This is an incredible struggle for you emotionally, as you can be pulled by pressure from the court to "do something" and by pressure from your client to get everyone to leave him alone. You are also likely to have your own opinion about the potential benefit to your client of having a relationship with the rejected parent. More than any other type of family law case, these have an intensity that is difficult to manage. Chapter 12 is focused on taking care of yourself when confronted with such challenges.

Intensive Psycho-Educational Programs

In recent years, the literature has shifted from once-a-week individual or family therapy to considerations of other more intensive interventions that bring family members together for a weekend or longer, sometimes together in groups of families, designed to teach families how to support relationships and heal the rifts in those relationships. These programs are in their infancy, and there is a considerable amount of controversy about many of them. One such program is Overcoming Barriers[226] (OCB), which has a summer camp program lasting several days that brings several families together to rebuild family relationships in a camp-like experience. OCB has trained various clinicians across North America, and there are many settings where a family can get an extensive camp-like weekend experience designed for the same purpose. Another such program in Northern California is Transitioning Families,[227] a weekend program also designed to help heal family dynamics. Such intensive programs are expanding around the

---

226. Overcoming Barriers, https://overcomingbarriers.org (last visited Nov. 5, 2017).

227. Transitioning Families: Creating Protected Space, transitioningfamilies.com (last visited Nov. 5, 2017).

world, although the research on the usefulness and success of these programs is limited at the time this book was written. Since 2014, OCB is attempting to research the effectiveness of its program, but we do not know about the research being conducted on the other intensive weekend programs.

Another program, but one with a great deal of controversy, is Family Bridges.[228] It is designed for situations in which the court has determined there must be a change of custody from the aligned parent to the rejected parent and there needs to be a period of transition to help facilitate this change. Placing the children in the Family Bridges program as part of the change ostensibly allows the children to learn, through a psycho-educational program, to understand why they became so resistant and to help heal the relationship with the rejected parent. Although the theory behind the program is a positive one, there is no independent research regarding its success, and in practice, courts also often order a lengthy period of no contact (sometimes up to ninety days) with the previously aligned parent. This is all forced on the children against their expressed wishes, and there is no understanding of how this affects the children in the program. Although we understand anecdotal evidence supports the use of this program in targeted cases of extreme unrealistic alienation without hybrid dynamics, we are concerned it is being used in cases where a more comprehensive approach is indicated, especially in complex hybrid cases.

It is important to remember these programs are extremely expensive, costing thousands of dollars per program. Thus, they are available only for cases in which the parents have a great deal of money. In other cases, more traditional therapy and a slower process are warranted, but in these extreme situations they are unlikely to be of value.

Conclusions

Lawyers are trained to be problem solvers. One of the biggest problems with cases involving resistant youth is that sometimes the problem cannot be solved, despite your best efforts and those of the courts. And sometimes knowing when to throw in the towel is also important—and goes against everything law school trained you to do and against what you believe might be correct for your client.

Imagine you are appointed in a family law case where the family is not financially wealthy. Father meets you and realizes you understand what alienation

---

228. Richard A. Warshak, www.warshak.com/services/family-bridges.html (last visited Nov. 5, 2017).

is, so he thinks you are amazing because, from his perspective, this is a case of alienation. You meet your 14-year-old client who tells you she would like contact with her father, and they have been having therapeutic visits for months.[229] Although there is a history of trouble between father and daughter, not the least of which is that Father is overbearing, the child wants to visit. Nothing strikes you as out of the ordinary except it would appear your client and father have grown through the therapy and are ready to begin unsupervised visits again. You go to court and ask for a shared parenting plan. Months later the child refuses to visit Father.

One day when the child refuses visits, Father calls the police, and your client is handcuffed and put in a police car until she agrees to go to Father's house. Your client calls you multiple times asking to change court orders so she does not have to go to Father's house. When you ask why, she states that she would like a relationship with her father, but her father has become too overbearing and will not leave her alone.

After the court order stands, the child runs away to a friend of her mother's on a day she is supposed to be with her father. Father takes the child without Mother's knowledge, and you cannot reach your client by phone. Mother calls you and the police because her daughter is missing, and she does not have her cell phone with her. Based on this information, you file a case in dependency court.[230] The case goes through a private dependency process where the judge, at the end, orders visits with Father again.

Those visits go well for a period, but eventually they break down again. The family court finally orders no visits with Father as the judge walks off the bench frustrated with the entire process. By this time, the child is 16 years old. Then six months before the child's eighteenth birthday, Father files a motion to modify parenting time. By this time, a new family court judge has been assigned to the case. Three months before the child turns 18, there is a trial at which Father testifies, as does the original therapeutic visit supervisor who still believes this situation is mostly the result of Mother's alienation. The child still tells you she ultimately wants contact with her father, but she is not ready for it today. Father testifies he and his daughter communicate through social media and that Mother

---

229. We understand therapeutic visits are controversial and not available in all jurisdictions. This could be family/conjoint therapy or some other form of contact between father and daughter that is in some type of therapeutic setting.

230. Not all jurisdictions allow for people other than the child welfare agency to file a dependency petition. In those jurisdictions, imagine you call the child welfare hotline.

is not aware of their communication and the child need not be concerned with what Mother thinks.

Imagine in this situation that you are a best interests attorney who must make a recommendation to the court about parenting time with Father three months before the child turns eighteen. Although the child denies Mother has ever alienated her, you know how Mother feels about Father and you know your client knows. In addition, the years of litigation have taken their toll on your client, and she is about to graduate from high school. Finally, you have your own biases about Father because of how he communicates with you and statements he has made to the court about you.

In cases like this, sometimes there are no "right" answers. You can do everything in your power, know your client very well, know the facts, and spend years on a case, but still there is no answer that solves the problem. And sometimes the trauma of the litigation becomes too much for the family, and it is time to cut your losses and allow the family to return to some sort of normalcy, hoping that your input in discussions with your client will pay off down the road. Know that in the moment, sometimes you and the court system need to let go of the family and let them get on with their lives despite the fact the court system has not resolved the problem. Be guided by the mistakes made by the Michigan judge and avoid overreacting, especially when it has the potential of putting children in harm's way.

Ultimately, with your good relationship with your client, you will then spend the next three months guiding her to heal her feelings toward both parents, take care of her own psychological and educational needs, and heal from the trauma of the high-conflict family dynamics. Most importantly, if you can, you will guide her to neutralize her polarized feelings and work to have independent relationships, on her specific and well-defined terms, with each of her parents as she moves into adulthood.

Special Circumstances 9

Representing children in dependency and family law is challenging. We already have identified critical areas in which you will want to know as much as possible, such as domestic violence, trauma and its impact, and high-conflict divorce. In this chapter, we will introduce you to a growing phenomenon, i.e., special circumstances confronting children in their day-to-day lives. Some of these are external issues caused by the child's environment and life circumstances. These include placement and immigration issues, among others.

Some of these are internal issues caused by the child's personal psychology or medical concerns, including but not limited to autism, cystic fibrosis, cerebral palsy or Down syndrome, ADHD, developmental delays, and severe mental health issues. When you have a child dealing with issues such as these, it makes your work even more complicated, as you will need to understand how the child's internal or external factors complicate his life and your work. Although this chapter will not provide a complete overview of these issues, it will begin to sensitize you so that you can identify critical variables, understand them, and know when you might need help from others in the process.

We will also provide resources to which you can refer when you see a child with these issues and need to learn more. Sometimes the most important part of the job as a lawyer is knowing when you do not understand something well enough and knowing that it is appropriate to ask questions. This chapter will give you a brief overview of the areas in which it is important to recognize there is a problem and that you might need to reach out for more answers in order to solve that problem.

In some ways, this chapter should be unnecessary because the same rules that we have been identifying still apply, including these: speak with each child at her level; learn from your child client, whether she is verbal or not; and listen and interact in a way that allows your client to feel your connection. Empathy, communication, and sensitivity are critically important. However, understanding the internal and external circumstances affecting your client directly will go a long way in helping you understand and then representing your child client more competently. In addition, we will have online resources from which you can gather more information about many of the issues we will discuss.

The following are important factors that require additional focus and knowledge to help you in representing your child client.

External Issues

This section focuses on the child's external environment and explains how it affects your client directly. Some are family-related; others are system-related. All have a profound impact on your child client. Although we are describing the issues and ways they might impact your client, as you listen and use your skills to understand your child client, your understanding of the particular client will improve.

Placement

Your child client may live at home with one or both parents, in a foster home, in a group home, or in out-of-home care with relatives. First, let us think about foster care. As a society, we ask foster parents to do the impossible—love a child as their own and then give them back at the end of the day to potentially less adequate parents.[231] When we say "less adequate," we do not necessarily mean

---

231. Phil's first book, *Children on Consignment*, was written for foster parents in 1987 (now out of print). This title reflected the fragile nature of the foster parent role in this regard.

they do not have the same resources as foster parents, but they still may be recovering from their own trauma and be less able, but still sufficiently able, to meet children's needs. While it can often feel as though foster parents are interfering with the reunification process, it is important to understand this point because of how children experience foster care differently than we do.

Imagine for a moment a preverbal child who has been living with one caregiver her entire life and then, for no reason the child understands, she is forced to live in a foster home. The child is terrified, does not understand what has happened, and must learn to rely on new people for her care. Over the course of the next one to two years, that child is seeing the original caregiver one or two times per week and then, without any explanation, is once again living with that caregiver. But during that period of time, the child has established a strong relationship with the foster family and, as his language skills start to develop, calls the foster parents "mom" and "dad."

Foster placements, like relative placements, become home to children. While children often understand who their biological parents are, many young children cannot logically comprehend why they have so many parents. Remember that logic comes from the prefrontal cortex, which is not developed in very young children. Children learn to love everyone in their lives who treat them with respect and love. Thus, it is not uncommon at the end of a case for children to feel conflicted about returning to their family of origin. It is not uncommon to think twice before removing a child from a foster home where he has lived his entire life to place him with out-of-state relatives because the law has a relative preference.

Rebecca has had multiple situations where, by the end of a case, particularly when the case has been in the system more than once, a child is conflicted about returning home. The child described in the Preface once said, "I want to go home this time, but if I get removed again, I am not going back to my mom." These loyalties can be even stronger when children are older and they have been placed with family members and sometimes when placed with foster families. These cases can begin to feel a little like a divorce situation where children feel torn between two people they love even when those two people are not biological parents and some of the issues from Chapters 7 and 8 begin to show up.

In these cases that have gone on for years and where children have a good relationship with foster parents, it is important to speak to the parents' attorneys, or the parents if you are allowed, to see if they are willing to allow the child to have ongoing contact with the foster parents once the case closes. Severing these ties completely, whether with biological or foster parents, can feel like a death to the child. That increases the risk of long-term consequences from an emotional perspective, as attachments are broken and the young child is not equipped emotionally to understand and manage her feelings of loss and confusion. At the more extreme end, these consequences would include but not be limited to insecure attachments moving forward, depression, poor self-esteem (remember, she will think it is her fault for this action), and failure to feel secure in her relationships and fear that any new relationships will not last.

Too often the system sees foster parents as a stepping stone to children returning home, particularly because they are not biologically related. From a legal perspective, that is absolutely what they are, but from the child's perspective, they are families with whom children have lived, sometimes for years, especially formative and important years, and they are usually families they have loved. This goes both ways, as foster parents often do not want children to have contact with the biological family once the case closes with an adoption. However, it is important to have a conversation with the foster parents and talk about why children typically need an ongoing connection to their biological family.

Relative placements are, in some ways, simpler, but they have their own dilemmas. First, we choose to place children with the people who raised the parents who were unable to raise the children in the system. Second, families often know the parents have issues, and they have tried to work with them for years. But by the time the system gets involved, the family is done with the parent and works to impede reunification. Sometimes families are too enabling of parents. But with extended family placements, children usually feel more comfortable, particularly at the beginning of a case. For obvious reasons, they want to be placed with family, and the law reflects the fact this is what most children want. Family often can help facilitate more contact with the parents as well as be a support to the parent to resolve whatever issues brought the case before the court. Family and nonrelated friends of the family can also be helpful to you in understanding the issues that brought the case before the court system.

Finally, group homes are where children end up if there are no foster placements or where they have such difficult behaviors that no foster home will take them. Group homes have staff. While some try to be more family-oriented, at the end of the day, the people in charge get vacation time and get to call in sick and not be there on certain days. Some children, adolescents in particular, enjoy the freedom they can have when they live in group homes, and some enjoy the outings and the ability to be around peers. For some children, being in a group home is easier because relationships are not as intimate and intense as in a family setting. Most of the time, however, the emotional outbursts of being around other adolescents become too much, and many of them begin telling stories of their personal belongings being stolen, people being in their business, there being no place for quiet time, and the bad influence some of the other children have on them. It is important to know how your client feels about his group home placement and you can expect him to describe both positive and negative elements. But remember that all children need a consistent, caring adult in their lives as resilience against the trauma they have inevitably experienced. Group homes rarely, if ever, have consistent, caring staff to provide the safety children need. Children in group homes are the most likely to have told Rebecca that they have no one in their lives to support them.

For these reasons, group homes are less desirable as placements for children, and in the case of very young children, they can be damaging. When children under the age of 3 are placed in group homes (often emergency shelter placements that drag on for months or years), they have a staff caring for them. As we learned in Chapter 5, children's development requires a warm, consistent caregiver. In group homes, where there is staff and the caregivers change frequently, children can end up having all the problems children raised in orphanages have faced.

Group homes are particularly damaging to young children, even if the buildings are clean and well maintained. Dr. Bruce Perry describes a child who was raised in a Russian orphanage in his book *The Boy Who Was Raised as a Dog*.[232] The orphanage told the parents how well fed the children were and how clean the location was, but as Dr. Perry discovered, "Peter and the other children who lived there had been profoundly neglected."[233] He described the neglect as follows:[234]

> Peter had been raised without adult attention for the first three years of his life. He'd been kept in what was basically a baby warehouse: a big, bright room with sixty infants in seemingly endless, straight rows of perfectly sanitized cribs. The two caretakers on duty for each shift would work methodically from one bed to the next, feeding each child, changing his diaper, then moving on. That was all the individual adult attention the babies received: roughly fifteen minutes each per eight-hour shift. The infants were rarely spoken to or helped other than during these brief intervals; they were not rocked or cradled or cooed at because there simply wasn't time for staff to do more than feed and change, feed and change.

232. PERRY *supra* note 149 at 215–30.
233. *Id.* at 216.
234. *Id.* at 218.

While many group homes that house infants are better than this description, the problem of staff vs. caring adult remains. Young Peter had a multitude of problems because of his time in the orphanage, including poor language skills, impulsivity, and outbursts where he lost control, which could last for hours. Peter's example, while extreme, illustrates the dangers of group homes for very young children. Although many of the staff in group homes that house very young children are trained better and engage well with children, the lack of a single or small number of consistent caregivers is likely to be detrimental to the developing child.

Thus, it is important to recognize there is no simple answer to the issue of placement, and it must be questioned and evaluated continually by the court and by you. Ask your clients how they feel about where they live. Ask them how they are cared for and how they feel about the care they receive. Ask them what happens if they get in trouble. Ask them what happens if they get angry and need to vent. Ask them what happens if they want to go to their room to be alone for a while. Understand that development and attachment mean that moving a child specifically because the law says you should may not be best for a child. If a child needs to move or if it is best for a child to move, determine what processes can be put in place to mitigate any harm caused by the move. This can include provisions for ongoing contact with the prior caregiver, appropriate therapy for the child, and a transition plan to help the child adjust to a new living arrangement. Asking the correct questions and understanding the impact of any potential move or termination of the relationship between a child and a potential caregiver will help you determine how best to serve your client.

Immigration/Refugee Status

Your child client's immigration status may also affect critical issues facing your client. Some children are refugees from a hostile country. For example, when Phil was a psychologist early in his career, he evaluated refugee foster children from Vietnam. Language and cultural issues permeated those evaluations, and sometimes no one knew how old the child was, as many did not have birth records. These children lived in foster homes, and many did not speak any English, creating a need for translators for basic communication with foster parents, medical and psychological personnel, and their attorneys. Understanding and having empathy for the traumas experienced in refugee camps outside Vietnam and the harrowing journey to the United States was also critical. Suffice to say, those were among the most challenging evaluations Phil has ever experienced.

When Rebecca was in law school, she worked with African refugees, and some of the same cultural and trauma issues applied. At least Rebecca and her African clients spoke French, solving some of the language issue. Most refugees come with few or no possessions, and they are unaccustomed to their new country's beliefs and practices, particularly about issues such as child abuse and domestic violence. What may be normal for them is illegal in their new country. It requires understanding these issues when dealing with these cases in order to walk the thin line between culture and safety and between culture and what you believe is appropriate.

Many youth experience immigration issues separate from refugee issues. During the time this book was being written, many families were being broken up by an immigration system that sent one or both parents to their country of origin, fragmenting families in the United States, or splitting up families within the United States. Many children experience fear and trauma worrying about whether that will become their experience because so many members of their families are undocumented. Regardless of your personal beliefs about undocumented immigrants, as a child's lawyer, it is important to understand how it will affect your client if a family member is deported and the overwhelming effects of the fear of immigration issues. Living with that constant fear can be as detrimental to the nervous system as all other forms of trauma we have discussed throughout the book and can lead to many of the issues described in Chapter 4. They are reluctant to talk to medical, legal, or psychological professionals for fear it will lead to problems with immigration. Because the abuse being suffered is less scary to the family than the fear of deportation, families often will not contact law enforcement in situations you may believe are necessary. Phil and Rebecca have worked on several cases where the reason parents were not in the same locale was because a parent had been deported or had a visa expire, forcing a relocation case regardless of which parent originally had primary custody.

If you know your client is undocumented, it is important to find out whether there are any visas for which they qualify, the most common being Special Immigrant Juvenile Status or U visas. The requirements for these visas may affect legally when you want a case to begin and end. If you do not work in an office or a county with systems in place to ensure these issues are addressed, make sure you know a local immigration attorney to whom you can refer these cases.

Being sensitive to such issues is critical when you work in the world of dependency or family court, and your representation of these children will be impacted by their immigration or refugee status. If these issues are unfamiliar to you, consult with an immigration attorney to help you understand them and how they may affect your child client and his family.

School

It is quite common for children in dependency or family court to have significant problems in school. For many children, they were very good students prior to the case beginning. Their grades suffer because they spend so much time worrying about the case. Some are diagnosed with ADD or ADHD (see elsewhere in this chapter), some have learning disabilities, some have behavioral problems, and some have missed so much school or moved so many times that they are far behind their same-aged peers academically. In addition, children in the court system often see many peripheral professionals, including you, and many of those appointments are during school hours, further disrupting their schooling.

As discussed in Chapter 5 on developmental issues, school is perhaps one of the most important environments for children between the ages of 5 and 18 from a developmental standpoint. Children who experience school failure and learning problems are at significant risk of a myriad of emotional problems, including but not limited to internal symptoms such as anxiety, depression, insecurity and limited self-confidence, poor self-esteem, and shame. External symptoms may include bullying, challenges with authority figures, symptoms of oppositional defiant disorder (described elsewhere in this chapter), or general aggressiveness.

Some children use school as an escape. Too much is happening in their home lives, so they turn to school as a distraction and coping mechanism. This is not necessarily a problem, and it certainly helps their school performance. However, it is important to ask questions of children who seem to be excelling in school to help determine whether they have emotional issues they refuse to face or that do not appear on the surface. Hiding from these underlying issues can be damaging to your clients' mental and physical health later in their lives as we have learned from the ACE study described in Chapter 4.

For these reasons, it is critical to understand your child client's school history, school functioning, and emotions related to school. Even though your main task is representing your child client in the court system, if you do not understand your child client's school functioning, your advocacy will suffer, as will your child client. Both authors often ask children who have poor grades what their grades were like prior to the case beginning. Because school is such an important developmental task for children, school performance can tell you a great deal about how your clients are functioning generally.

Neglect

Neglect can take many forms, but we will focus on two main issues. The first is obvious neglect of the child's basic day-to-day needs, i.e., food, clothing, shelter, medical/dental care, and basic hygiene. In dependency court, you are likely to experience children whose basic needs have rarely, or intermittently, been met. Of course, when children experience this type of neglect, there can be significant consequences in other aspects of their development. For example, children whose dental needs were neglected may have rotten teeth that need to be removed; children whose medical needs were neglected may need immunizations and care for specific physical issues; and children whose hygiene was ignored may need significant assistance in learning self-care of their hygiene. For such children, if their parent caregivers did not meet those needs, placement in any out-of-home care setting will likely lead to adult caregivers who do an adequate job of meeting those needs, but you may need to be proactive and facilitate getting those needs met and ensuring the ramifications of the neglect are addressed quickly. For example, every state has an agency that addresses developmental disabilities. It is important to have these children evaluated by that agency as soon as the case begins.

In contrast, emotional neglect can be much more challenging, and it often appears where there has been physical neglect. Serious attachment issues challenge children and caregivers alike. As identified in Chapter 5 on child development, when there are attachment challenges such as insecure or disorganized attachment, children have significant problems in relationships and later have a higher likelihood of trauma manifestations because they do not have the ability to self-soothe and regulate. Many cannot function in intimate placements such as with a family or relative, needing the more impersonal placement of a group home. The more severely traumatized may experience what is commonly referred to as reactive attachment disorder (RAD). According to the *DSM-5*, children with a diagnosis of RAD, which is now in a group of trauma- and stressor-related disorders, just like PTSD, experience criteria including:

A. A consistent pattern of inhibited, emotionally withdrawn behavior toward adult caregivers, manifested *by both* of the following:

- The child rarely or minimally seeks comfort when distressed.
- The child rarely or minimally responds to comfort when distressed.

B. A persistent social or emotional disturbance characterized by *at least two* of the following:

- Minimal social and emotional responsiveness to others
- Limited positive affect
- Episodes of unexplained irritability, sadness, or fearfulness that are evident even during nonthreatening interactions with adult caregivers.

C. The child has experienced a pattern of extremes of insufficient care as evidenced by *at least one* of the following:

- Social neglect or deprivation in the form of persistent lack of having basic emotional needs for comfort, stimulation, and affection met by caring adults
- Repeated changes of primary caregivers that limit opportunities to form stable attachments (e.g., frequent changes in foster care)
- Rearing in unusual settings that severely limit opportunities to form selective attachments (e.g., institutions with high child-to-caregiver ratios)

In addition to these criteria, RAD can be diagnosed only after the child has a developmental age of at least 9 months, must be evident before age 5, and must be distinguished from autism spectrum disorder. This is a severe form of attachment trauma, and whereas some believe in medicating children with this disorder, we believe interventions for RAD should be specialized and trauma-based and include child-parent psychotherapy and other forms of trauma therapy.

There are many problems with a RAD diagnosis, but similarly to the PTSD diagnosis described in Chapter 4, the important issue for you is to recognize these symptoms are not reflective of an aggressive child; they are a symptom of neglect and trauma. At that young age, because trauma is in the nervous system, emotional neglect shows up as forms of trauma, and instead of treating the trauma, children often get a diagnosis of RAD. These children need intensive neurorelational therapy.

Less serious forms of attachment difficulties also require therapy that focuses on helping the neurorelational trauma and development. Therapists who are experienced in providing these children with a steady and consistent presence in their lives will work with the child and her caregivers to facilitate the development of a secure base for the child and her relationships.

Expect your child clients with problematic attachment issues to have no trust for you or other adults in their life, perhaps act aggressively or withdraw and avoid you, or alternate between various challenging behaviors. When you see such symptoms, know that your child client has been traumatized and ensure that she gets the necessary services to learn to trust and feel safe with strangers and adults in caregiving roles. It can take time for you to build a relationship with these children if they are older. If they are young and nonverbal, you can look to their behaviors to see how they respond to you and others in their lives to help you understand how the neglect has affected them. Ask how they are eating and sleeping, whether they tantrum "normally" or have long or dangerous tantrums, whether they jump or startle at loud noises, or whether they cry when they have needs.

One of the more common forms of neglect we see in dependency is a dirty or filthy home. These are not cases where there are clothes piled on the floor because everyone is too tired to clean. These are cases where there are animal (and sometimes human) feces on the floors and walls, dishes piled in the sink for weeks, rotten baby bottles, a fridge with rotting food, mold in the home, or roaches everywhere. Often we hear lawyers and courts say that when the home is cleaned up, it is safe for the child to go home. Many people believe these are the easiest cases to handle. In reality, because of the underlying neglect issues, these can be some of the most difficult cases because (1) you have to determine the reason for the filthy home, (2) you have to solve that underlying issue, and (3) you have to deal with the symptoms of the neglect while your client was in the home and ensure that the parents can parent effectively, both physically and emotionally.

Neglect is often the most misunderstood issue a lawyer encounters because it is a lack of action, rather than an action, that causes the harm. When an action causes the harm, we can see the problem, implement services, and determine when the problem has been resolved, at least ostensibly. But with neglect, the issues are far deeper, and the symptoms can take time to appear; the ramifications, however, are some of the most extreme we experience and include brain and emotional development. Thus, it is imperative to think about how your client is being neglected, both physically and emotionally, in every type of case you see. It is also important to reflect back on the trauma manifestations from Chapter 4 and the development issues from Chapter 5 and ask whether your client exhibits any of the problems mentioned. If so, getting to the root of the neglect is imperative for helping your client.

Coming to Court

As noted throughout this book, representing children is different. Whereas parents are usually required to come to court, professionals still argue whether children should come to court. In many jurisdictions, children are not parties to a private family law matter; in dependency, they are parties, but many people still believe it is inappropriate for children to be in the courtroom when painful issues are discussed.

Even before the passage of the United Nations Convention on the Rights of the Child, academics have questioned the wisdom of children coming to court to address their voice, especially in dependency and family court. Although the United States is now[235] the only country in the world with an established

---

235. At the time of this writing.

government capable of ratifying the Convention that has not ratified it,[236] the rest of the world has come to terms that, per Article 12, children's voices must be heard when their issues come before courts. Even in the United States, however, it is common for children to be in dependency court, although few children under the age of 14 are heard in family court settings, except for a few jurisdictions. Although the academic arguments about this issue are beyond the scope of this book and chapter,[237] suffice to say that your client's voice is important to the court when reaching decisions about your client's best interests, regardless of the court.

For purposes of this chapter, we think four issues are important. First, we think a significant part of your job is understanding and helping your child client express her wishes and perspective, independent of whether you are a client-directed advocate or a best interests attorney. Of course, this goes beyond the superficial of what your child client wants to the more nuanced why your client feels as she does.[238] In family court, an alienated child might express a desire for no contact with one parent even though it is not in her best interests. In dependency court, your client might want to return to her biological family even though it is not in her best interests. Your client needs to have a voice, you need to understand that voice in depth, and yet the court makes the choice.

Second, we believe when your client expresses her voice, she can validate her feelings and understand them. Part of becoming an independent and functioning adult is learning to explore, understand, and express important values and feelings. By giving your child client the opportunity to express herself and explore the depth of her feelings, she is becoming better prepared to make adult choices. Although you are not a caregiver to the child, as an adult in the child's world, you play a role in her scaffolding to become an adult. Working through these

---

236. *Convention on the Rights of the Child*, UNICEF for every child, https://www.unicef.org/crc/index_30229.html (last visited Nov. 5, 2017).

237. *See, e.g.*, Rebecca M. Stahl, *Don't Forget about Me: Implementing Article 12 of the United Nations Convention on the Rights of the Child*, 24 Ariz. J. Int'l & Comp. L. 803 (2008); Patrick Parkinson & Judy Cashmore, The Voice of a Child in Family Law Disputes (Oxford University Press 2008); Nicola Taylor, *What Do We Know about Involving Children and Young People in Family Law Decision Making? A Research Update*, 20 Aust. J. Fam. L. 5 (2006).

238. Additional issues of best interest vs. client-directed representation will be discussed in the next chapter. Here we are using it only as a focus on children's voices in the courtroom.

issues helps a child grow and learn, and as the child is already in an adult world, you can help facilitate that process by understanding her views.

Third, coming to court introduces your client to the judge. Whereas this is common practice in some other countries, meeting the judge is far from the norm in the United States. In New Zealand, judges often meet with children; in Ohio, if any party requests it, the judge must meet with the child in a family law case. Simply meeting the judge and knowing who will be making the decision can ease your client's anxiety and give her a greater sense of comfort. We believe it is important for judges to see the children about whom they are making decisions. Even if the judge never speaks to the child about the allegations of the case, it is important the judge knows what the child looks like and that the child is a real person. Rebecca has a case, perhaps one of the most difficult factual cases she has ever had, where there are allegations of sexual abuse against the father by the child. There are many reasons to believe the allegations are not true,[239] and when a new judge came onto the case, his first statement was, "Am I releasing the child to the father today?" It was not until he saw the child walk into the courtroom, start shaking, and break into tears at the sight of her father that the judge took a step back and realized that regardless of whether he believed the allegations, the child had a genuine fear of her father. Thus, having your clients come to court and allowing the judge to see the impact his decisions have on the child can be very beneficial.

Fourth, coming to court may help your client understand the system and, more importantly, understand how the judge will be making the decision regarding her life. Many children only know about court from shows like *Law and Order* or, even worse, *Judge Judy*. Children can be very fearful of court, and once they understand what really happens, it can feel less intimidating. If allowed, your client can hear the reasons for the decision from the impartial person who is making the decision. It is usually better for children to hear the decision and the reasons for that decision from neutral professionals, and if the judge provides that information, your client is more likely to accept it even if it goes against her wishes.

There are, of course, many people who believe it is harmful for children to come to court. While at times being in court can be damaging to a child, not being there and making up stories in her head about what is happening is likely far worse than what is really happening and can be much more damaging to a child. Rebecca always gives children the option of whether they want to be

---

239. Whether they are true or not is not important to this discussion, and we would never advocate disbelieving your client.

in court. More importantly, the first decision does not have to be the final one. Frequently Rebecca's clients come into the courtroom, and if it gets to be overwhelming, they simply walk out. No judge has ever had a problem with a child walking out of court when it became too much for the child to handle. And just because a child is crying or showing emotion does not mean the experience is overwhelming. Sometimes it is simply sad, and they are expressing that sadness. Court cases are difficult, and hiding that difficulty outside the courtroom can be more damaging for the child and allow professionals to forget the impact of their decisions on the children they serve.

Finally, there is always the issue of whether children should testify in court. There is almost no research on the effects of children's testimony in family and dependency court. Each jurisdiction has its own rules about whether children should testify, but generally we believe it can be harmful to a child unless the child wants to do it. Rebecca once had two children testify because they desperately wanted to tell the court why they wanted to go home. Another wanted to testify to help protect her siblings. These situations are different from family court, where a child may be asked to choose between his parents. In many family court jurisdictions, children can meet the judge in chambers. While there are due process issues with this, sometimes it can be beneficial as a meet-and-greet for the reasons stated above—the child gets to know who the judge is, and the judge gets a feel for who the child is as a person. That way, the judge is not making a decision about someone she knows only from paper.

Ultimately, whether your client comes to court to testify or you advocate for her voice or a psychologist evaluator understands her feelings and the basis for them, know that it is valuable for her to have been heard. However, even if she does not testify or speak to the judge, there may be other benefits to your client in understanding who is making the decision affecting her life and why.

Internal Issues

This section focuses on the child's internal medical, psychological, and developmental issues and how those issues might be affecting your client and your representation. Understanding these issues is critical for your effective advocacy. Many of these internal issues can be misdiagnosed as ADHD, oppositional defiant disorder, or severe mental health issues when children are experiencing trauma symptoms. We will address this in each section below, but it is important to remember that the trauma symptoms are similar to many of the diagnoses we address here. Traditional verbal therapies often do not address the underlying issues; they only inhibit the automatic responses.

In other words, verbal therapies can help block the impulse to act from becoming an action, but they cannot resolve the underlying impulse to act from the nervous system trauma. Therefore, with all the issues below, it is important to solve the actions, but even more important to solve the nervous system trauma. Some verbal therapies have begun to incorporate more tools that work with the nervous system, including mindfulness and breathing techniques, but even those generally fail to get to the root of the nervous system trauma in a systematic way.

Attention-Deficit Hyperactivity Disorder (ADHD)

Attention-deficit hyperactivity disorder (ADHD) has been diagnosed in some form or another in children for nearly 250 years. In its earliest days, symptoms of superficial attention, impulsive judgments, and lack of patience were seen as problematic. By the early 2000s, there was a sense that small numbers of children experienced problems with sustained attention and self-regulation, sometimes being aggressive and defiant, and had difficulties learning from the consequences of their actions. In those early years, these problems were seen as some type of unknown brain disorder. When Phil began practicing in the early 1970s, children were diagnosed with "hyperkinesis," "minimal brain damage," "learning disabilities," or "hyperactivity."

The primary treatment for ADHD is stimulant medication, which started with Ritalin in the 1970s. However, medication for ADHD symptoms skyrocketed in the 1990s with a variety of medications introduced to replace or provide alternatives to Ritalin. At the time this book was written, controversy continued about not only the diagnosis but also possible interventions that might be more appropriate for many of these children.

Both of us believe children are often misdiagnosed with ADHD, having experienced poverty, neglect, significant attachment problems, overly permissive parenting, trauma, family violence, problematic diet, emotional dysregulation, and other experiences that lead to symptoms that might be consistent with ADHD. Although a small subset of children do benefit from ADHD medications, the majority of children in the court system are more likely to benefit from a variety of other interventions that can help calm the inner child.

Trauma symptoms that manifest as ADHD are mostly hypervigilance. If a child's nervous system is so hypervigilant he never feels safe, of course he will not be able to sit still. While some children have a brain chemical imbalance that causes ADHD, as the child's lawyer, you should understand that trauma therapy may be a more effective intervention before a diagnosis and medication are begun. Many people involved in the court system would rather diagnose and medicate than find the appropriate help, especially because many of the treatments that work best for ADHD-like symptoms but are not ADHD are not treatable with conventional therapies. There are, of course, other interventions for ADHD than medication, but this is not a book about ADHD interventions. Instead, it is important to ensure your client is also getting treatment for the trauma he experienced, remembering that many Medicaid-based therapy programs are behavioral health systems but not mental health systems.

Oppositional Defiant Disorder (ODD)

Oppositional defiant disorder (ODD), grouped in the category of "Disruptive, Impulse-Control, and Conduct Disorders," is defined by the *DSM-5* as "a pattern of angry/irritable mood, argumentative/defiant behavior, or vindictiveness lasting at least six months." These children often outwardly blame others for their mistakes, may act vindictively and in ways to deliberately annoy others, frequently lose their temper, and may actively avoid following rules. These ODD symptoms affect relationships, especially relationships with parents, teachers, and peers, and may contribute to learning problems. Commonly, these children experience family dynamics that impact negatively on their functioning.

For the most part, interventions for ODD include various types of therapy, including cognitive behavioral therapy and social skills training. Often these children will be put into group therapy. Younger children always need parents participating in the interventions, and older children may also benefit from anger management. This diagnosis is less common in younger children, but if they receive it, a form of dyadic therapy is more beneficial. The particular interventions you will want for your child client depend on the etiology of the dynamic, including whether significant attachment problems are contributors. Note, however, that ODD is differentiated from RAD generally because of the age of the diagnosis. Both involve similar problems for children later in life because it may be more difficult to find adoptive homes for children diagnosed with either disorder, and these children live with the stigma of both diagnoses. But similarly to ADHD, these aggressive behaviors often are the result of severe trauma, and the diagnosis is based upon a list of symptoms rather than an underlying cause. With appropriate trauma-based therapeutic intervention, it is possible to help resolve these issues without the need for these diagnoses.

Severe Mental Health Issues

Some of your clients will have severe mental health issues, severe depression, bipolar disorder, delusions, and dissociative disorder. The symptoms of many of these severe mental health issues can feel overwhelming for a lawyer without training in mental health issues. Children exhibiting many of these extreme emotional problems can be emotionally draining and present challenges in addressing their emotional and behavioral difficulties. It is important to consult with a mental health specialist when looking for guidance in how to help these children, particularly one who knows what resources are available in your jurisdiction.

The most important aspect to remember is that while it is very important you know your client well and understand his mental health issues, you are not your client's therapist. This does not mean you cannot be therapeutic in your conversations and have a good relationship with your client, but it does mean you cannot be your client's only go-to about issues in his life that require therapeutic intervention. Unless you are well trained in therapeutic intervention, it cannot fall on you to try to talk a child out of suicidal behavior.

Severe depressive disorder and bipolar disorder can make conversations with clients very difficult. These clients often become suicidal or evince self-harm, often by cutting. This can lead to ongoing hospitalizations, which is likely to disrupt their placement, which then interrupts social connection, thus causing a downward spiral of further depression and disconnection. It can also be scary as a lawyer to have a child tell you he is suicidal.

Not included in the sections about attachment problems and oppositional or other emotional problems are those children who appear to have significant psychiatric problems such as childhood schizophrenia or dissociative disorders. The *DSM-5* identifies childhood schizophrenia as involving at least two symptoms, including delusions, hallucinations, disorganized speech, grossly disorganized or catatonic behavior, and negative symptoms. Childhood schizophrenia is considered a neuropsychological disorder. Dissociative disorder includes criteria in which two or more distinct identities or personality states are present, amnesia must occur, and the person must be distressed by the disorder. Dissociative disorder is considered a Trauma-Related Disorder. Both are rare, but when they occur, you must ensure your clients are properly diagnosed and help them receive the services they need. Both disorders must also rule out substance abuse or other medical conditions.

It is beyond the scope of this book to discuss more details about these severe mental disorders, but if you suspect that your child client is experiencing symptoms of either, a comprehensive evaluation by a trained child psychiatrist is indicated. Your interactions with your clients who have more severe mental health disorders can be challenging. These clients tend to require extensive time, and when they have more psychotic disorders, it can be more difficult to communicate with them. One day they are easily engaged and communicate well, and the next day you can barely get them to say their name. For someone without therapeutic training, it can be confusing and difficult to help these clients with their legal issues. As with all children, getting to know them and what matters to them is increasingly important, especially getting to know *who* matters to them. This can help ensure there is a strong family or friend unit to help support your client through these difficult times and on the more difficult days of communication, you have a place to go back and pull from knowledge about their entire life.

Autism Spectrum Disorder

Autism was first described in 1908 to identify a subset of children who were especially withdrawn or self-absorbed. In later years, it evolved to include Asperger' syndrome, which was considered a milder form of autism in boys with troublesome social interactions or obsessive behaviors. By the latest version of the *DSM-5*, all categories of autism were folded into the category of Autism Spectrum Disorder (ASM). According to the *DSM-5*, ASM is now in the category of "Neurodevelopmental Disorders," and it identifies two primary sets of symptoms: impaired social communication and/or interaction and/or restricted and/or repetitive behaviors.

More than likely if you have a child client who has ASM, you will learn about the multiple symptoms that client experiences. Typical symptoms include disconnection from others, active avoidance of eye contact, apparent lack of empathy and emotional disconnection, delayed language, repetitive behaviors, emotional dysregulation and outbursts, extreme sensitivity to external stimuli, and difficulty understanding figurative language.

You are likely to interface with the school system and other ancillary professionals (e.g., occupational therapists and speech therapists) to facilitate interventions for your client. If you are operating in dependency court, you are likely to take a very active role in ensuring sufficient services are provided. If you are operating in family court, you will likely facilitate parents in accessing those services and communicating with each other about them. In family court, you are also likely to be engaged with the parents and their conflicts over how to manage the ASM symptoms and interventions. In family court, it is common for parents to disagree about the diagnosis and management of your child client's ASM.

Many of these children are nonverbal or lack sufficient verbal skills to direct counsel properly. So, it is important to remember what you know about representing any nonverbal or less-verbal clients and notice how they interact with you, with caregivers, with other people, and certainly with their parents. These children often have difficulty with a change in routine, and by definition, the cases in which you are involved have been a huge change in routine. It is important to learn about your clients' needs for routine and try to get it reestablished as quickly as possible. These cases, therefore, take some time to understand how parents and other caregivers operate and may require thinking outside the box in terms of parenting time orders and in terms of transitions between homes, in both family and dependency courts.

Medical Conditions

Many medical conditions children have can interfere with your representation. First, many children can suffer serious medical conditions from abuse, e.g., abusive head trauma (formerly called "shaken baby syndrome"), that results in severe brain damage, or cases may come to you involving very serious physical injuries that require extensive medical knowledge to understand. Some children are born with medical conditions, including cerebral palsy and Down syndrome. This book is not designed as a medical textbook. While we believe it is very important to have at least a cursory understanding of these issues, and in the case of abuse cases, a more involved understanding of how injuries occur, this book is not the place to address that.

Instead, it is important to know you have access to a doctor or another medical professional who can help you analyze these cases. In terms of medical issues from birth, the most important thing is to ensure your clients' needs are being met. As discussed previously, states have agencies that work with developmentally delayed children and adults, and it is important to make sure your client is receiving those services and his caregivers are following through with the suggestions of those agencies.

In terms of physical abuse allegations, it is necessary to ask medical personnel why a particular injury may be non-accidental or why an injury may be more typical of accidental injury. Be curious, ask questions, and ask them often. It is not your job to determine the veracity of claims, but it is your job to know the correct questions to ask of medical personnel to have them help you with their expert opinions. Many jurisdictions have children's hospitals, and it is helpful to know the doctors there so when you have cases with severe medical issues, you have someone to whom you can turn with questions.

Sexual Abuse

Similarly to physical abuse allegations, it can be very difficult to know whether your client was sexually abused. Forensic evidence of sexual abuse is rare, and because it happens in secret, it can be difficult to prove. In both family and dependency cases, the accused parent often says the sexual abuse allegations are an attempt to have custody removed despite the falsity of the claims. Recently, the Arizona chapter of the AFCC created a document to help lawyers evaluate sexual abuse claims.[240] While it is somewhat Arizona-specific, it has useful information for sexual abuse claims overall.

As a child's representative, we believe there are a few issues you need to consider. First, you represent the child, and regardless of what is objectively true, your client has emotions that need to be addressed. This means it is rarely your job to decide what is true, only to understand what is true for your client. Second, although some jurisdictions have children's advocacy centers or other forensic interviewing protocols where children are interviewed only once, many jurisdictions still interview children multiple times about the same incident. As we discussed in Chapter 5, this can lead to problems in terms of the veracity of children's statements. As a children's representative, you can ask for a court order that children be interviewed only one time and by a trained forensic interviewer. This means it is not always appropriate for you to ask children about the incident. While you must do your job, you must also be cognizant of how continuing to ask children about the abuse can be both legally problematic and traumatic for the child.

Third, sexual abuse is the ultimate boundary violation. This means children will often put up walls and choose not to discuss the allegations for quite some time. While writing this book, the #metoo and Times Up movements both took off, and these global conversations can be quite beneficial to your representation and conversations with your clients. Because of these movements there is an entry point into helping children recognize they are not alone. But these global movements cannot fix the boundary crossing these children feel. You must, therefore, be extra careful to hold boundaries with these children and give them more choice in the conversation and in your representation as was discussed in Chapter 4. Most importantly, remind these children what confidentiality means—it means you as the lawyer cannot disclose what is discussed, but the child is free to tell anyone what you discuss. Remind your client that she has a voice in this process, and it is a voice that will be heard, but at her own pace.

Children who have experienced sexual abuse tend not to want to discuss it, and they often have freeze-state responses as we discussed in Chapter 4. One of the reasons children who have experienced sexual abuse tend to cut is because

---

240. *Child Sexual Abuse: Assessment for Early Intervention for Alleged Abusers, Protective Parents, and the Child Who Alleges Sexual Abuse*, AZAFCC (2017), *available at* azafcc.org/wp-content/uploads/2015/12/2017-AZAFCC-Summit-Project_FINAL.pdf (last visited Nov. 5, 2017).

they want to feel something because they have become so dissociated from the feeling in their bodies or because it releases the holding tension they have been feeling while attempting to hold themselves together. It is important to get a baseline about how these children communicate about nonsexual abuse issues before discussing the allegations.

Overall, clients who have experienced sexual abuse tend to begin as withdrawn and rarely want to speak about the abuse. Beneficial therapy can include group therapy so that the child knows she is not alone, as well as individual therapy to deal with the specific trauma. Most importantly, take your time speaking with these children. In sexual abuse cases, you are asking a child to discuss one of the most sensitive topics imaginable with you, a complete stranger. Getting therapy in place early can provide you with an additional professional external to the family with whom you can discuss the family dynamics and the ultimate issue of the sexual abuse. Further, these children often need extensive therapy to unwind the layers of trauma sexual abuse creates.

Reproductive Health, Sex, and Trafficking

If you represent teenagers, you will encounter teenagers having sex. There is nothing abnormal about this, and just as with all other aspects of their lives, it is important to hold a space of nonjudgment. Although this book is about representing children, sometimes your older clients will have children of their own. While you are not their parent or even the social worker, you may be the only adult that children trust, meaning you might be the one having the "how not to have children" conversation. Speaking to children honestly about reproductive health is important to your legal representation as well as to their growth. It can be helpful to speak to local doctors who are willing to meet with teenagers and answer their questions. While in many jurisdictions there are children's hospitals and doctors who specialize in reproductive health for teenagers, we understand there are also jurisdictions where this is less available. We hope that lawyers in those jurisdictions take the time to understand better the reproductive issues teenagers face and have these open conversations with them as well.

Youth in foster care are at a much greater risk of being trafficked. Entire books can be written on trafficked youth, so here we just want to raise your awareness enough to ask questions. We believe it is vital you learn about youth in sex trafficking, and we have put some resources online. The layers of trauma and secrecy and fear that envelops trafficked youth are far too great for an explanation here. But as always, the reminders from Chapter 4 about trauma— take the time to listen to your client without judgment and create as safe a place as you can for her to communicate with you. In addition, many jurisdictions have group homes and agencies designed specifically to work with youth who have been sexually exploited. It is important for you to ask questions to determine whether your client may have been sexually exploited but to do so in a trauma-informed way.

Finally, if your client does become pregnant, or impregnates someone else, there are legal issues you must begin working with during the pregnancy. You can ask that the child welfare agency help with parenting classes and prenatal appointments and transportation prior to the birth of the child to help reduce the risk of the child being removed upon its birth. Further, if you live in a jurisdiction where there are placements that will take children and their minor mothers, you can ask that your pregnant client be assessed for placement in one of these homes. You can also ask for court orders that the social worker look for placement with a foster home or relative willing to provide a home to both the minor parent and the baby. If these issues are dealt with prior to the baby's birth, it can reduce the likelihood the baby will be removed upon his birth.

For teenagers who have babies, there are family law issues that must be dealt with prior to the child's birth. It is important to ensure both parents have access to the child unless there is a reason one parent should not. Whether your client is the mother or the father of the child, you may need to direct your client to the family court to file the appropriate paternity paperwork.

Delinquency

Many of your clients will have ongoing delinquency cases as well. Obviously, it is important to remind clients with multiple ongoing cases that they have different requirements through probation than they do through child welfare. But it can also be helpful to work with your client's probation officer and defense attorney to determine what her requirements for probation are and whether the child welfare agency needs to be ordered to provide necessary services through the child welfare agency instead of probation. Depending on your jurisdiction, one agency may take a lead on cases, or the agencies sometimes work together. It is important to know how your jurisdiction operates.

One of the most common frustrations people have with youth in both the delinquency and dependency systems is placement. Probation and the child welfare agency will argue over who will pay for placement, and certain placements are sometimes available to only one agency and not the other. Other times the child welfare agency will attempt to place a delinquent youth in a probation placement because the youth tends to go AWOL or because the youth has behaviors the child welfare agency cannot control. Sometimes youth remain in juvenile halls because the child welfare agency does not pick them up. When these issues arise, it is imperative to get before a judge immediately to ensure a child does not remain in a more restrictive placement than is ordered simply because the child welfare agency has not followed through on finding placement. These children tend to be the most difficult to place, so child welfare agencies sometimes take longer to place these children. It becomes important for you, as their dependency lawyer, to get the issue before a judge for an emergency order regarding placement. Working together, these two separate courts can better serve crossover youth.

Involvement of Other Professionals

Recognizing the impact of these internal and external issues is critical for your court-related advocacy on behalf of your client. In addition to resources identified in the References section at the end of this book, you are likely to benefit from consulting with or gathering information from various professionals. This section will identify the common professionals with whom you are likely to interact and the information you will need to help your client. As a child's attorney, it can be very helpful to have a list of professionals across a variety of practices with whom you can consult on your cases, especially if they are not directly involved in that case.

Mental Health Providers

If you are representing a child in family court and your child client is in a high-conflict family, you are likely to be interacting with a psychologist or another mental health professional along the way. Typical roles for these mental health practitioners include but are not limited to family therapist, adult individual therapist, child individual therapist, family mediator, custody evaluator, and parenting coordinator.

Therapists provide counseling for family members, and depending who the client is, there may be issues of confidentiality with them.[241] For the most part, you would want access to the child's therapist, if there is one, but it may very

---

241. *See, e.g., AFCC Guidelines for Court-Involved Therapy*, Association of Family and Conciliation Courts (2010), *available at* https://www.afccnet.org/Portals/0/PublicDocuments/CEFCP/Guidelines%20for%20Court%20Involved%20Therapy%20AFCC.pdf (last visited Nov. 5, 2017).

well be that if the parents cannot agree, you will hold the therapeutic privilege on behalf of your child client. In some jurisdictions in dependency cases, you automatically hold the therapist-client privilege until a child is of a certain age. You likely will not have access to the parents' therapists unless the parent signs a release of information. It can be helpful for you to have that access, but unless you have a valid reason for it, it is unlikely a parent is going to agree. In dependency cases, parents often are required to sign releases for their therapists to speak to the social worker, so it is possible to gain information about parents' therapy using that route.

There are two main issues that arise with therapists involved in court cases. First, therapists are often asked to make recommendations to the court. When therapists are performing therapy, even if they are forensically trained, providing recommendations to the court puts the therapist in a dual role and is usually against their ethical duties. It is never appropriate for a therapist to make recommendations about the safety of a parent if the therapist is the child's individual therapist. Even the parent's therapist does not have all the information necessary to make such recommendations. The therapeutic relationship is one of support, encouragement, some education, and healing. It is not an evaluation of the person's ability to parent. Therefore, if you are in a jurisdiction where judges and other lawyers believe it is appropriate for therapists to make recommendations, sometimes it is an unfortunate requirement to have therapists come to court to testify about their ethical duties and explain why they are not the appropriate people to be making those recommendations in either dependency or family court.

Second, individual therapists are often asked to do conjoint or family therapy. While this is not inherently unethical, it is usually unfair to your client. Your client deserves to have an individual therapist, someone whose sole job is to support and help heal emotional trauma and other emotional issues. If that person also becomes the family therapist whose job is to help solve familial problems, your client loses a very important support in this process. In some cases, this is less damaging than in others, but we have found that the typical practice is to use the individual therapist as the conjoint therapist. We believe it should be the exception, and it often falls on you, the child's lawyer, to ask the court to order the individual therapist to be different from the conjoint therapist.

Finally, most therapists dislike testifying and being involved in the court process in any way. Despite the fact many of them know they are taking cases that are in litigation, they want little or nothing to do with the actual court proceedings. Rebecca has found that just stating her recognition of this to therapists has a profound impact on their willingness to work with her. Many of them are incredibly standoffish until she lets them know she understands why they are uncomfortable and does not want to interfere in the therapist-client relationship. Therapists, when your allies, can be incredible allies who provide insight into your client and the case situation like no one else can. Like you, they tend to have no agenda other than helping the child, and for that reason, they can be your best support in helping your client. Unfortunately, many of them are so scared of the adversarial nature of the court proceedings they do not want to be involved in any way until you reach out and affirm you are only there for their help and you respect them enough to ask for their help.

Mediators

A mediator may provide confidential assistance to parents regarding resolution of a parenting plan, and given that it is likely to be confidential, you probably will not communicate with the mediator.[242] Some jurisdictions allow children's lawyers to participate in confidential mediation. If you are working in dependency court in some jurisdictions, you might also be participating in child protection mediation with a variety of stakeholders in your child client's life.[243]

Mediation can be beneficial to you and your client. First, you have a better understanding of what the other parties want and who they are. Mediation is a time for everyone to sit at the table. It is an opportunity to bring your client's concerns to the table without an adversarial context. In dependency cases, it can help you identify the issues the case needs for a better resolution and can help you articulate a more specific case plan for parents than a form approach common to cases that do not participate in mediation. We believe if you are in a jurisdiction where mediation exists in either family or dependency court and you can attend, it might be one of the most important meetings for you to attend in the entire case.

In dependency, mediation can also provide an opportunity for everyone to sit together and devise the best plan for moving forward. In a system where families so often feel they have no voice, mediation provides them the opportunity to be heard. At the beginning of a case, it can help everyone create a more meaningful

---

242. *See, e.g., Model Standards of Practice for Family and Divorce Mediation*, Association of Family and Conciliation Courts (2000), *available at* www.afccnet.org/Portals/0/PublicDocuments/CEFCP/ModelStandardsOfPracticeForFamilyAndDivorceMediation.pdf (last visited Nov. 5, 2017).

243. *See, e.g., AFCC Guidelines for Child Protection Mediation*, Association of Family and Conciliation Courts (2012), www.afccnet.org/Portals/0/Guidelines%20for%20Child%20Protection%20Mediation.pdf (last visited Nov. 5, 2017).

and specific case plan, and in the middle of the case, it can help with transition plans or getting parents back on track in their services if they have fallen off track. At the end of the case, mediation can help with creating a parenting plan in line with all the issues in the case.

Most importantly, regardless of the type of court system, mediation creates a safe place for everyone to be heard. You, as the child's attorney, can provide invaluable information to everyone about the needs of the child whether it be his wishes about reunification or the fact he cannot sleep at Father's house on Thursday night because he cannot take the child to basketball practice. Sometimes, the most practical issues get overlooked, and mediation is an opportunity to slow down enough in the process to ensure the practical questions can be answered as well as the deepest questions of whether it is safe to reunify a family. We believe the participation of children's attorneys in mediation, regardless of the court, is vital and should always be encouraged.

Custody Evaluators

A custody evaluator, if appointed by the court, will be evaluating all family members and gathering sufficient information to make a recommendation to the court about the parenting plan. Phil has been doing child custody evaluations for nearly thirty-five years and has written several books about the process of conducting custody evaluations.[244] In different jurisdictions, you may see someone appointed to do a brief focused assessment, which is a more limited scope process, generally focused on gathering more limited information and providing limited recommendations to the court.[245] A more comprehensive evaluation will likely be used in more complex family dynamics and when more data are needed before making recommendations to the court.[246] More comprehensive evaluations would likely be needed in complex matters such as exist with very high-conflict families, when children are resisting contact with one parent, or in cases involving domestic violence, substance use/abuse, relocation, or a combination

---

244. *See, e.g.,* Philip M. Stahl, Conducting Child Custody Evaluations: From Basic to Complex Issues (Sage 2010).

245. *See, e.g., AFCC Guidelines for Brief Focused Assessments*, Association of Family and Conciliation Courts (2009), *available at* www.afccnet.org/Portals/0/PublicDocuments/Guidelines/BFATF2009final.pdf (last visited Nov. 5, 2017).

246. *See, e.g., AFCC Model Standards of Practice for Child Custody Evaluation*, Association of Family and Conciliation Courts (2006), *available at* www.afccnet.org/Portals/0/ModelStdsChildCustodyEvalSept2006.pdf (last visited Nov. 5, 2017).

of more than one of these complex issues. Note there are special expectations for child custody evaluators conducting comprehensive evaluations in domestic violence cases.[247] You may be talking with the custody evaluator as a collateral witness depending on the laws in your jurisdiction and depending on issues of privilege.

Parenting Coordinators

A parenting coordinator is usually appointed by stipulation of the parties to assist parents in resolving day-to-day areas of conflict.[248] Parenting coordinators help the parents improve communication, provide education about the impact of conflict on children, may serve to coordinate with other professionals in the case, and help the parents work out disagreements and resolve conflicts. When parents cannot agree on critical differences, even with parent coordinator efforts, the parenting coordinator is typically empowered to make decisions or at least make recommendations to the court.

Recognizing that each of these professional roles is unique, it is important for the same mental health professional to avoid engaging in multiple roles.

Child Protection Social Workers

In dependency court, you are likely to be interfacing with the child protection social worker. Sometimes you will deal with them in family court when there have been calls to the hotline but the child welfare agency has not filed a dependency petition in court. In some jurisdictions, because you are a lawyer and the social workers are represented parties, you are unable to speak to the social worker without his lawyer being present. In other jurisdictions, that privilege has been waived. If you can communicate with the social worker, it is important to remember that he is another party in the case and, if you have a concern about the case, reaching out to the social worker's lawyer is usually the way to handle any conflict.

---

247. *See, e.g., AFCC Guidelines for Examining Intimate Partner Violence: A Supplement to the AFCC Model Standards of Practice for Child Custody Evaluation*, Association of Family and Conciliation Courts (2016), *available at* http://www.afccnet. org/Portals/0/Center%20for%20Excellance/Guidelines%20for%20Examining% 20Intimate%20Partner%20Violence.pdf (last visited Nov. 5, 2017).

248. *See, e.g., AFCC Guidelines for Parenting Coordination*, Association of Family and Conciliation Courts (2005), *available at* http://www.afccnet.org/Portals/0/ AFCCGuidelinesforParentingcoordinationnew.pdf (last visited Nov. 5, 2017).

In family court, you usually may speak to the child protection social workers because they are not parties to your case. It can be helpful to speak to them about what has transpired in the family during the course of the investigation, but remember that in most jurisdictions it is illegal for the social worker to disclose who made a report about a family. Sometimes, after your work on a family law case, a social worker may contact you regarding your representation if the report has been made after you completed your work.

Medical Professionals

To the extent your child client has significant medical issues, it is likely you will be interacting with the pediatrician in the case. Significant medical issues can include but not be limited to Down syndrome, cystic fibrosis, and cerebral palsy. If nothing else, you are likely to facilitate any necessary medical appointments for your child client's benefit. Asthma, failure to thrive, and obesity are also issues affecting children involved in the court system. Dr. Nadine Burke-Harris's research on adverse childhood experiences and medical issues suggests that these, and many other, medical conditions are a result of trauma. Her book, *The Deepest Well: Healing the Long-Term Effects of Childhood Adversity*, was published during the writing of this book and provides a wonderful overview of how childhood trauma affects medical conditions and behavioral issues. While the research on these issues is new, the medical community is beginning to recognize the crossover between trauma and medical issues. As both the medical and legal communities begin to focus on that link, your relationship with the child's pediatrician becomes even more important.

Child Psychiatrists

As noted elsewhere in this chapter, if your child client experiences various types of significant mental health disorders, you will likely need a psychiatric evaluation to understand more fully the etiology and nature of the symptoms. This will be especially true if you are concerned about your child exhibiting symptoms of childhood schizophrenia such as psychotic or delusional thinking. You might also benefit from knowing a child psychiatrist who can provide general information and consultation if you need it for some of your clients.

School Personnel

Finally, it is likely that you will want to be engaged with your child client's various school personnel, advocating for her educational needs. This might include your client's teacher(s), aide(s), speech therapist, and occupational therapist. You might need to attend Individualized Education Plan (IEP) meetings if your client is receiving special education services, and you might need to advocate for services that you believe your child client needs. The IEP is required by law for students receiving special education services and outlines the steps the school will take to help the child with her learning problems. Knowing a good education attorney is beneficial as well because sometimes school districts need a little push to implement the IEP process properly and within the confines of the law.

School personnel can also be a source of support for you in cases where you worry about a child's safety at home. You can call the school and provide the teacher or administration with your contact information if anyone at the school has any concerns. Similarly, you can ask that person to allow the child to call you anytime she wants to speak to you away from her parents. Sometimes children do not want to talk to you with their parents present but may want to reach out, so having a relationship with someone at your client's school is an effective way to ensure your client can reach you to talk without her parents overhearing.

Conclusions

This chapter has focused on potential external and internal issues that are likely impacting your child client's functioning and needs. As we described at the beginning of the chapter, regardless of what your child is experiencing, you need to approach your work the same. Skills such as listening, understanding, relating with your client, and advocating for her needs are your major tasks in your role.

As you can see from all the issues described in this chapter, there is a strong likelihood that you will be confronted with several "non-legal" issues and some extraneous but important legal ones, such as immigration and your client's education. Each family and each child is unique, and those unique characteristics will determine what issues you will confront in any given case. Multiple resources exist to help you and your child clients get the necessary help you and they may need to address your client's best interests.

Although we know that it is not your job to get the services your client needs, we believe it is part of your job to be sensitive to those needs and advocate for them within the context of your role.

Finally, we are certain that you will be exposed to issues that have not been identified in this chapter. Using the guidelines we have described in other examples, we urge you to learn as much as you can about the particular issues in that case and use that information to better advocate for your client's needs.

Professional Issues |||

This final section addresses issues specific to being a children's representative—but those that affect you as a professional more than those that affect your child clients specifically, including ethical issues you will face in your work, your own biases, and the effect this work has on you personally.

We will look first at the ethical issues you face as a lawyer for children. These are the ethical issues unique to this work, not an overview of ethical issues all lawyers face, in terms of interacting with your child clients, other professionals, and issues involving siblings. These ethical issues are not solely about ethics, but fall under the general idea of professional responsibility as it pertains to representing children of all ages.

We then turn to your own personal and cognitive biases. All people have personal and cognitive biases, and this chapter will focus on how these affect you in your representation and how to work with them. We also discuss how to recognize whether other professionals involved in the case are influenced by or are correcting for their own bias(es) and whether you, as a lawyer, need to ask different questions to ensure your clients receive appropriate services.

Finally, we will look at how this work affects you. Representing children is some of the most rewarding and wonderful work we can imagine. And it is a great honor. It is also trying and difficult and, at times, overwhelming. In the final chapter, we examine how this professional toll affects you specifically as a children's attorney and provide some ideas for mitigating the more damaging effects.

The final section, therefore, will be a chance to step outside of the effects this work has on your clients and take a broader look at how you fit into the process and how this work affects you. Much of this book has had you as the observer, but in this section, we will ask you to become the active participant in your work with children.

Ethical Issues in Representing Children

10

This chapter focuses on the specific ethical issues that are part of representing children and how the specific psychological issues children face may affect these ethical issues. This chapter is not a full overview of ethical issues, only those most affected by family and dependency law and what we have covered in this book.

The ethical issues you face as children's representatives often have no simple answer. The direct duty to the client is usually different from that with adult clients; the issues in family and dependency law are different from those in a business setting; and as representatives for children, you often have multiple clients per case. In addition, in family law cases, it is not uncommon for the children's representative to be the only legally trained person on the case, except the judge, because parties are so often self-represented. Thus, there are many ethical issues unique to representing children.

Meeting the Child Client

The first ethical issue arises in meeting with the child. Because children's representatives often, although not always, have a duty of confidentiality, you may often speak to children alone. Therefore, the first interaction with children is one society says should never happen. As a society, we teach children not to speak to strangers and certainly never to speak to them alone. You, however, as their representative, are a stranger who speaks to children alone all the time.

In dependency cases, you are often the last in a long line of people meeting these children. The first people they have met are usually the police or social workers who took them from their families. Thus, they are often not excited to meet you. In all types of representation, adults often speak to your clients before you meet them the first time, often telling them what to say to you. You are in a likely uncomfortable situation with a child who has no reason to trust a stranger and who may have been instructed to tell you something other than how he genuinely feels about the given situation.

This is not news to anyone who has represented children, but there are ways of handling the situation better to help children feel more comfortable, and in turn, that can help you do your job. First, introduce yourself and your role in front of people with whom the child feels comfortable. In her first few months practicing, Rebecca went to visit a 5-year-old who was living with his father at his uncle's house. She walked in and asked to speak to the child alone. When the conversation ended, the uncle gave her a piece of his mind. And he had every right to do so. She had barely said hello to the uncle or the father, and she certainly had not asked to speak to the child. She had just assumed that as his lawyer, that was her right, and his, so she acted upon it. When representing adults, and sometimes even older children, it is not uncommon to introduce yourself as a lawyer and have people want to speak to you and other family members. But with children, and particularly young children, the extra step can be necessary for both their comfort and that of their families.

Ever since that encounter, Rebecca altered her approach a great deal. No matter where she meets children, if they are with adult caregivers, she introduces herself to everyone there, explains her role, and finally explains the duty of confidentiality, in age-appropriate language, of course. Upon completion of the explanation of confidentiality, she asks the child if it is okay if they speak together alone. Only if the child says yes does that first conversation take place. The child gets to decide, always. Later in the chapter we will discuss what happens when a child refuses to speak with you.

Now that you have introduced yourself and walked away from the child's caregivers (if the child feels comfortable with that), how do you begin the conversation? Remember, these children have experienced a great deal of trauma, so the goal is to create a safe space for them. Perhaps the most important aspect is to give the child some semblance of control over the situation. Allow children to sit wherever they feel comfortable if the room is set up in such a way they can sit in multiple places. Some children even choose not to sit. As a lawyer for children, you likely interview children in their homes, in their foster homes, at court, at school, in offices, and probably other places as well. This nomadic legal lifestyle has its advantages. You likely are not stuck in a rut about where you sit and where children sit when you speak to them.

If you are involved in a child's life, that child will likely feel out of control. Children tend to have less control over their lives than do adults, but in situations where they are involved in the court system, they often feel as though they have no control. Something as simple as allowing them to choose where to sit begins to shift their thinking that you are not like other adults and that you are going to have a different relationship with them. Adults often ask children to sit still and look at them when they are talking to children, but that is not usually how children operate. Sometimes the best conversations with children involve drawing or spinning or playing on the floor. You can give them more control by asking them where they would like you to sit or whether it is okay to sit in the chair you would like to use.

These questions serve two purposes. First, they respect the child's autonomy and give her the smallest amount of control in an otherwise uncontrollable situation. Second, and perhaps more importantly for your clients, allowing a child to choose where to sit lets the child set boundaries. Remember that trauma is often the result of a boundary violation, giving child clients the ability to begin to set boundaries helps reduce the re-traumatization your appearance in their life may cause. Many of your cases begin in both family and juvenile court because of a lack of boundaries or when children's boundaries have been violated by the family or the system itself. Safe boundaries are essential for everyone, and you are going to be able to communicate with your client only if she feels safe in your presence. Children are not used to being in a position with adults to say when they feel uncomfortable. While it is important to consider these issues when representing adults as well as children, the fact that children have fewer cognitive faculties means these issues are even more important when dealing with children and deeply affect your professional relationship with them. And all of this happens before you get to the initial conversation with your clients.

Communicating with Your Child Clients

As we discussed in Chapter 5, children's development and language are crucial to understanding the conversation you are having with them. Children's developmental issues, and their competency, go hand in hand. Many people are afraid of children and have difficulty interacting with them; this is the most common argument against judges interviewing children. In many jurisdictions, lawyers representing children do not do so full-time, particularly in family law. Thus, one of the most fundamental issues children's representatives must face is learning how to interact with children and ensuring they have the proper training to do so.

Of course, with nonverbal children, this becomes even more important. Many people argue that it is impossible to represent a nonverbal child's wishes. And to some extent, that is correct, but in many ways, it can be easier to know what nonverbal children want than verbal children whose words may be influenced by others. The nervous system does not lie, so by watching how children respond to a variety of circumstances, you can learn much more than by just listening to the words they say. As we discussed in Chapters 4 and 5, these children's actions, development, regression, etc., have a profound impact on what they are saying to you when you take the time to listen and to know what you are watching for. Most likely, you are not being unethical by not noticing and considering it, but you may not be fulfilling your job of presenting the entire child to the court if you are not noticing his behaviors and emotions. It should underlie everything you do in your practice.

Rebecca was once asked by a new lawyer how she interacts with children. Without thinking, she responded, "I know I have gotten through to a child when I can make her laugh." That had never been a conscious decision, but it makes perfect sense. Laughter can only happen when someone feels comfortable and safe, and you can only interact with your client once she feels comfortable and safe. Laughter is a form of letting down a guard and connecting on another level. It indicates both people understand each other and agree that something is funny. It does not even matter what makes someone laugh, as the act of laughing is an act of connection. And as we discussed in Chapter 4, a lack of connection is one contribution to trauma, so using ways to connect with your clients can help pull them out of their trauma responses, at least momentarily making it easier to communicate with them. We must mention, of course, that some laughter is nervous laughter, but this comment about laughter as connection is when the laughter is about connection and not when it is nervous laughter.

What do you do if a child refuses to speak to you alone? It does happen, and it creates problems for you as the child's representative. Can you trust what he says to you if you never have that confidential communication? What if a child will speak to you only with siblings present? With a caregiver present? Young children and older children alike sometimes choose not to speak with you, albeit usually for different reasons.

While it is more difficult to represent children who will not speak to you, or at least will not speak to you alone, the very fact they will not do that is informative. And you can work with that. The first issue is to recognize what your job actually is. You are not a forensic interviewer attempting to get at "the truth." Phil is a forensic interviewer in his custody evaluation role, and he recognizes that some children do not want to speak with him about the family's issues. Not being a forensic interviewer, your job is to present the child you represent to the court process in all her elements. That does not mean just her words. If that were your job, then anyone could walk in, ask the child some questions, walk out, and provide that information to the judge. The real question for you as her representative is how to present critical information about the complete child to the court.

Therefore, knowing what words a child is going to tell you in private is sometimes less important than watching the child in all contexts. Learning to notice the subtleties of what children tell you without words is as important as having the confidential conversations with them. While all people communicate nonverbally as well as verbally, children do so even more. We have had children turn their backs to us when talking about difficult topics, get up and hide behind a couch, and walk in and put their heads down so as not to talk at all. Phil recalls a teenager who refused to say anything about her views of her family in the context of a custody evaluation, although when the topic of her younger autistic brother came up, she had plenty to say. Those moments stay with us far longer than the words children say. Those are moments of feeling, and nothing an external source tells a child can affect how a child acts in the moment.

The child who put his head down on the table is one of the best examples of talking without words. That was one of Rebecca's clients, and she had an established relationship with him. She knew his mannerisms, had worked with him about a year, and generally knew his position on the case and about certain other aspects of his life. Usually, this child was exuberant, silly, and chatty (arguably as part of his trauma response, but that was his general way of being with Rebecca). Although he and his older brother thought they would be going home that day, for legal reasons, it was impossible. Rebecca had informed his brother of that fact, and in the thirty seconds between the time she said goodbye to the older brother and the younger brother walked in, the older brother told the younger one they were not going home that day. The younger one, despite his personality, walked in and put his head on the table and would not speak. Weeks later when there was a question of whether he should go home, and even a question of whether he really wanted to go home (he was not at court and was unreachable the day the decision was made), Rebecca thought of that moment. That was a moment he could not fake. Children can *tell you* anything. Actions, however, can only express truth, and that moment was a powerful one for knowing just how much the child wanted to return to his parents.

An important issue is how to explain your job to your child clients. As noted above, this should probably happen in front of anyone who is with the child when you meet him. That serves two purposes. First, it allows the family an opportunity to feel comfortable with you and know you need to speak confidentially with your client. Second, this gives family members information about what your role is and what it is not. You are the *child's* lawyer, not the family's. Many caregivers and relatives try to get you to represent them instead of the child, but if you clarify your job in front of them from the beginning, you can help reduce that problem, although you will rarely get rid of it entirely.

There is no set standard for how to explain your job to children. We believe there are four key aspects about your job you must explain to your clients and a fifth in best interests jurisdictions. First, your job is to get to know your client. As mentioned previously, you get information about your clients from a variety of people, and your clients need to know you want to get information directly from them, as long as they want to share such information. Letting children know you want to get to know them is, we believe, important to creating a solid and trusting relationship. This is also how you help children understand that you want to listen to them tell their story, which helps create a level of trust.

Second, your job is to answer their questions. You can help them understand how different people are going to try to tell them what is happening, but your job is to give them an honest answer. Within that context, it is important to let your clients know you will not lie to them. Third, your job is to tell the judge what your clients want. In jurisdictions where statutes require it, you must also tell your clients your job includes telling the judge what you think will keep them safe or what you think is best for them.[249] Your other job is confidentiality if your jurisdiction requires it and an explanation of the limits of confidentiality in all jurisdictions. Confidentiality will be discussed more fully later in this chapter.

Many books and trainings specifically address how to speak with children. The most important issue to remember, however, is that representing children is not the same as playing with your own children or other children who are in your

---

249. We will address the difference between these roles later in the chapter.

life. There is still a legal process with legal goals. There are still requirements of obtaining information and providing children with age-appropriate information. Also, as we discussed in Chapter 4, and will discuss again in Chapter 12, your own self-regulation is important for having a safe and open conversation with your clients. If your own nervous system is not regulated, then your client will not be able to feel safe. Remembering to take a moment to check yourself prior to entering a conversation with a child will help you and your child client communicate better. We will discuss how to self-regulate in Chapter 12.

As noted above, one of your jobs is to answer the child's questions and provide the child with information about the case. But what if you know something sensitive you do not know whether the child knows? For example, what if a father is not the biological father or a parent is incarcerated? Sometimes children already know the information, so your job becomes easier. Sometimes they do not know the information, and you must determine whether it is appropriate to share it with them. Unlike other situations in which society may try to protect children from the truth, as their lawyer, you have an obligation to provide information to children, but you also have a moral obligation to do so in an appropriate manner. When the child must have information but you do not believe you should be the one to provide it, you may need to tell the parents that they provide the information by a specific date or you will do it for them.

The information to provide your child clients becomes a bigger issue in families where children are a variety of ages. For example, in a case that involves teenagers and children under age 10, the information provided to the teenager is different from the information provided to the younger children. And sometimes it is necessary to have that conversation with the older child. Some children ask whether their younger siblings will hear everything. Others are grateful when you tell them you will not be providing all the information to the younger children. While you cannot tell siblings what each of them has said, you can tell older children what information you will be providing to younger children or even ask the older children if their younger siblings know certain information.

Just because you do not provide all information to children does not mean you lie to children. We have both been involved in cases where people lie to children about what is happening in their families or what is happening in the court process. For example, children have been told parents who are incarcerated are simply out of state working and Phil has evaluated families where the children do not know parents are divorcing or that one of the parents is planning to move to a different state. Rebecca once had a forensic interviewer tell two children on a case the cameras in the interview room were to keep children safe. We believe none of that is acceptable and there is never a reason to lie to children.

There are ways of omitting difficult information without lying. You can tell children the court does not believe they are safe, or you can tell them that because parents cannot always decide what to do, judges must get involved. If the children are young and do not already know this information, you do not have to tell them their parents are drug addicts or that their parents have been involved in years of custody litigation. Other times it is important to tell children the specific issues that brought the case before the court. Some children need to hear a specific reason. Doing so in a way that is both compassionate and age appropriate is key. Chances are the children already have some inkling of the truth anyway. Know that children can usually handle more information than you may have thought and that they always handle the truth better than deceptions or no information. When children are not told anything about what is going on, they begin to think the worst, and their thoughts are often much worse than the truth. Children need to know the truth about their family situations, albeit in an age-appropriate and sensitive way.

When speaking with your clients about the case, even though it is not a legal issue, it can help to ask a child, "What do you do for fun?" It is easy to forget that the first goal of family and juvenile law is to make a child's life as normal as possible despite being involved in the legal system. The best way to do that is to allow them to be the children they want and need to be by having fun. Sometimes this also provides you with the best information about the child's legal issues, but usually it is a way to connect and help children have as normal a life as possible. That should be your ultimate legal goal for each child. This question can also help bring children out of a specific trauma response if their emotional state or agitation feels to you like it is becoming too much and they are shutting down.

The question of fun serves an additional aspect as well in that it allows you to see how your clients talk about issues they enjoy. While it is very helpful as a baseline when your clients do engage with this question, it is just as important when they tell you they do nothing for fun. As discussed in Chapter 9, it is not uncommon for your clients to withdraw or be depressed due to the trauma in their lives, but it also is not uncommon for children to become depressed simply because of their involvement with the court. A child who tells you he does nothing for fun or he does not know how to answer the question is telling you far more than the lack of an answer would suggest.

In terms of speaking to child clients, part of your job is to normalize children's situations. Rebecca was once doing a visit with a child at a fast-food restaurant, and they were in the play area. She overheard her client ask another child if he had an attorney. The client was approximately 10, and this was his second time in the dependency system. While that moment broke Rebecca's heart, there have been others where she helped children understand they are not alone. One of them was on a flight with a child traveling to another city to see her father, not in an attorney-client relationship. Although not her client, the child said to Rebecca, "I'm weird—my parents live in different cities." Rebecca smiled and informed her that many children were just like her, and Rebecca knew many of them. Having their situation normalized can be very healing for children, just knowing there are other children who are in a similar circumstance.

Similarly, some children expect you to be shocked by their circumstances, as though they are the only client who has had a particular experience. One client showed Rebecca the cuts on her arm asking, "Is this the first time you have seen this?" Obviously, the answer was "no," and that client was a little surprised that she could not shock her lawyer. That desire to shock is rare, but it is a piece of your client trying to normalize her experience. That is different from you thinking your clients are just like someone else you have represented previously. They are unique individuals with unique needs, but they do not have to feel alone as though they are the only people to have experienced what they are going through. This is particularly helpful when children feel conflicted about loving everyone in their lives when they believe someone does not want them to care about someone else or when they are angry at but still love a parent and want to go back home. Helping children understand that these are normal feelings can help them know it is okay to feel what they are feeling.

Client-Directed vs. Best Interests

As we mentioned in Chapter 3, this issue has been debated for decades, and here we only reference it with respect to the ethical issues it raises and the ways you can use both models to assist you in the issues addressed throughout this book. What seems to matter most is *how* we act using either model. You can have very similar outcomes if you take a step back in either model.[250]

There has been a great deal of discussion that representing children's wishes means just that—you do what your client tells you regardless of the consequences.

---

250. Rebecca's own thinking (and writing) on these issues has evolved significantly over the years. There was a time (in her teens) when she believed children should have the final say in basically everything that happens in their lives. Then she was a firm believer in only "client-directed" representation. She still believes that is the better model, but from a more nuanced place, and there are times it may not be.

And some people believe best interests representation means that you get to be paternalistic and ignore your clients and their perspectives. Research done in Arizona, however, demonstrates the people who practice have a more nuanced view of both models.[251] The research found, "Many representatives report feeling that what the child wants may also be what is in their best interest[s]."[252]

A "client-directed" model is the more natural legal model. And the American Bar Association Model Rules of Professional Responsibility would suggest it is the appropriate model for lawyers to undertake. Rule 1.14 states, "(a) When a client's capacity to make adequately considered decisions in connection with a representation is diminished . . . because of minority . . . the lawyer shall, as far as reasonably possible, maintain a normal client-lawyer relationship with the client."

Too often in practice, people use this role as a cop-out. The mentality is "your role is to walk in, ask a child what she wants, and walk out, and then present that to the court." Even in jurisdictions where you are appointed in a client-directed capacity, this is not your only job. It would be bad lawyering for any lawyer to ask his client what she wants and then follow it blindly. This role, on its surface, appears simple and straightforward, but it can feel incomplete when not examined from the context of family and juvenile law. It is very easy in a business setting to ask a client what he wants and advocate for that within the confines of the law and your understanding of how to navigate the legal system. The legal system was designed for business. And in a criminal setting, no one questions this is the proper role, even for juveniles. But family and juvenile law are different. As described elsewhere in this book, family and dependency court issues are about family stories, not solely legal issues. Further, there is rarely a single end point in the case, and there are multiple hearings with a variety of outcomes, so the client-directed model that works in a single issue case is very different than one that works in a long-term dependency or family law case. You can advocate for what your client wants over time even if you advocate for the steps to help achieve it along the way. Or, if it is feasible, you can advocate for the ultimate goal at the first hearing. The point is that you must consider all these options and not only a single focus outcome at a single hearing.

Regardless of your appointed role, you remain a counselor at law. You have an obligation, as any lawyer does, to advise your client about the potential ramifications of her position and the likelihood of the court agreeing with her position.

---

251. Duchschere et al., *supra* note 61.
252. *Id.* at 39.

Further, while in court, you may advocate strongly for your client's position. However, if you believe it is not legally feasible or there might be a danger in following that path, nothing prevents you—and we would argue you have an obligation—to inform your client of your position. This is, of course, much easier with a teenager than it is with a 6-year-old. In Rebecca's experience, the most difficult age for client-directed representation is 4- to 7-year-olds. Moreover, all the psychological issues addressed in this book demonstrate that children's words are only a piece of the puzzle, and the client-directed model ignores the fact that children tend to "speak" from multiple avenues.

The arguments against the best interests model begin with the ethical implications. Lawyers have a duty of loyalty to clients, and the best interests model is antithetical to that duty. Further, the arguments go, it undermines children's autonomy to question their own beliefs about their lives, particularly by the person appointed to represent them to the court. The fact is, legislatures have created the best interests model, which begs the question of whether statutes can undermine your ethical duties as lawyers admitted to a state bar. Whether you agree or not, the fact remains there are statutes appointing lawyers in a best interests role and it then becomes the lawyers' duty to fulfill that role. But what does that really mean? There could be an entire book on that issue, so we will not go too deeply into it, but we will scratch the surface of how it plays out.[253]

First, to address the question of undermining your clients' autonomy, this is, of course, a valid and strong argument. We believe, again after years of struggling with this, when you follow the imaginary friend model and take the time to understand your clients, develop your relationships, and focus on more than just the actions in court, you help to create a bond and a feeling of autonomy in your child clients. Your ability to see your clients from their point of view and to take the time to connect on that level is the gift of autonomy you give them. When you honor their position, even if you ultimately are barred from arguing for it, you have started to provide that space of healing. And most importantly, if you are honest with your child clients about why you cannot do what they ask and you honor their feelings and do not lie to them, they tend to understand; some may even be grateful.

---

253. The academic discussion about the difference between these two roles is interesting and beneficial to the growth of the profession, but it can also get us lost in what it means to do this work daily. As this book is designed for practice, much of the academic debate will be left out, knowing that others have done fine jobs writing about it.

The fear by many lawyers appointed as best interests representatives is that they will use their own biases instead of listening to the child client. We will address biases in the next chapter, but here the concern is that the paternalistic view of the lawyer will take over. While it is the lawyer's job to determine the *how* of representation, it is not the lawyer's job to determine the "what." So why is it appropriate for a legally trained person to be determining what is in a child's best interests when appointed as her lawyer?

Over the years of representing children, speaking to hundreds of people who represent children, and participating in research on the role of representing children, one thing has become clear to both of us—there is only one simple answer. The answer is that you, as the child's lawyer, must do everything you can to know your clients thoroughly. In many ways, the best interests model requires you to work even more diligently because before you can take a position in court, you must understand how it will affect your client.

Rebecca once had a case where, upon reading the report from the child welfare agency, she was convinced she would have to ask for the child to be removed from her parents. There were allegations of physical abuse as well as emotional abuse. The child welfare agency had not, however, removed the child. Upon meeting the child, Rebecca asked about her feelings about not living with her parents. The child's eyes began to bulge, she started shaking, and her muscles tightened. Instead of asking for removal, Rebecca and her client discussed a safety plan. The interaction with the client was different from what the paper trail suggested it would be. This child also was just at the age where these discussions become more difficult; she was 10. Had she been younger, the outcome might have been different, and although Rebecca initially believed 10 was too young for such a discussion, in that case after speaking with the child, Rebecca's position changed.

Similar to that example, we believe it is important when representing children in a best interests jurisdiction that you give your client the opportunity to convince you that your opinion about the situation is incorrect. They might prefer being hit with a belt once a month to living in a group home and being afraid for their safety a good part of the time. Some children are so worried about the breakup of their family that they cycle into a severe state of depression and cannot function in school or with friends, for example, and even have been hospitalized once or twice. If being home can help remedy those problems, it is important to recognize that being in a less-than-ideal home may be necessary.

Ask your clients if they have seen a change in their parents. Ask your clients how they have grown throughout the process. In a family law case, ask children why they feel the way they feel about everything they say. Only then can you begin to comprehend what is in their best interests. At the end of the day, it is the children's life, not yours, and it must work for the children, not you. In family law matters, Phil engages with children directly by reminding them that the ultimate decision is about their life, not Phil's, which is why Phil wants to know what they think, if they want to talk about it. Then, of course, if they do express their wishes, Phil wants to know why they feel the way they expressed and then explores the nuances of how well thought out their ideas are.

In addition, one of the benefits of the best interests model is you can take the blame when your client's position is one he does not want to reveal to others. While this is not the reason for the best interests model in most jurisdictions, it is a positive side effect and one Rebecca has used frequently. As noted in other chapters, children often feel conflicted about their positions or do not want parents to know specifically how they feel. As a best interests lawyer, you have the opportunity to understand your client's position and protect him from it. Your child client benefits by telling an angry parent the child has to do something because that is what her best interests lawyer recommended and what the judge ordered. In that way, she does not have to take the blame for what might be her position but a position she does not want her parents to know. This can be especially true in very high-conflict matters where parents despise each other.

Sometimes children give implicit permission for this when they do not want you to know the truth of their fear. Rebecca once had a case where a child adamantly stated she wanted to go home but knew all the allegations of physical abuse her siblings were making about Mom. She continued to deny the abuse to Rebecca but had told her therapist and her caregiver she was afraid to go home. There also was evidence the mother was telling her children what to say to their lawyers. Rebecca told this child that she would tell the court the child's position that the abuse did not occur and that she wanted to go home but then asked the child if it was okay for Rebecca to advocate that she not go back to her mother yet. The child readily agreed with a look of relief on her face. Remember, children are influenced by both internal and external reasons to state certain things. In a case like this, it is likely that the internal reason was that she did not want to feel guilt, and the external reason was the pressure Mom was placing on the child to state that she wanted to come home. Knowing your child client well helps you make sense of all of this.

Therefore, despite the decades of debate about the differences in roles and which one is better, when you come to these roles from the imaginary friend model based on the psychological issues described in this book and take time to understand your clients' positions from all angles, the best interests vs. client-directed models are less distinct than most people believe them to be.

Sibling Issues

Perhaps the strangest ethical conflict you will face as a children's lawyer is multiple-person representation. Unless there is a direct conflict, you often represent all the siblings on a case. In an ideal world, each sibling would have her own lawyer, but financially and logistically that is usually not feasible, especially in dependency court. In any other area of law, multiple-party representation is allowed, but it is rare and frowned upon, and it requires specific consent from all parties involved. With children, you are likely appointed to the entire sibling group. The ABA Guidelines on representing children in child welfare cases state that if you are appointed as a best- interests attorney, there is no conflict because the representation is a best interests role. While we disagree with this blanket statement, it raises an interesting question about your role with your sibling clients. How do you determine conflicts? How do you navigate cases when there is no legal conflict but children have different positions and different situations? Obviously, the laws of your jurisdiction will affect the answers to these questions, but here we present what we believe are the most important issues to consider.

The most obvious conflict is when children state that one of their siblings is harming them. It is nearly impossible to represent children when they are in significant conflict and risk of harm toward one another. The problem for you, however, is determining when conflict becomes too much. Siblings fight and argue. But at what point does it cross a line and become an actual risk of harm between them? An obvious one is sexual abuse between siblings. Another simpler situation is in a dependency case where the sibling relationship is one of the allegations in the case. What is less easy to determine is when siblings just do not like each other. This can be resolved only on a case-by-case basis, but it helps to ask the children how commonly the conflict erupts, whether one child fears another, whether the parents are aware of and stop the conflict, and sometimes asking the children themselves whether they believe you can represent both of them. In a family law matter, you will also want to know the extent to which siblings are influencing the wishes or views of each another. While you do not have to get written agreement to represent both siblings like you do in other legal matters, getting verbal consent can be beneficial to you as the children's representative.

What about siblings who have different positions? While there are no specific rules about this, one good barometer is whether you can argue both positions in good faith. Often you can argue that children are differently situated and therefore can represent both children despite the fact they want different outcomes or you believe different outcomes are in their best interests. As such, in a family law case, it can be possible to represent multiple positions if children have different needs. It is more difficult when you get to a point of no return in the case, such as termination of parental rights. If you have verbal clients who want to go home and nonverbal clients who you believe are better where they are in a jurisdiction where you are client-directed, how can you cross-examine a parent and demonstrate her failings as a parent to the younger child while still arguing that the older children can return in a client directed jurisdiction? These specific issues may not happen for you, but they are good guidelines for how to think about these issues as they arise.

What about siblings who call each other liars? This can be one of the easier answers. Your job is not to question the validity of your clients' positions, so if your potential sibling clients diametrically disagree about the facts pertinent to your representation and pertinent to the legal issues in the case, you cannot represent all of them without having to disbelieve at least one of them. This is a corollary of the above problem where children want different outcomes, but it has an easier answer because the underlying reason is not that they are differently situated, it is because they do not believe one another.

What about siblings who blame the others for problems in the home or the cause of the dependency? This is usually another simple answer; it is difficult to represent people who dislike one another and blame one another for problems in the home. When these issues are central to the issues in the case, it often, if not always, becomes a conflict for you. But sometimes the blame is not apparent or it is not specific to the issues in the case. In those cases, you must determine whether you feel comfortable representing all the siblings.

Each jurisdiction has its own rules and its own analysis regarding conflicts between multiple parties, but the unique nature of your job representing children and the unique nature of family and dependency proceedings in general make these issues more nuanced than some. Ultimately, you must determine your own comfort level with the situation before you.

What about Confidentiality?

In most jurisdictions, lawyers are not mandated reporters. Lawyers are usually prohibited from reporting information obtained from a client without that client's direct consent. If you are appointed as a GAL without a duty of confidentiality to your client, this section does not apply. If, however, you are appointed and have a duty of confidentiality, the questions we discuss are some of the most difficult you will face as a lawyer.

It is important to know that because of your position and duty of confidentiality, children often feel safe telling you information they have not told anyone else. This has its advantages in that you can get to the heart of what is happening in your client's life and try to help him work through the issues. As noted above, it can allow you to have frank conversations with your client about how she feels about a situation without the need to reveal it to anyone else. In that case, your client can feel comfortable being honest, and together the two of you can work out a plan to achieve your goals without harming your client in the meantime.

The problem with the limits of confidentiality exists when you learn something about your client's safety, particularly if it is a current issue. Sometimes this includes information about physical or sexual abuse going on in the home or your client having suicidal ideation. If a child is suicidal, many jurisdictions allow you to tell someone. It is important to be open and honest about whether you can keep this information confidential because in some jurisdictions, you cannot. But if you are allowed, or required, to tell someone, it does not mean that is your only recourse. You still can speak to your client about it and see if there are other ways of handling the situation than immediately divulging that specific fact. Each situation is, of course, different, so you must know your client in that moment to know how to resolve the situation.

Some of the most troubling moments as a lawyer for children are when a child tells you she is being abused and you are not allowed to mention it. We do not know any lawyers for children who have done this work for a significant amount of time who have not encountered this scenario. If you are the first person a child tells, you can ask about specifics, including how often, in what manner, by whom, and who knows about the abuse. But remember, you are not a forensic interviewer trying to figure out the entire truth, and depending on the age of the client, if you ask too many questions or ask them inappropriately,[254] you could hinder a later investigation because you asked too many or the wrong types of questions. Be careful in your questions and be sure to determine why the child is telling you the information in that moment. There could be a reason a child discloses at that time. Remember to think about and understand "why" you are now hearing this information.

What do you do, though, if a child tells you he is being abused and he is in the home with a parent or is about to be in the home with a parent and then says you cannot tell anyone? The answer differs depending on the type of role you have,

---

254. Remember the issues described in Chapter 5 under the heading Children's Memory and the Question of Suggestibility.

but even in a best interests jurisdiction, if you cannot provide the evidence to back up your suspicions, you may not be able to stop the child from going home. And remember, from the child's perspective, the abuse may feel less troublesome than the alternative. Thus, it is often important to create a safety plan with the child. You can also try to see if the child will let you speak to the parent's lawyer about what is happening. You might be able to ask for additional services, including therapy for the child, so the child has a place where he can express a problem to someone who is a mandated reporter. For younger children who are not yet in school, you can ask for an order that the child be in day care.

These situations can feel overwhelming and scary.[255] This is not something law school prepared you to do. Law school prepares you to understand confidentiality and the dangers that come with it, but rarely does it prepare you to know a child is being harmed and there is nothing you can do about it. We do not want to diminish the feeling of fear you will likely experience each time a child tells you he is being harmed and you cannot say anything about it. But we hope the skills discussed throughout this book will help you take a step back from that fear and discuss options with your child clients. The better you get to know your client in these situations, the more likely you are to find a solution, even if it is not the ideal solution from your perspective. And remember, the better your relationship with your client, the more likely she is to call if, at some point, the abuse becomes too much and she finally wants you to tell someone. We believe the imaginary friend model helps encourage such actions by helping you become a safe professional for the child to speak to about the abuse.

Safety plans can include knowing whom to call and where to go; identifying a friend the child can call; or identifying a safe place to go, such as a friend's house or a church. You can ensure the child has a list of phone numbers to contact and that she can take them to school. You can get permission to call the school and tell the administration who you are and if the child needs to reach you, she be allowed to do so any time. From a child's perspective, there may be hundreds of valid reasons the child would rather be in a potentially dangerous situation than in the situation you perceive as being less dangerous. So discovering these reasons and helping the child (and maybe yourself) see there are other ways to handle the situation may provide some reassurance about the child's safety in the home. Finally, with time, some children choose to disclose the information to others. They learn that you really are trustworthy in that you did not tell anyone

---

255. In Chapter 12, we will address how to deal with your own feelings when they become overwhelming and scary.

when you said you would not, but they have found their voice, or the abuse became too much, and they ask you to tell someone.

Confidentiality is the cornerstone of lawyering. There are few, if any, other professions that can learn this type of information and be prohibited from sharing it. You likely learned in law school the reason for this duty is to ensure an open and honest relationship with your clients. When these more difficult situations arise, we encourage you to remember why the duty exists and remember these cases are not finite in time; facts change and children and families change, and you will continue to have a relationship with your client while she is in the potentially dangerous situation. Knowing all that can may help you mitigate some of the fear that comes with these difficult situations.

Collateral Sources

As a children's lawyer, you interact with countless collateral sources. Some of these were discussed in Chapter 9, but here we discuss potential ethical hurdles of these interactions. As noted above, you likely have a duty of confidentiality with your client. This means you can learn from others about your client, but you should not be giving them much information unless it is necessary for the care of your client and only with the permission of your client.

One of the most awkward aspects of representing children is that people will tell you what your client thinks and wants. Parents and their lawyers will tell you that your client wants what they want. Therapists will tell you children tell them about fears the children have not discussed with you. Caregivers will tell you about the child's thoughts, feelings, and behaviors. School personnel and social workers have their own thoughts about your clients and what your clients want and need. Even physicians and child custody evaluators may have information necessary to the representation of your client.

But at the end of the day, while you should do your best to collect all this information, you also must know your client as she presents herself to you. With the involvement of these people, it sometimes is important to remind them that your job is to represent the child, not them. Caregivers and social workers, in particular, may try to manipulate children's attorneys to their positions. They do this not necessarily because they are doing something inappropriate but because they tend to be the people who think they are looking out for the children's best interests. In family law cases, when you are allowed to speak to the parents, they often try to manipulate your position as well and tell you not only what the child wants but also what they believe is best for the child.

But as the appointed lawyer in these cases, you are limited as to the people with whom you can speak. Know the law in your jurisdiction. For example, lawyers representing children in California family law matters may not speak with the child custody evaluator unless the judge has specifically authorized it. As a lawyer, you must remember you cannot speak to a represented party without permission. In family law cases in many jurisdictions, it is common practice for the child's attorney to be allowed to speak directly to represented parents. But sometimes it may be in your own best interest to communicate only through the parent's attorney if the parent is difficult or is trying to influence your position.

Similarly, in dependency cases, each jurisdiction has different rules about communicating with represented social workers, but remember they are represented in every jurisdiction. It is our belief that particularly when you want to discuss anything more than factual information, you should involve the social worker's lawyer. These lines for children's attorneys are easily blurred, but in jurisdictions where you are appointed as a lawyer, you should continue to act as a lawyer and follow the ethical rules all lawyers must follow regardless of whether they represent children.

Getting to the Truth

Many of the ethical issues we face as representatives for children boil down to a simple question: What is our job as children's representatives? Is our job to know "the truth" of the situation? More importantly, is there one simple truth? When dealing with children and families, truth becomes a muddle of emotions and alignments and changing memories. Judges, not lawyers, are the fact finders in dependency and family courts.[256] But in some jurisdictions, particularly those in which representatives are appointed in a best interests model, the role can feel more like a fact-finding mission—how can we advocate for best interests when we do not know the truth?

As professionals in these systems, many of us have come to learn that truth is often in the eye of the beholder. Usually, the objective truth does not match anyone's story exactly. This happens for a multitude of reasons. First, some people distort facts or lie. Sometimes parents distort facts or lie. Sometimes social workers distort facts or lie. And sometimes even lawyers distort facts or lie. But there

---

256. We recognize that in Texas and Georgia, juries might hear elements of family law matters, but we also recognize the rarity of this.

are other reasons someone's subjective truth may be different from the objective truth. We discussed memory in Chapter 4, and trauma greatly affects memory. Trauma exists in all your cases for all the parties, not just the children. Therefore, people may remember something differently from what really happened. They may have only a feeling of what happened and filled in the story to fit that feeling. Furthermore, memories can change as we remember them over time, particularly if the memories involve intense emotions.[257] As humans, we all tend to have an "illusion of memory," despite the fact that it can be very difficult to remember events, especially those with overwhelming emotion attached to them. This illusion and others will be discussed in the next chapter.

Knowing that you may never know the objective truth, what is your role in these situations? We believe your most important task is to understand your client's truth. Yes, it is vitally important to know whether neglect has occurred in a home. Yes, it is vitally important to know whether there has been domestic violence in the home. But it is also vitally important to know what your client thinks is true. To help the court understand your client's truth is the main focus of your representation.

One way this necessity manifests is when the objective facts tell you something did not occur but your client believes it did. What if your client has been so alienated, or has a delusional disorder, that he believes abuse happened that did not occur? Does that mean it is not true to that child? Does it mean we do not act accordingly? If a child believes she was sexually molested by her father and there is objective evidence that the molestation was unlikely, do you place the child with the father? Your role in a situation like that is to explain how, despite the lack of objective truth, harm can still come to your client if the judge requires your client to live with a parent who the child believes has harmed her.

These situations can be some of the most difficult we face. Sometimes we will never know what is objectively true in a family or juvenile law case, but we can know what is subjectively true to our clients—and it is imperative that subjective truth becomes part of the record. At the end of the day, you are representing the child, and regardless of your statutory duty in that context, your only duty is to the child client, meaning you have a duty to present your client's truth. It is not your job to decide whether it is true for you or even true for the court.

---

257. Mark Fischetti, *Why Do Our Memories Change*, SCIENTIFIC AMERICAN (Feb. 201, 2017), https://blogs.scientificamerican.com/observations/why-do-our-memories-change-video/.

Conclusions

Representing children is different from representing adults. Despite the years of debate about how all children should be treated the same, it is impossible to deny there are factors inherently different in the role of representing children. But many of these ethical, and somewhat odd-for-your-practice, issues fall away when you go back to the basic tenets set forth in this book: be your client's imaginary friend. Remember you are there for the child. You are there to be the child's advocate, regardless of whether you are advocating the child's wishes or the child's best interests. You get to be that advocate because your relationship with the child is different from anyone else's. You get to keep the child's confidences even when it is difficult to do so. You get to learn about the child from a multitude of people, including the child. And you get to help this child navigate a scary, tumultuous, and maybe even healing process. In fact, for all these reasons (and more), Phil and Rebecca have worked these many years with children to help them navigate and heal through their challenging world.

Recognizing Risks of Bias and Illusion in Your Work

11

In recent years, there has been an emphasis on various types of biases and how they influence your work. Biases can be of various sorts, including implicit bias that affects you without awareness but also cognitive biases that reflect how humans tend to oversimplify complex issues. Furthermore, there is growing research that humans regularly operate with various illusions about their skills and abilities, not because of any emotional reasons but because of the way the brain is wired. This chapter will identify some of those issues and help you think about ways to control for various biases and reduce the illusions in your life.

Cognitive bias is particularly problematic for children's attorneys and judges in the dependency and family court because other lawyers simply represent their clients' positions with some help guiding those positions along the way. As we have discussed throughout this book, however, children's lawyers are different. Sometimes children's lawyers must take a position that is independent of their client's position, and even if they are client-directed, children's lawyers have a great deal of influence over their child clients and the system. Therefore, children's lawyers need to be more aware of their cognitive biases and how those biases may affect their representation.

The Neuroscience of Cognitive Bias

According to Daniel Kahneman,[258] humans have a strong tendency to oversimplify complex matters and are at risk of using heuristics in that process. Heuristics are defined as shortcuts in logic and reasoning that describe how people make decisions or reach conclusions when faced with complex problems. Heuristics allow us to make complex decisions easier from a point of view that works for our own lives. But as a lawyer, particularly a lawyer for children, we cannot make informed legal decisions for our child clients using shortcuts, even ones that might work in our own lives. From a holistic perspective, there is no more complex legal work than in dependency or family court, so the risk of making errors of judgment using one or more heuristics is great. The complexity is because these areas of the law are rarely about the law and are much more about what matters to the people involved. What are their values? What are their biases? What are the family dynamics that have led to their life situations?

Kahneman describes two types of thinking: System 1 and System 2. System 1 thinking is rather impulsive and does not require reflective thought; System 2 thinking is more reflective and analytic. All too often, we use System 1 thinking when we should be using System 2 thinking. This is natural for day-to-day life and saves people time and energy that can be spent elsewhere.

For example, suppose you go to the grocery store and want to buy a few staple foods. With or without a list, you can go through the store and gather what you need with effortless System 1 thought. Suppose instead you need specific items for a party you are hosting and need to make sure you have enough of several different items. You need to slow down, think through the menu, check and recheck your items, and be certain you have enough of each item before leaving the store, i.e., System 2 thinking. Of course, the consequences of getting either of these trips to the grocery store wrong are small when compared with the work you do in family and dependency court. In your own life, System 1 thinking can be helpful because you know what you want and need, and you know what matters to you, so you can make more impulsive decisions even when the decisions seem larger. Of course, there are times when larger decisions need more System 2

---

258. Daniel Kahneman, Thinking Fast and Slow (Macmillan 2011).

thinking in your life, but your biases can be important motivators in what information you find necessary for your personal decisions.

Decisions about someone else, however, require you to stop and reflect far more often. What you may believe is important may not matter to your child clients. Even with all the research, years of experience, and information from your colleagues, there is always more information to learn about a particular case in front of you. This chapter will discuss how your own biases can interfere with representing children and then provide some ideas for how to limit the influence your own biases have over your decisions and representation.

Regarding family law, child support is fairly automatic in many jurisdictions, as parents fill out financial affidavits explaining their respective financial income and relevant expenses, factoring in parenting time, and a computer program determines the support one parent must pay to the other.[259] We can think of this as the computer having created System 1 logic and reasoning. In contrast, consider a case with allegations of domestic violence, high conflict and alienation, and perhaps even one parent wanting to relocate with the children to a different state several hundreds of miles away from the other parent. Gathering and holding data associated with each of these issues while formulating recommendations for your child client will require System 2 logic and reasoning. However, if you have a bias against relocation, perhaps because you believe children benefit when both parents are in the same geographic area, you might be using System 1 logic and reasoning and ignoring data about the possible domestic violence or alienation, while discouraging the court from allowing the move. In your work, faulty logic and reasoning in a case such as this, or the myriad other family or dependency cases, can have serious consequences for the children.

Kahneman and others have written extensively about different types of heuristics that have the potential of influencing our work in complex matters of logic and reasoning.[260] We will provide a list of common heuristics seen in our work and discuss how they may affect your work with child clients.

---

259. Of course, there are cases where child support is difficult to calculate because of a variety of factors, but generally speaking it is an algorithm without too much nuance.

260. For a more extensive description of many types of heuristics, *see, e.g.,* Chapter 4 in PHILIP M. STAHL & ROBERT SIMON, FORENSIC PSYCHOLOGY CONSULTATION IN CHILD CUSTODY LITIGATION: A HANDBOOK FOR WORK PRODUCT REVIEW, CASE PREPARATION, AND EXPERT TESTIMONY (American Bar Association Section of Family Law 2013).

Anchoring Heuristic

Anchoring heuristics are those through which you analyze data as you analyze the case because you have a particular position about one major aspect of the case even if it is not the only aspect. Families are rarely of "a single story." As a result of anchoring, you sometimes minimize or even ignore data that could undermine your anchored position as it has been defined. Considering the case of allegations of domestic violence, high conflict and alienation, and relocation, it is easy to anchor yourself to certain data or certain issues. For example, if you are against the relocation, you might anchor to that, and any evidence you gather would be filtered through that anchor. When you hear allegations by Mother about domestic violence and her request to move is, in part, to feel safe and free of her ex-husband's control, you might not consider that evidence because you are anchored to the idea that Mother should remain near Father so that the children can have two parents in the same city.

Confirmatory Heuristic (Confirmatory Bias)

Confirmatory bias is looking for data supporting your position rather than taking in all the data available and using those data to take a more nuanced position. It is a step further than the anchor heuristic. If anchored to the idea that both parents should be in the same city, you will avoid looking for evidence that might support the relocation; then, because no evidence has been found, you confirm the relocation will not be in the children's best interests. In such a scenario, you ignore the data that support a relocation or that support findings about domestic violence because those types of data might disconfirm your chosen hypothesis. This is an heuristic of exclusion; you exclude data from your analysis by only focusing on data that confirms your first opinion about what should happen in the case.

Availability Heuristic

In contrast, suppose you observe there are data supporting a finding that Father has occasionally been a perpetrator of domestic violence although Mother does not live in fear. Mother and her attorney continue to bombard you with these allegations, making it difficult to find room to explore or observe Father's allegations about Mother inappropriately influencing the children to say bad things about Father. You only have so much energy and time, and if most of it is taken up with one type of data, it will be difficult to develop hypotheses and gather data about the rest of the picture. It is easy to forget that most families are not of just one story, i.e., the story you are bombarded with, but rather multiple fragments of some elements of domestic violence, some elements of parental alienation, and some elements of trauma or attachment problems. Thus, the availability heuristic is when you cannot receive all the available information because you get overwhelmed by certain types of information provided to you by people with an agenda, i.e., the parties or their attorneys. This is particularly damaging for children's attorneys because, as we discussed in Chapter 9, everyone external to your client tries to provide you with information, and they all have their own biases.

Hindsight Bias

Hindsight bias is basing too much of your experience with this new case on a similar case from the past despite the fact these are new people with different, although in some ways similar, issues. Perhaps you have had several cases in which previously abused children who went home suffered additional abuse and came back into the system. You start to believe, in hindsight, you could have predicted these problems. Once such hindsight bias creeps into your reasoning and logic, you become reluctant to send the next child home because you expect her to be back in the system anyway.

For example, Rebecca had a case where the father was about to have his child returned to him and was doing very well living in a sober living facility. She consistently had to question her hindsight bias because previously she had experiences where such facilities, but not even that one, had covered up their clients' substance use. It is important to know there is potential for a problem, but it is unfair to clients if you are not open to new information. This can be particularly problematic the longer you practice. From a professional perspective, it is easy for cases to begin to look and feel the same as cases you experienced before, but from the family's perspective, they are their own unique family unit, and professionals need to recognize how this family might be different from families in previous cases. There is benefit to having experience, but when experience blinds us, it risks becoming hindsight bias.

Primacy Bias/Recency Bias

Similar to anchoring, primacy bias reflects a strong tendency to focus mostly on information you hear first in the case. Thus, hearing from Father that Mother is emotionally unstable and hearing from a pediatrician that a child appeared to have a small bruise, you focus primarily on that information; you ignore the "facts" of the case that Mother's instability was solely around the time of separation two years earlier and the bruise was likely the result of a fall rather than anything Mother might have done. The primacy bias means all the information you learn later gets filtered through the lens of the information you learned first.

In contrast, recency bias refers to overly focusing on those data that come in last and influence your logic and reasoning so that you begin to ignore everything you previously thought you understood. Both types of bias interfere with complex reasoning and logic. Your mind focuses on specific pieces of information not because they are the most important but because of the timing of when you received them. And the timing of the information provided to you is based solely on when you had the opportunity to receive the information, not on its importance to the case. Thus, these biases have little to do with the facts of the case and more to do with how your memory works.

Affiliative/Disaffiliative Bias

An affiliative bias is one in which you are influenced by characteristics a parent has that are similar to those you hold. Conversely, a disaffiliative bias exists when you and the parent have different characteristics. This could be an affiliation due to:

- Shared or different interests, e.g., when a parent describes that he likes taking his children camping and you enjoy camping and taking your children camping as well;
- Shared or different philosophies, e.g., when a parent describes herself as a conservative person politically and you have more liberal beliefs;
- Shared or different religions, e.g., when one parent is of a religion similar to yours and the other parent is of a religion different from yours.

Such affiliations should never affect how you do your work. Although you need to understand your client, and the adults in her life, if you learn too much about the adults and their traits and interests, it is all too easy to like or dislike the adult according to his interests. Phil was once involved in a case where the father enjoyed skiing. The evaluator involved in the case also liked to go skiing and seemed to ignore the father's drug use and his limited parenting skills when recommending for a 50-50 parenting plan and against the relocation, and that Father have primary custody of the child if the Mother moved. In recommending in favor of Father's position, the evaluator was influenced by the shared interest, which led him to ignore data that did not support Father's position.

Professional Biases

Professional biases are different from cognitive biases in that they are not based on how you perceive information; they come from the fact you are a professional in this field and have learned specific information along the way. They are more learned biases than cognitive biases. There are many areas in which different professionals might use research to form opinions about issues in a case before seeing any of the family members.[261] For example, some psychologists and attorneys appear to have the view that very young children need all their overnight parenting time with one parent, usually the mother, or that various forms of equally shared parenting are best for all children. In other cases, these professionals might have a view that relocations are generally harmful for children and usually try to force parents to live in the same community, regardless of the legal issues in the case.

In still other types of cases, these professionals might have a view that children must be protected from unsupervised contact with a parent anytime there has been domestic violence in the case, despite the fact domestic violence manifests itself in different ways in different families (see Chapter 6). In dependency court, some professionals believe children should be removed from their parents automatically whenever there is evidence of substance use or family violence, even when these may be one-time incidents and not patterns of behavior that bring harm to the children. In a similar vein, some professionals never advocate out-of-home placement until conditions are extremely severe and toxic for the child.

The problem with taking such rigid positions is two-fold. First, social science research is not very precise. For example, a nuanced understanding about relocation shows the potential harm is somewhat limited, that some children will function better after a relocation and others will function worse; and that a change in primary custody from one parent to another to protect against a relocation may create more harm than the relocation itself. Another example is the research about overnights with young children. Few studies even address this issue, and attachment is not the only consideration in this debate. At the time of publication, the most recent research literature on the topic identified certain factors that are likely to increase the risk of *high-frequency* overnights with the other parent, including but not limited to high conflict between the parents, logistics

---

261. Irwin Sandler et al., *Convenient and Inconvenient Truths in Family Law: Preventing Scholar-Advocacy Bias in the Use of Social Science Research for Public Policy*, 54 Fam. Ct. Rev. 150 (2016).

of work and residential location, qualities of parenting, and the child's temperament; there is no research that supports no overnights with one parent as an automatic position. There is also significant research that removal from a parent is traumatic, as well as significant research on the long-term effects of the trauma experienced in the home. Research cannot, therefore, always provide the answer in your cases.

The second problem with such professional biases is that such biases lead directly to the oversimplification and risk of cognitive biases identified in this chapter. For example, a child custody evaluator who has a "research bias" that relocations are harmful will likely look only for data that support such a conclusion even though the conclusion was formed before the gathering of any data. Phil once reviewed a report in which the custody evaluator had recommended against a relocation. In reviewing the evaluator's notes, Phil saw that the evaluator had written "moves are always bad" in the margin of the first page of notes with the parent who was opposing the relocation. Upon inquiry at a deposition, it was revealed that the evaluator had this research bias and applied it to this case as well as many others. Anchored to this belief, the evaluator never looked for data that might support or reduce the risk of the move in a particular case. The important task is to recognize one's professional beliefs and suspend them while gathering all data necessary to reach a conclusion about the outcome in the case.

Illusions Regarding Our Abilities

Perhaps one of the bigger challenges facing professionals who work in family and dependency court is they often believe they have better skills than they really do. According to Christopher Chabris and Daniel Simons,[262] as humans, we experience many illusions that tend to inflate our belief in our abilities. For example, research supports the idea that humans have a strong belief that they attend to relevant and important details when observing children and families. It is common, however, for many of us to miss critical features when we are meeting with family members. For example, if you focus on the substance use/abuse of Mother, you may not pay attention to other issues in the case. This may cause you to miss critical parenting variables, such as problems with domestic violence with Father, or critical variables associated with your client's trauma response.

---

262. Christopher Chabris & Daniel Simons, The Invisible Gorilla: How Our Intuitions Deceive Us (Harmony Press 2011).

Another illusion is that you will remember critical details when you learn them, regardless of note taking. For most people, however, without notes, they might forget critical information even though they think they have a great memory and will remember everything. Chabris and Simons, however, focus on the reality that humans are likely to forget substantial information if they do not write it down and point out that when humans forget information, they tend to use shortcuts, such as the heuristics described earlier in this chapter. Most of the heuristics described above are based on including or excluding particular data based on your bias. Thus, if you forget to take notes, when evaluating your position for the court, you likely will be at risk of being influenced by biases rather than a complete overview of information.

This problem worsens when humans are overconfident in their positions. Chabris and Simons state that humans are frequently overconfident, especially about things they know little about. This is called the Dunning-Kruger effect. Research on the topic suggests that humans are at risk of believing they know more than they do about things they know little about. What is interesting is the less someone knows about a particular topic, the more that person believes he knows. The colloquial phrase is that someone knows "just enough to be dangerous." When you think you know more than you do about critical issues, e.g., family dynamics, and you are overconfident about that alleged knowledge, you remain at risk of oversimplifying complex information. Given the complex family dynamics in family and dependency court, all of us are at risk of oversimplifying issues, especially because we think we know more about them than we really do.

Debiasing Strategies

One would expect the simplest strategy to avoid being influenced by heuristics and these illusions should be to understand them and consciously work to avoid such influence. Of course, that is a necessary first step, but according to various research, it is insufficient. Awareness alone, even when combined with efforts to avoid such heuristics as anchoring or confirmatory bias, typically fail. Just as most humans have the illusion that they are more capable of critical tasks, and hence are at risk of overconfidence, awareness of these issues alone only increases the risk of overconfidence in their ability to avoid being influenced by these biases and illusions. In other words, humans tend to think they are doing a better job of eliminating bias than they actually are, including the bias that they think they know more than they actually do.

In contrast, other strategies actively counteract these influences and are necessary for your work as a children's lawyer. For example, to avoid the risks of anchoring and confirmatory bias, it is necessary to develop multiple hypotheses and then, as data become available that support certain beliefs or outcomes, look for data that will both confirm and disconfirm those beliefs. Remember, if you stop your inquiries because you believe you have settled on the correct conclusion, you are in the process of oversimplifying. If you have taken complete and thorough notes of your interactions, it is easier to review those notes and ensure you are at risk of neither primacy nor recency bias. If you are investigating a family's domestic violence, rather than being inattentive to the issues, you must look to understand the nature of parent-child relationships and the qualities associated with good parenting.

As a children's lawyer, you are inundated with information from a variety of sources, not the least of which is your client, whose information and position may change as the case moves along. As such, your job mining through all this information becomes more difficult. Your cognitive and professional biases can overwhelm your beliefs about the case. Thus, it may be critical for you to speak to others about your cases, particularly those you know have a different point of view. We are not suggesting you violate your duties of confidentiality, but you can reach out to colleagues about the critical issues and ask how they might weigh different factors. Tell them the information that supports the conclusion you have reached as well as the information that may not support your conclusion. Very often in the cases you see in family and dependency courts, reasonable minds differ about the "correct" outcome. So periodically talking through your cases with other professionals can help ensure your own biases are not becoming the defining characteristic of your own processes.

For example, when Rebecca began representing children, physical abuse was something she could not tolerate in parents. After years of listening to children describe it, talking to professionals who experienced it as children, and seeing the effects of physical abuse versus other forms of abuse, Rebecca now has a more nuanced understanding of what physical abuse means in a case. Rebecca's initial response, the nervous system response, is that physical abuse is still wrong, but the higher brain functioning kicks in sooner and stops that reaction to allow for a discussion of all issues in the case and not focus solely on the abuse. The underlying bias still exists most of the time, although less and less strongly, but the response to that bias has become more System 2 thinking over the years.

Identifying Bias and Illusion in Other Professional Work

In your role as child representative, you are likely to read reports from child custody evaluators, psychologists, therapists, social workers, and others who have contact with and provide evaluations of your client and/or her family. We urge you to review the work of these professionals in the context of information identified in this chapter. Phil spends much of his professional work reviewing the work of other professionals. He has seen many child custody evaluation reports that are thorough and well done and show that the evaluator managed and controlled for both professional and cognitive biases. On other occasions, he has seen poor work reflective of professional biases, as described earlier in this chapter, e.g., that relocations are always harmful to children, that a young child of divorce should not have overnight parenting time with one of his parents, and that a parent who engaged in one incident of SIV should not be allowed supervised visitation with his child until he has completed a BIP[263] and cognitive biases including those described earlier in this chapter. Phil also has seen testimony by experts that reflects an incredible overconfidence in their conclusions, failing to consider the potential limitations of their data.

In your work, you will want to look for the potential influence of any of these dynamics. To do this, consider whether the report writer used a multi-method process, including interview data, observational data, collateral data, and perhaps psychological testing data and/or home visits, in gathering information about the child and his family. It is important to consider more than one source of data when performing forensic assessments. Next, you should look for evidence that the professional considered multiple hypotheses and gathered data about all elements of the child and his family, not just single stories such as domestic violence or attachment. Third, you want to look for a risk/benefit analysis of the multiple considerations, e.g., risks and benefits of primary parenting with Mother, primary parenting with Father, and shared parenting and if shared parenting, the benefit of a balanced 50-50 plan vs. a plan that is not "equal" but has substantial time with each parent. Remember, there is no research supporting the fact that a 50-50 equal parenting plan is better or worse for children than a parenting plan that provides substantial parenting time with each parent. Finally,

---

263. Note that it is the automatic nature to which we are referring and the fact that it was one incident of SIV. Of course, with a perpetrator who has an established pattern of CCV, a recommendation of supervised access might be the right choice.

you should look for an analysis identifying the evaluator considered multiple hypotheses and the risks and benefits of various custodial options, as well as evidence of the debiasing techniques described earlier in this chapter.

While this book is not a trial skills book, we want to point out how important it is to examine and cross-examine witnesses who have written reports about their debiasing methods whether you believe they have done a very good job or have allowed their biases to overtake their work product. When Phil is hired by one side of a case, he is routinely cross-examined about how he manages potential for retention bias. He explains all the issues described about cognitive biases, acknowledging the ever-present risk of retention bias, despite his attempts to control for them.

Conclusions

It is important to remember that in an area as imprecise as family and dependency court, and with vague determinants such as the best interests of the child or imprecise concepts such as attachment, bonding, alienation, or domestic violence, it is even more critical that those who work with children and families be more careful when reaching their conclusions and recommending outcomes. In your own work, take careful notes, develop multiple hypotheses, look for information that is not directly in front of you, consider all aspects of the parent-child relationships, and understand not only your client's wishes but also the bases for those wishes. Reach out to people you know who have perspectives different from you. Ask them to challenge you and your beliefs in a particular case. When looking at professional reports, try to find evidence the other professional did the same.

And remember your biases are not your client's biases. Your child client may value aspects of her life differently than you do. The difference between being a children's lawyer and any other professional who must take a position on a case is that you are required to consider your client's biases. While you may believe all physical discipline is inappropriate no matter what, your child client may prefer to be spanked once in awhile than live in foster care where he is "safe." Your child clients, particularly as they age into adolescence, might prefer a less ideal home situation with one parent than an objectively better home situation with the other parent because they have friends in one community and not the other. At the very least, you must know your clients' biases and perspectives no matter what your role in the case is.

As humans, it is natural and necessary to value certain aspects of our lives more than others. What we do with that information is what matters. Only when you have gone through your own debiasing process can you reduce the risks inherent in the human tendency to oversimplify or be overconfident, becoming reasonably confident that others working in your case are acting likewise. Finally, remember this work is important to your client and the families you serve. Stay humble, recognize the limitations of your knowledge and the research regarding children and their voices, and strive to do the best job possible in every case. Although you cannot erase all biases, and may not be able to avoid influences from within (as described in this chapter), strive to serve all your child clients and the court to the best of your ability. That will help reduce the risk of any biases interfering in your efforts.

The Professional Toll | 12

Most of this book has discussed the impact of being involved in the legal system on your child clients and your relationship with them. The previous chapter was about how to recognize and reduce the risks of being influenced by various cognitive or professional biases you personally hold that affect your representation. This chapter, however, is about how this work affects you. Of course that will affect how you do your job, but ultimately this chapter is about you and only you. As lawyers for children, you likely have encountered or will encounter some of the most horrifying issues imaginable. Over time, these stories can take their toll on you. This chapter is an overview of what that toll looks like, what aspects of being a lawyer make it a unique experience compared to other healing professions, and what you can do to help yourself when facing these issues.

Until recently, the legal system paid little if any attention to the emotional and physical effects on you of the work you do as a professional and as a human being. As the rest of the professional world got better at noticing the effects of being in a healing profession, lawyers were left off the list of those affected by what they see every day. People rarely think of lawyers as being members of a healing profession, but those who work in family court and dependency court systems understand that is exactly what lawyers are, particularly in family and dependency systems, which aim to be systems of healing and forgiveness, not systems of fault and punishment. Fortunately, the mentality has begun to shift, and now the terms *vicarious trauma* and *compassion fatigue* are becoming ubiquitous at family and dependency law legal conferences as well as in larger organizations that work in these fields. But there also is something unique about being a lawyer that affects these issues.

Lawyers, in general, experience depression and substance abuse at a higher rate than the general population.[264] One lawyer who visited multiple states and participated in discussions about these issues discovered there were "deep feelings of shame and isolation" about these feelings.[265] There are multiple reasons for these numbers, and many of them exist in the world of Big Law, which is not where most children's attorneys work. This chapter will not cover all the professional problems lawyers face. Instead, this chapter will cover two reasons for these higher rates of anxiety, depression, substance abuse, and even suicide, particularly in those who work in family and dependency law. There are others, of course, which include long hours, demands of the job, the need to respond to clients consistently, and inappropriate bosses. But in the field of representing children in dependency and family law cases, compassion fatigue and vicarious trauma are two of the biggest factors affecting lawyers' work. How the other issues that affect all lawyers relate to vicarious trauma and compassion fatigue will be addressed but not as stand-alone issues.

Although the terms are not always clearly demarcated, we are going to discuss vicarious trauma and compassion fatigue as two distinct, although interrelated, issues. Vicarious trauma is exactly what the name suggests; it is trauma you experience vicariously from your clients' lives. As discussed in Chapter 4, trauma is stored in the nervous system. Vicarious trauma is similarly stored in your nervous system and can affect you in much the same way as primary trauma, but it develops over time instead of resulting from one distinct event. Vicarious trauma can have much the same effect on your nervous system as primary trauma does in your child clients. It is also part of the new diagnostic

---

264. Jenna Cho, *Can We Finally Talk about the Elephant in the Room? Mental Health of Lawyers*, Above the Law, https://abovethelaw.com/2016/02/can-we-finally-talk-about-the-elephant-in-the-room-mental-health-of-lawyers/.

265. *Id.*

criteria for PTSD in the *DSM-5*. This means that experiencing trauma vicariously in a professional setting is sufficient to be diagnosed with PTSD when the
other criteria are met.

Compassion fatigue is more about the external aspect of how you begin to
see the world. It affects how you view the world more than how your nervous
system responds to the trauma you see every day. This is the feeling bubbling up
inside you making you think the families you see every day are the norm, losing the optimism you have for life, and seeing work-related situations in places
they do not exist. It can also be described as what people call "burnout," in
which you have given so much of yourself that you have nothing left to give.[266]
For example, in one training Rebecca attended, the speaker told a story of how
she was on vacation with her family. She was on a mountain looking out over
a beautiful canyon, and as she stepped toward the edge of the cliff, her first
thought was, "I wonder how many people have jumped off this cliff." Her family was admiring the view. Compassion fatigue can sneak up on you in those
moments you least expect.

Finally, although not discussed as much, primary trauma, as opposed to vicarious trauma, is happening in courtrooms all the time. Being in these fields and
under extreme stress, lawyers and others can act in ways they would not normally act outside the courtroom. People can become mean and petty and yell
and be disrespectful when, in their "real" lives, they are kind and compassionate
beings. It is natural to be hurt when a lawyer you believed was a colleague treats
you with disrespect. It can be just as painful when you find yourself acting in
ways you would not normally act and find yourself being the inappropriate and
rude person.

Phil has been in family court situations in which attorneys argue, yell, and
become rude with one another, largely because the dynamics of the case include
this same behavior between parents. Sometimes as cases move through the system, attorneys find themselves acting like their difficult clients. But as we saw in
Chapter 4 and throughout this book, trauma can cause people to act in ways
they otherwise would not. When you and your colleagues experience trauma
day after day, everyone's actions can be affected, and it can be a downward spiral until you take conscious steps to change it. Thus, vicarious trauma becomes
primary trauma, and the spiral continues.

---

266. Some people would describe burnout as something different from compassion
fatigue, and in many ways, it is. But to keep this chapter simple, we are putting them in
one category because they are similar in how they manifest.

Another form of primary trauma cannot be ignored, although it is rare. Family and dependency cases sometimes have dangerous parties. If you watch the news, you know that family law attorneys have been shot and sometimes killed. These events seem to be increasing. While even the most violent people tend not to bring that violence to the courtroom and the professionals involved, it does happen, and it is imperative you be conscious of it and protect yourself accordingly. If you know a party is dangerous or you have been threatened in any way, alert court security. If people harass you on the phone or in person, tell them your only communication will be written. This work is stressful enough, and sometimes your job is to tell courts certain parents should not be allowed to parent their children. So take any precautions necessary if you believe your safety is compromised.

Manifestations of Vicarious Trauma and Compassion Fatigue

Vicarious trauma acts in the nervous system similarly to regular trauma. Therefore, people who experience vicarious trauma can have responses that are similar to those who experience primary trauma. For example, people can become hypervigilant and hyperaroused, as often occurs in fight-or-flight responses. But more often, particularly with vicarious trauma, people find themselves in a state of chronic freeze. We described the physiological signs of fight, flight, and freeze in Chapter 4 regarding trauma generally. As a professional, the physiological signs and symptoms are similar when you are experiencing them because of vicarious trauma.

We will provide a brief overview here of symptoms of vicarious trauma to help you notice when they arise in you so you can help yourself and be better available to help your clients feel safe in your presence. Fight-or-flight symptoms, or an overly active sympathetic nervous system, appear as increased heart rate, difficulty breathing, cold sweats, a tingling sensation, muscular tension, an exaggerated startle response (jumping at loud noises), an inability to fully rest or relax, tendency toward anxiety or panic attacks, rage outbursts, racing thoughts, worry, or hypervigilance. Freeze symptoms, or an overly active parasympathetic nervous system, appear as low energy, exhaustion, physical or emotional numbness, low muscle tone, low heart rate or low blood pressure, poor immune system function, depression, dissociation, apathy, and under responsiveness.

Although more difficult to track, others can find themselves in a state of fight/flight and freeze together, as though the accelerator and the brakes of a car are used at the same time. This can be very confusing and difficult to track because the symptoms of fight, flight, and freeze appear to be happening together. This may seem counterintuitive, but it tends to show up where you go, go, go and then, when you finally sit to relax, you fall asleep. There is nothing between sleep and running on fumes. You feel as though some muscles are always tense but you have very low muscle tone in others. Where a healthy nervous system oscillates between sympathetic and parasympathetic responses within a range, a nervous system with the brakes and accelerator on at the same time lives mostly in extremes—rage and apathy or a racing heart and low blood pressure.

We frequently see lawyers in these states. Notice how many lawyers are tapping their feet or fidgeting much of the time. But notice them again after experiencing a very intense encounter—their eyes are blank, and they appear as though they are not present. These are people in fight, flight, and freeze at the same time. Furthermore, there is evidence that patterns of chronic pain are types of freeze. How many lawyers do you know who have chronic pain, particularly in their backs?

In addition, as noted above, people's personalities can change because of vicarious trauma. People begin to have a shorter fuse and can begin to react rather than respond to situations. When people are stuck in fight, flight, and freeze, they are less able to take a moment, breathe, stop and think, and then respond. As you may remember from Chapter 4, the fight, flight, freeze responses are automatic. The higher brain functioning, which allows for reflective thinking, has shut down, and the system is capable only of immediate reactions and not thoughtful considerations. Thus, when people experience vicarious trauma every day and the system becomes overloaded, the ability to respond with thoughtfulness diminishes. As mentioned in Chapter 11, to have your own biases affect your work less, you need to think carefully and respond rather than react. Thus, your ability to care for your own vicarious trauma is important for your work as well as your health.

Further, when the nervous system gets stuck, many health conditions intensify. Remember the findings of the ACE study outlined in Chapter 4; research is clear that emotional trauma can affect physical health. Although the ACE study only examines childhood trauma, one can extrapolate how these issues affect you even later in life. The immune system is weaker, the body is physically tense all the time, and emotions are difficult to control. These factors make it more difficult to function every day. In addition, the sympathetic nervous system shuts down the immune system because when you are running from a tiger, protection from the common cold is of little importance. You might find yourself getting sick more frequently. You might find yourself having sleep problems, and if you are noticing, you might recognize an increase in the outward stress you feel. To combat these problems, you might find yourself drinking more heavily, isolating yourself from friends, and having more challenging interactions in your personal relationships. All of this creates specific challenges when vicarious trauma takes hold.

Thus, vicarious trauma settles inside you and manifests as immediate reactions rather than reflective responses. It becomes more difficult to slow down without crashing entirely and more difficult to show up in life with your clients, colleagues, friends, and families. As physical symptoms begin to appear, you may try to treat them as medical conditions, but until you resolve the underlying nervous system over- and under-reactions, the physical symptoms may not disappear.

Compassion fatigue manifests differently than vicarious trauma. Compassion fatigue leads to a distorted view of broader reality because you spend your life seeing humanity at its worst. It is easy to forget there are families without domestic violence, substance abuse, and severe mental health issues. It can be easy to forget the majority of people do not harm their children. It is easy to forget a significant number of separated families do so without much conflict and without an increased toll on children.

One of the more insidious aspects of compassion fatigue is how it has a tendency to sneak up on you when you least expect it. You can be having a nice evening with a friend and become distracted by people in the room you believe are fighting. If you are single, you might never feel comfortable dating, assuming all potential partners are dangerous. Phil has a friend who worked in rape counseling and believed all men were potential rapists. She was reluctant to date anyone until she quizzed him about his history of resolving conflicts and relationships with women and how he felt about children. This clearly affected her relationship life, at least until she met a gentle person who answered her queries and ultimately became her husband and the father of her children. When you work in family or dependency court, you may find yourself expecting the worst in situations because that is what you see every day.

Compassion fatigue can also manifest as difficulty in being with friends and family who are experiencing their own discomfort in life. As we have stressed throughout this book, we do not believe in comparative trauma; everyone's trauma affects them, and just because someone experienced something "worse" than someone else does not mean it is going to affect them more. That said, it can become increasingly difficult to have the same compassion for a friend going through her third breakup in a year as you do for the child who was beaten with a belt by her mother. You can literally get too overwhelmed by the trauma you hear every day to show up for your friends and family in ways they need you and in the ways you want to show up for them as the compassionate, caring person you likely are.

There is an interesting ancillary benefit, however, to all the trauma you hear every day. While it is not really a manifestation of compassion fatigue, we can think of nowhere else to address it. Because you see and hear the worst of humanity, you may find your friends and family know you are going to be able to withstand their stories as well. You can become a solid friend to these people because there is little left in the world that will shock you. So many people do not want to hear about tragedies that befall their friends and families, but because you have a gift in doing this work, you usually have the capacity to hold these stories for people when others cannot. While you can easily get overwhelmed by them, which is what most of this chapter addresses, there is the piece where it can bring you closer to your friends and family because you have capacities others may not have.

Burnout shows up similarly to compassion fatigue as being too overwhelmed to handle any aspect of your life. Burnout is a symptom of compassion fatigue and vicarious trauma. It is when everyday activities become monumental tasks. You are unable to find the passion for the job you began because you wanted to help children and families. You may stop returning phone calls and responding to e-mails. Burnout is strongest when your ability to show up as an empathetic imaginary friend for your clients becomes diminished, if not nonexistent. We have both seen, and expect you have seen, people who have reached this point in their professions. People who you know once cared a great deal about their clients and the children they serve reach a point at which they cannot get anything done. Once burnout sets in, the problems addressed above set in as well. These include higher rates of depression, suicide and suicidal ideation, and substance abuse than in the general population. Without properly addressing the underlying vicarious trauma and compassion fatigue, these issues continue to grow. We will address the ways to help. But first, what is it about being a lawyer specifically that makes vicarious trauma and compassion fatigue feel so menacing?

Difference about Being a Lawyer Than Other Healing Professions

As noted above, few people outside of the profession think of lawyers as members of a healing profession susceptible to the effects of compassion fatigue and vicarious trauma. In the minds of the public, the professions that usually fit that description are therapists, first responders, and doctors. Until recently, we did not think of judges and jurors as being susceptible to the effects of vicarious trauma. But Phil has taught judges about the impact of vicarious trauma and compassion fatigue unique to their world, and some of the most interesting research on vicarious trauma has been done with jurors who sat in courtrooms and listened for days and months to evidence associated with traumatic events. From that research, it is apparent how these issues affect us when we least expect it.

Rebecca was once speaking to a firefighter about the trauma they see every day. As they continued to talk, he stated he thought lawyers had the more difficult job. He sees a situation and gets out, and while he sees traumatic events and their immediate aftermath, he does not have to see what happens afterward. Rebecca was surprised by his statements because she had never thought about the pain children's representatives experience in that way. The wounding in the family court and dependency law profession is deep and profound. Lawyers do not tend to see the blood and gore that first responders do, but the firefighter was correct; lawyers see the aftermath and the pain and the effects of ongoing, never-ending trauma. Children's representatives both see and literally feel how it exists in the children and families they serve.

Another difference between lawyers and other healing professionals is the reaction lawyers receive in society. Few people do not have an opinion about lawyers, and often those opinions are negative. It is difficult to do a job when many in society generally view your profession as a group of lying sociopaths. Rebecca rarely tells people she is a lawyer; instead, she says she represents children in family court and foster care. It is interesting that her conversation happened with a firefighter. Firefighters are universally loved. The reactions that lawyers receive in society matter, and it affects lawyers' mental health. The response Rebecca usually gets? A look somewhere between shock and horror on the recipient's face and then, "Oh that is such difficult work. I could never do that" or "That must be both so difficult and so rewarding." Society tells you how you should feel, and it shows up as vicarious trauma and compassion fatigue.

Because you work with children, you see these issues as they affect those who are the most vulnerable in our population. In research done in Tucson, Arizona, among children's lawyers, one lawyer stated he had to leave the full-time practice of representing children because it became too much to be with the abuse and neglect of children all day long.[267] It is human nature to want to protect children; otherwise, our species would not still exist. But the types of people drawn to working with children tend to be more empathic, and this leads to a higher risk

---

267. Duchschere et al., *supra note 61.*

of vicarious trauma and compassion fatigue. The more you can feel of the world around you, the more difficult it can be to protect yourself from its harmful effects.

Brené Brown has a short video on YouTube about the difference between empathy and sympathy available, and it helps explain how and why those in healing professions, lawyers included, end up with vicarious trauma.[268] In the video, Dr. Brown describes the four qualities of empathy as (1) perspective taking, (2) staying out of judgment, (3) recognizing emotion in other people, and (4) communicating that you recognize their emotion. These are the very qualities this book has stressed—how can you put yourself in the shoes of your clients, without judgment, and understand them from their perspective while holding space for them to feel all their emotions despite those emotions being so overwhelming? For what it is worth, such traits are common in very good psychotherapists and, while you are not supposed to be acting as a therapist, having those qualities is important to forming a relationship with your clients. As we have stated, when you work in family and dependency courts, you are a healer as well as a problem solver, even if you do not think of yourself as a healer and typically think of yourself as a problem solver. This entire book has been about connecting to children, and Brené Brown describes empathy as connection, whereas sympathy is really disconnection.

But that deep, open, and honest connection to another person, particularly a person who has experienced intense and/or chronic trauma and is in pain, requires you to find within yourself the place where you have felt that pain. It requires you be willing to connect with the pain, sit with it, and maybe feel it yourself. Dr. Bruce Perry writes, "Human social life is built on this ability to 'reflect' each other and respond to those reflections with both positive and negative results."[269] This means besides experiencing what your client experiences, at the nervous system level, you trigger the feelings you experienced previously.

Science seems to suggest, perhaps controversially, that humans can feel what they see. If you see someone being touched, your brain lights up as though you

---

268. Brené Brown on Empathy, https://www.youtube.com/watch?v=1Evwgu369Jw (last visited Nov. 5, 2017). It is difficult to put a link to a video in a printed book, but we believe this short video provides a very concise and very necessary explanation of empathy vs. sympathy. Therefore, we provide it knowing it is difficult to link to a video in a printed book. It can also be found by doing an online search for "Brené brown empathy video."

269. Perry, *supra* note 149 at 67.

are being touched. And some people may feel it more than others.[270] It also would seem possible that humans can experience the emotions others are experiencing. Have you ever felt an angry person walk into a room? How about a confused and scared person? This sort of empathy makes you a better lawyer but also more susceptible to the vicarious trauma in this field.

There are many ways lawyers in general are susceptible to these conditions. First, legal training does not prepare lawyers for emotional connection, even though those who work in family and dependency court need to connect emotionally with their clients. Instead, lawyers are taught they should be devoid of emotions in their legal work. But that mentality does not work in dependency and family law (or, arguably, in any other area of law). Therefore, lawyers must learn how to recognize the effects of working with these intense emotions despite being taught for three years they are unnecessary to the practice of law. Lawyers representing children must navigate the sometimes difficult line between too much emotion and "just the facts," devoid of emotion as required by the legal process. This requires a great deal of patience and awareness of how it affects you.

When working with children, this specific aspect of legal training can create difficulty in connecting with your clients. For example, many lawyers are trained, even in dependency and family law cases, to ask children about the "facts" of the case. As we have discussed throughout the book, even knowing what facts are true is difficult. But here, what is important is knowing that part of your job is to (1) ask children to talk about deeply painful and emotional aspects of their lives in a factual way and (2) repeatedly ask them to have conversations about aspects of their lives that cause them pain. While you are not the one causing them pain, you may feel that your conversation has caused the child pain, particularly in that moment. As a way of describing the difficulty of a particular day, Rebecca has told people how many children she made cry during a day. Certainly, Rebecca is not causing the child to cry, but that feeling of being the instigator can loom large in your life as a lawyer, particularly because lawyers are not trained to navigate the emotional discussions the way other healing professions are.

This lack of training in emotions is one reason lawyers are less able to help each other while experiencing vicarious trauma and compassion fatigue. After a rough day, psychotherapists who go to their colleagues for help may be met with

---

270. Jakub Limanowski, *How You Feel What Another Body Feels: Empathy's Surprising Roots in the Sense of Touch*, Scientific American (June 26, 2012), https://www.scientificamerican.com/article/how-you-feel-what-another-body-feels/; Perry *supra* note 149 at 67.

support that is appropriate to helping with the symptom manifestation. Lawyers, by contrast, are trained to be problem solvers. Rebecca recently experienced such an event. She had a client who needed to be put on a psychiatric hold. The client was screaming, "I want to die" in public and banging her head against a wall. Eventually the paramedics arrived. and her client was transported to the hospital. Rebecca, not surprisingly, was slightly dissociated after this event. While the person she spoke with after the event is a kind and warm-hearted person who meant well in that situation, the person's immediate response was to offer solutions to a problem that no longer existed—how to de-escalate a client in that situation. Lawyers are problem solvers, so of course that was the response. The person did nothing inherently wrong, but in that moment, a more useful response for someone who just experienced that level of trauma is to offer her the space to feel what she is feeling. We will discuss more of what to do in these situations later, but it is important to remember that legal training is part of the reason lawyers are less able to support one another through the throes of vicarious trauma and compassion fatigue despite being caring, compassionate people.

As a corollary to the above, as a lawyer, you often are not allowed to respond naturally to your client in pain, particularly a child client. As we discussed in Chapter 10, you are already in an awkward position with this child, often alone in a room having a conversation about topics not generally discussed with strangers. If your friend or partner is crying and telling you an awful story about trauma, your likely response is to comfort that person with words or a hug. While you can offer children some words of comfort, hugs are more controversial, particularly in that room without windows and without a camera. Further, you must hold some level of professional disconnect from what is happening, as though you are not affected by it. In a relocation case, Phil was interviewing a 9-year-old child who broke down in tears, upset because one of her parents wanted to move 1,000 miles from the other and fearful that she might upset one of her parents by what she had to say. He had to remain detached, give her space to cry, say some comforting words, and continue the evaluation. In a more natural environment, you would likely show your own emotion and shock, horror, or pain at hearing what the child told you, especially given the nature of trauma you deal with when representing children. With your child clients, by contrast, you just get to sit there and listen and take notes. Your own process gets stuck. Your own nervous system cannot resolve the trauma it is experiencing in that moment, increasing the risk of your own vicarious trauma and compassion fatigue.

Next, the confidential nature of your jobs causes two main problems. First, it makes it more difficult to discuss these issues with others. Remember from Chapter 4 that the best way to heal trauma is to allow it to move through the nervous system. If you are unable to discuss the trauma you see and deal with every day, it has no place to go but to get stuck in your own nervous system. As a corollary, many of your friends and family do not want to hear about the trauma you see every day, even if you could talk about it. While you may be able to discuss your cases without too many specifics, why would you want to pass on the trauma to others? There is no reason to do so to those who are not used to experiencing it in their daily lives. Even Phil has difficulties when Rebecca talks about some of her traumatic experiences, especially when he is dealing with his own difficult cases. Although this is normal, it does little to help the one experiencing the vicarious trauma or the listener respond.

As we discussed in Chapter 10, sometimes you learn information about your clients you would like to share for their safety, but you cannot share it because you are a lawyer and must keep it in confidence. This can take its toll on anyone. You may know information about a child you believe should be shared for her safety, but because you cannot share it, you know the child is in potential (or known) danger, and there is nothing you can do about it without losing your job. Such conflicts are incredibly challenging and increase the risks of developing your own vicarious trauma. Essentially, you want to help, but you cannot and then you end up worrying about a child you know may be in danger.

It is important to put a huge caveat here. In most jurisdictions, if you know your client is experiencing harm or you know your client is a danger to himself or others, you may (and sometimes must) tell someone. While this is not true in all jurisdictions, it is true in some. But more importantly, you can have a frank conversation with clients about the need to share information for their safety. When children were suicidal, Rebecca told them she would rather lose her bar license than lose a child. It rarely happens, but in those moments, you may be able to find ways to protect yourself from holding that information as well as your client. However, learning to take such actions in a child-focused way takes experience and requires you to know how it is affecting you.

Regardless of your role as a client-directed or best interests attorney, sometimes decisions with long-lasting repercussions are made, and sometimes you disagree with those decisions. In one of her first cases as a client-directed lawyer, Rebecca had a client who repeatedly said to other professionals that he did not want visits with his mother but told Rebecca he did want to see his mother. During visits, he did well. This was before she understood all the reasons a child could act in these ways. She argued for visits to continue, and ultimately that child went home. When the case reactivated a couple of years later, Rebecca wondered whether she had originally read the signs correctly. Or what about the child who you believe says that he wants to go home only because Mom has started buying him toys at every visit? Or what if you are a best interests attorney and you make what you end up believing is the wrong call? What if a client is further harmed or, worse yet, dies? It is important to remember that some cases have no good answer. Although ultimately the decision is the judge's responsibility, lawyers for children have an inordinate amount of influence on the courts. If you enter this profession because you care about children and want to help them, feeling like you have failed even one of them can be one of the most difficult aspects of the job—and one lawyers are not trained to navigate.

Finally, although relatedly, there can be a feeling in the legal profession that you are just a cog in the wheel and can do nothing to alleviate the suffering your clients face. This is one of the biggest differences between lawyers and members of other healing professions; they get to do what they can to heal, while lawyers sometimes end up just having to provide bad news. You are unable to force a parent to participate in services to allow a child to return home. You are unable to force parents to stop fighting long enough to put their children first. As a child's lawyer, sometimes your job is to provide bad news. And when you repeatedly give children bad news, it can become difficult because you likely entered the profession wanting to help children and families. That can wear on you and your well-being. You cognitively know you are not the cause of the child's despair, but it can be painful to know you must give the child news that causes her pain.

Thus, being a lawyer is different from other healing professions. You probably are not well trained to deal with the emotions you see in your child clients, yet you must force them to speak about their traumas in a non-trauma-informed way; you work with colleagues who are less capable of offering the support you sometimes need during times of intense trauma; and you see awful things happening to children, sometimes without the ability to help your own clients navigate their pain and suffering. And at the end of the day, you must keep it to yourself and act "professional" while speaking with children, so your own pain is less likely to be expressed.

There Is Hope: The Importance of Self-Care

This chapter is not meant to be a "doom and gloom" chapter. In fact, by providing you with information about the signs and symptoms of vicarious trauma and compassion fatigue, we hope you will be able to alleviate the symptoms earlier and faster. You can do this work without having the pain and trauma you see every day affect every aspect of your being, and you can find yourself living a joyful life with appropriate nervous system regulation. This section is an overview of ways to help you do that from changes in your lifestyle to the moment-by-moment tools to help you navigate your work day.

If you take nothing else from this chapter, remember this: the most important and helpful dynamic in your life to help you with the risks of vicarious trauma and compassion fatigue is your close friends and family members, i.e., those relationships in which you feel supported and loved. Interestingly, this is no different from what we seek for our very young clients. Our needs as humans to connect do not change because we turn 18 and become professional adults. As we discussed in Chapters 4 and 5, children learn to feel safe through healthy relationships in which they learn to navigate the effects of trauma. Despite the fact you are a professional with a fully developed brain, those social connections are just as important to your own feeling of safety and emotional security. Unfortunately, one of biggest problems with compassion fatigue and vicarious trauma is people tend to isolate themselves. That is why it is so important for you to notice if you isolate and instead reach out to those you love.

Some people go so far as to say the cause of addiction and symptoms that mask addictions, such as avoidance of emotion, is isolation. This work, as we mentioned above, can be very isolating. Johann Hari, who traveled the world to learn about the war on drugs, found it is isolation that leads to addictive drug use.[271] He references the study where rats were caged individually and given two containers of water, one plain and the other containing heroin or cocaine. The rats would eventually drink only the drug-laden water and eventually die. Rats that were in a cage with other rats and had interesting activities to do, would choose to drink only the regular water. None of them died despite being offered the drug-laden water in the same manner. Further, rats who began being isolated in cages and were later moved to the social cage, would eventually stop drinking the drug-laden water.

What does this tell us about humans? Connection heals. Phil has seen this daily in his psychological work. Perhaps one of the most poignant examples of an explanation of loneliness and the importance of human connection came from a scene at the end of an episode of *Mork and Mindy*. In it, Robin Williams, as Mork, states,[272]

---

271. Johann Hari, *The Likely Cause of Addiction Has Been Discovered, and It Is Not What You Think*, HuffPost (Jan. 20, 2015), https://www.huffingtonpost.com/johann-hari/the-real-cause-of-addicti_b_6506936.html.

272. Francis Whittaker, *Mork Talking about Loneliness Seems Incredibly Poignant after Robin Williams' Death*, Buzz Feed (Aug. 12, 2014), https://www.buzzfeed.com/franciswhittaker/mork-talks-about-loneliness?utm_term=.nmNoQl2j4#.tgVYDv9rO.

Mork: This week I discovered a terrible disease called loneliness.

Orson: Do many people on Earth suffer from this disease?

Mork: Oh yes sir, and how they suffer. One man I know suffers so much he has to take a medication called bourbon. Even that doesn't help very much because then he can hear paint dry.

Orson: Does bedrest help?

Mork: No because I've heard that sleeping alone is part of the problem. You see, Orson, loneliness is a disease of the spirit. People who have it think that no one cares about them.

Orson: Do you have any idea why?

Mork: Yes sir, you can count on me. You see, when children are young, they're told not to talk to strangers. When they go to school, they're told not to talk to the person next to them. Finally when they're very old, they're told not to talk to themselves; who's left?

Orson: Are you saying Earthlings make each other lonely?

Mork: No sir, I'm saying just the opposite. They make themselves lonely—they're so busy looking out for number one that there's not enough room for two.

Orson: It's too bad everybody down there can't get together and find a cure.

Mork: Here's the paradox, sir, because if they did get together, they wouldn't need one.

What makes this quote even more touching is that Robin Williams took his own life years later. Although we do not know all the reasons he had his addiction problems and ultimately took his own life, we do know that he often felt isolated from others. It is easy to become lonely when you work with such emotionally difficult cases. Remember that having a support system in place can help alleviate your loneliness and help connect you to the healing power of your community. Many of the other following "cures" for vicarious trauma and compassion fatigue become less necessary, sometimes even unnecessary, when you have a community of supportive friends and family.

And it is important to say that you need not overwhelm your friends and family with the pain you experience every day. But you may need to tell them what you need from them. Many people like to help and give advice. They often want to tell you there is nothing more you can do to help your clients than what you are already doing. But if Rebecca has learned anything from years of studying trauma from scientific to ancient to new age realms, it is that simply being present with someone is healing. On that issue, all the teachings agree. You can talk about the most mundane issues; as long as you are together and you feel safe, healing happens.

It can be very helpful to you just to ask your friends to show up, to be with you, and sometimes to let you cry. As professionals, we are often taught that crying is a sign of weakness. It is actually a great way to let energy move. If trauma is stored in the nervous system, one way to move it out is to cry. That is why it is our natural response. Sometimes a good cry is all you need, and sometimes having a friend willing to be with you while you do it is all the healing you need. It also is okay if crying does not work for you. Similarly, laughter moves energy, so getting together with friends and laughing can also help, even if you never mention why you are upset in the first place. We hope that after reading this book, you are left with the knowledge there is no weakness or shame in releasing emotion in any way that works for you.

While healthy relationships are the most effective antidote to vicarious trauma and compassion fatigue, several other ways can help as well. One way to look at this is to ask yourself what your resources are. One somatic experiencing practitioner/trainer has defined a resource as "anything that makes you stronger or calmer without having a cost."[273] In other words, if the activity you choose helps you calm down or makes you feel stronger and there is no cost to your system to engage in that activity, it is a resource. Resources can be as big as taking a trip to the other side of the world and as small as holding your hands or crossing your legs a certain way. Knowing your resources is vital to your health in this work, and the rest of this section will examine different types of resources to help get you thinking about what yours might be.

A general rule of thumb is to do activities you enjoy. Just as the most important question you can ask a child client is what he does for fun, it also is the most important question you can ask yourself. When you are experiencing the effects of vicarious trauma and compassion fatigue, it can be easy for you to lose interest in whatever used to give you enjoyment. Rediscovering these parts of yourself can help you come out of the overwhelm caused by vicarious trauma and compassion fatigue. As a psychologist who has experienced and dealt with vicarious trauma and compassion fatigue risks for many years, Phil has found

---

273. Rebecca heard this quote from someone who took the training. The trainer is Gina Ross. Rebecca has been unable to find a written example of the quote, but it so perfectly explained the concepts of this chapter, she decided to use it. If you are interested in Gina Ross's work, visit her website at http://www.ginaross.com/ (last visited Nov. 5, 2017).

that teaching, traveling, taking part in social physical activities such as golf and going to the fitness center with a friend, and having social relationships are fun for him. Ensuring that he engages in all of that allows him to manage the potential risks of vicarious trauma and compassion fatigue.

With issues related to vicarious trauma specifically, remember that it will get stuck in the nervous system if you let it, so getting yourself physically moving can help. Many people find physical exercise such as walking and running or yoga classes based on postures help them move the energy that would otherwise get stuck in their bodies. If you find yourself suffering more from compassion fatigue, it can be very helpful to do activities that remind you of the good in the world, especially if it involves being in beautiful parts of the world for hiking, or seeing movies you enjoy, or traveling to fun places.

Besides these general suggestions, people may find that other activities are beneficial to them when experiencing symptoms of vicarious trauma, including being in nature, finding a spiritual path, meditating, and going to therapy. Besides trauma, another buzzword is mindfulness, and mindfulness techniques can be invaluable, particularly when you are just beginning to notice the effects of the working environment.

You can do many things during the work day to help mitigate and eliminate the effects of vicarious trauma and compassion fatigue as they arise. One of the most effective is to get away. Using the concept of pendulation of the nervous system, you allow the nervous system to activate and then pull it away to something else, allow it to activate again, and then repeat the cycle. Without thinking, you probably do this when you can, but with a demanding job, you may not think to take the time to do it. But you can make the time. On those days you get overwhelmed, go out for lunch or take a walk around the building or chat with a coworker about something inconsequential to your job. Although somewhat ridiculous, a favorite technique of Rebecca's recently has been to find joke memes on the Internet and send them to friends. This fulfills two objectives: (1) It is a distraction from the overwhelm, and 2) it is a connection to a friend, albeit through texting but still a connection. You can take a few minutes to pull yourself away from the overwhelm long enough to reregulate the nervous system. Then you can get right back to work with a more refreshed outlook.

If you notice yourself dissociating at work, e.g., walking into objects or spacing out, it can be helpful to consciously notice yourself sitting in a chair or to silently identify objects you see. Look at your computer and say to yourself "computer." Look at the lights and silently say "lights." Notice what draws your attention and focus on it for a few seconds. Then feel what it is like to be where you are, likely sitting in a chair: How does your back feel on the chair? How do your feet feel on the floor?

If your heart begins to race or your foot is shaking or you have butterflies in your stomach, try to find a place in your body that feels less jumpy. Most people like to hold their hands a certain way that is comforting to them. Notice how you usually hold your hands when you sit. If your nervousness increases and your hands are not in that usual position, try putting them there and see how it affects your nervous system. These are little tricks that can help. Everyone has her own tricks, and it is helpful to know what makes you feel better when you are not in that state of overwhelm. Then when you feel that state coming on, you have the tools to help and just have to use them.

These are all useful tools, but as the pressures of vicarious trauma and compassion fatigue begin to mount, it may be necessary to reach out for professional help. There are many forms of psychotherapy, but one of the most effective for these particular issues, because it works on the nervous system and the meaning people associate with their circumstances, is somatic experiencing. Somatic experiencing can also help give you ways to recognize when your nervous system is beginning to experience overload and provide you with strategies to self-regulate. This can help not only with a momentary experience but also with responses to colleagues. Rebecca has begun teaching a meditation class at her office based on the ideas from somatic experiencing. Not every workplace offers such a program, but Peter Levine's books, listed in the online resources, have invaluable tools for such self-learning.

Other than your own addiction or isolation, there is no incorrect way to help yourself with the manifestations of vicarious trauma and compassion fatigue. As long as you find something you enjoy that has nothing to do with your work, the activity can be healing. If you do the activity with other people, it becomes even more healing.

Meaning Making

Tangential to the question of what to do to help yourself heal is an attempt to reframe some of the meaning of what you do. One of the most important aspects of healing is changing the meaning of the pain you experience. As humans, we can bring our own meaning to any event and any circumstance. Therefore, what if we look at some of these issues from a different perspective? Rebecca recently had an experience that exemplified this perfectly. She was with a wonderful group of friends and felt overwhelmed by emotion. When away from that group of friends, Rebecca had been doing incredibly well and feeling positive about most aspects of her life. She said to a friend, "I don't understand why every time

I'm here, no matter how great my life is, I find myself falling apart." Her friend responded, "What if you look at it differently? You're doing great out there because you have a safe place to fall apart?" The meaning changed, as did the entire situation.

You can do this in your job as well. If you must give bad news to a child client, be grateful your client is hearing the news from someone with compassion who will be honest rather than from a variety of people who may not provide the full story or may have their own interests at heart. Even though your words may lead to your child client crying, your words, coming from a place of your child client's best interests and said with heart, compassion, and empathy, is what your client needs. Knowing you are doing good for your child client, even in difficult circumstances, can give your life positive meaning. And knowing that simply being present is one of the most healing ways to show up in the world, you can learn to be present with your child clients and to help them with the process of healing when the painful information is provided. They may not remember you consciously later in life (and often you hope they do not), but they will remember how you made them feel. That feeling of safety you create will stay with them in their nervous systems the same way trauma does.

Thus, even some of the most difficult aspects of your job can be reframed so they feel more like opportunities to do good for your clients. As the throes of vicarious trauma and compassion fatigue become even more intense, it can be difficult to reframe the meaning of what you do. That is one of the manifestations. But talk to someone new to the profession. Talk to someone who remembers why you started the work you do. Sometimes just talk to your clients about their lives. Somewhere in all of that there is a new meaning for you to see. Know that if you connect with and listen to your child clients and are able to help even some of them with the trauma in their lives, you are doing good despite all of the challenges in your work. Then remind yourself of that every step of the way.

Importance of Compassion for Everyone in the Process

Besides the importance of community, perhaps the most important aspect of working with vicarious trauma and compassion fatigue is to have compassion for everyone in the process. This includes yourself. Dr. Perry discusses the guilt he felt when seeing where his patient lived. He states, "I felt guilty. Guilty about the luck, the opportunities, the resources and the gifts I have been given, guilty about all of the times I had complained about working too much, or not getting credit for something I had done."[274] It can be easy to fall into this trap, especially when you work with poor families who have not been given the opportunities you have had. It can be easy to fall into the trap of feeling that your problems are not as bad as theirs. But as we stated above, pain and trauma are not comparative. What hurts you hurts you. What hurts them hurts them. For your own mental health and for your ability to help your clients, you must continue to recognize this, over and over again.

Maintaining compassion for the others with whom you work is important. Rebecca often says one of the most difficult parts of representing children is having compassion for the parents, whether they are drug addicts or have personality disorders that cause them to put themselves and their own needs before their children's, understanding why they act the way they do based on their own traumatic histories, and still understanding their actions may not be safe for their children. But that first step of compassion is important. Understanding peoples' histories helps you understand how to help them, and understanding how to help them can ultimately help your clients. Then understanding how all of this affects you can help you continue helping more clients over the course of your career.

And do not forget to have compassion for the lawyer who snaps at you. This is a small profession, and everyone has moments when he loses his temper. Everyone has moments when she gets angry, has bad days, and does something she will regret later. The important piece of this is to learn why you and the other attorney responded a particular way and to help her and yourself through it. Phil recalls a time when, during a very contentious trial, and after not responding to a cross-examination question the way the attorney wanted, the attorney, whom Phil generally likes, raised his voice quite loudly at Phil. Phil was startled, despite the fact that the case had both lawyers raising their voices at different times. When Phil's testimony was over, the lawyer who yelled at him came over to apologize, and Phil, recognizing how unusual this was for their typical interactions, said he understood and thanked the lawyer for apologizing. Taking the high road always helps one's compassion. On the other hand, as lawyers, you may ultimately have an ethical responsibility to talk to a colleague who appears to be too overwhelmed by the issues addressed in this chapter.

You likely entered this profession because you have deep compassion for people. But that is often the first human emotion to get lost. Seeing the world as black or white makes your job easier. If you always make someone the wrongdoer, then

---

274. Perry, *supra* note 149 at 17.

the difficulties of the job seem easier. It is easier to fall into the trap of relying on biases because the nuances of family and dependency law can get overwhelming. But if you lose your compassion for others, you lose your compassion for yourself, and if you lose compassion, you lose the ability to connect to people you love. Then the vicarious trauma and compassion fatigue get worse. Remember that everyone in this process is struggling and everyone in this process is human. Compassion for everyone is vital to the process and to the profession and to your own overall health.

Concluding Thoughts

There is no doubt this work is difficult at times. For most of the people who represent children, sometimes days, weeks, months, and even years can feel overwhelming. We hope it is not like that for you, but we want you to know that these tools can help you navigate those days. There are ways to take care of yourself and heal from the pain you see and experience every day. If you are struggling, reach out to friends, family, and professionals. Remember there is no shame in being vulnerable. In fact, it is a great sign of strength. You are going to be a better lawyer if you are healthy, and you are only going to be healthy if you acknowledge when the work becomes too much.

We hope you never forget why you began this work. Most people who represent children do it because they want to help—and, importantly, help children who are in need. It is often a thankless and underpaid profession, but the rewards are in your child clients. We ask you to remember the privilege and honor you have been granted to share this time in your child clients' lives. As we have reiterated throughout this book, in these cases, you are the only person whose only role is to be there for the children, to present the children to the court, and to help the children navigate these rough waters. It is a huge responsibility, but it is also the opportunity to touch and help bring healing to children's lives. At some level, we want them to forget us. But at another level, we want them to remember the feeling of being seen, of having their feelings understood, and of having someone care about their feelings. If you can help your child clients experience that, you have helped them in ways that are far greater than what happens in the courtroom. And if you are helping them, know that their experiences need not define them forever. We hope you take this responsibility seriously and with the honor that we do. And we hope this book has made it just a little easier to help yourself navigate this rewarding, yet challenging work.

Index

professionals (*continued*)
   mediators, 189–190
   medical professionals, 192
   mental health providers, 187–189
   parenting coordinators, 190–191
   school personnel, 192–193
psycho-educational programs,
   161–162
Psychology Today, 30
pushing, 110

Q
questioners, 101
questions, 99–101

R
reactive attachment disorder (RAD),
   173–174
realistic estrangement, 151
recency bias, 223–224
reflective functioning, 123
refugee status, 170–171
rejected parent, 150
relatives, 168
repair function, 123
reparations, xvi
reproductive health, 185–186
reptilian brain, 57–58, 71
resilience, 75–80
responsibility, 123
rest and digest response, 55
Ritalin, 179

S
schizophrenia, childhood, 181
school, 172
school-aged stage (ages 6–11), 91–94
school personnel, 192–193
self-care, 245–250
self-destructive behavior, 119

self-esteem, 92, 130
self-regulation, 75
self-soothe, 87
separation instigated violence (SIV),
   109–110. *See also* domestic violence
   parenting problems and, 122
   pattern, 122
severe mental health issues, 180–182
sex, 185–186
sexual abuse, 183–185
   allegations of, 97–98, 183–184
   issues to consider, 184
   therapy for, 185
   as ultimate boundary violation,
     184
shaken baby syndrome, 183
shame, 131
shock, 74–75
shoving, 110
siblings, 156–157, 210–211
Simons, Daniel, 225–226
situational couples violence (SCV),
   110–111. *See also* domestic
   violence
   intervention, 125
   parenting problems and, 122
   pattern, 122
socialization, 91
social work, xii–xv
social workers, 191
   child client's meeting with, 198
   child protection, 191
   child's experience of removal and,
     74
   as collateral sources, 214–215
   interviews by, 98
   therapists and, 188
somatic experiencing, 78
somatic issues, 72